Second Millenium B. C.

SEA

CASPIAN SEA

ASSYRIA

MITTANI

Haran

Tigris River

Nineveh

Asshur

Euphrates River

Ugarit

Byblos

Mari

ELAM

Damascus

Jerusalem

Babylon

BABYLONIA

Ur

PERSIAN GULF

ARABIAN

DESERT

RED SEA

Authoritative detail makes this a thought-provoking general introduction to Hebrew history and religion.

Dr. Booth feels Jesus and the events of the New Testament cannot be understood apart from the Old Testament faith; therefore, considerable attention is given to historic development of it. The reader gains, too, an appreciation of Old Testament literature as a collection of books written by a diversity of authors.

Format and content make "The Chosen People" not only an excellent text for college students, church school students and ministers, but also an invaluable resource book for church school teachers.

". . . FOR I GIVE WATER IN THE WILDERNESS,
    RIVERS IN THE DESERT,
  TO GIVE DRINK TO MY CHOSEN PEOPLE,
    THE PEOPLE WHOM I FORMED FOR MYSELF
  THAT THEY MIGHT DECLARE MY PRAISE"
                    —ISAIAH 43:20-21

THE CHOSEN PEOPLE

A Narrative History
of the
Israelites

by

OSBORNE BOOTH

THE BETHANY PRESS

© 1959 BY

THE BETHANY PRESS

ST. LOUIS, MISSOURI

Library of Congress Catalog Card Number: 59-13168

Printed in the United States of America

To my wife, Ruth

PREFACE

This book has been written for the average reader who would like to know something of the commonly accepted results of devout scholarship in the Old Testament field. The aim has been to present an account as readable as possible, with an absolute minimum of footnotes. There is very little that is original. In fact, most of the opinions given are so generally known that they could be accredited to any one of several authorities, were there any desire to authenticate them.

I wish to acknowledge my indebtness to the administration of Bethany College, especially President Perry E. Gresham and Dean B. R. Weimer, to my colleague Professor B. C. Shaw, who discussed matters of history, and to my typists, Barbara Gould who began the task and Charlotte Myers who completed it.

In the editorial field I am grateful to Ambrose Edens and George Fowler, both of the faculty of Texas Christian University, who read the manuscript and made a number of suggestions which I believe markedly improved it. I am particularly grateful to Darrell K. Wolfe, Director of the Bethany Press, and to one of his editors, Dorothy K. Eicks, for guidance.

Ultimately, however, much of the credit should go to a long list of great teachers. Those in the immediate field include Professors George A. Peckham, Frank Chamberlin Porter, George Dahl, Charles Cutler Torrey, A. T. Olmstead, J. M. P. Smith, and particularly my faculty adviser, Professor Millar Burrows. I did not have the privilege of studying under Professor William Foxwell Albright, but it is becoming increasingly evident that no one can write today in the field of the Old Testament without admitting indebtedness to him. It is quite apparent that most of the items of value in this book should be accredited to one of those listed above. My mistakes are my own.

With the single exception of a change of one word in Amos 3:12 the Revised Standard Version has been used. May I express my gratitude for its use.

To me, the history of these chosen people is a thrilling narrative, starting with nomadic shepherds, rising to a great empire under a few talented rulers, and then sinking back into obscurity, to find in its religious faith and literature a substitute for temporal power. The story of the growth of that faith and that literature is carried down to the birth of Jesus of Nazareth and, nearly a century later, the selection of the books of the Hebrew Scriptures. It is hoped that for some people the Old Testament may, as a result of this book, be somewhat more readable, and somewhat more read.

CONTENTS

Page

Part One

Introduction

CHAPTER I THE OLD TESTAMENT
Why Are We Interested? 15
What the Old Testament Is 17
CHAPTER II THE LAND AND THE PEOPLE
The Land of Palestine 19
Adjacent Lands 25
The People of Palestine 26

Part Two

The Early Days of Israel

CHAPTER III THE ANCIENT TRADITIONS: Sources 31
CHAPTER IV THE ANCIENT TRADITIONS: Stories of Origins 34
CHAPTER V THE ANCIENT TRADITIONS: The Patriarchs 43
CHAPTER VI THE ANCIENT TRADITIONS: Moses and the
Exodus 52
CHAPTER VII THE SETTLEMENT OF PALESTINE: The Story
According to Joshua 64
CHAPTER VIII THE SETTLEMENT OF PALESTINE: The
Story According to Judges 71

Part Three

The Monarchies

CHAPTER IX THE UNITED KINGDOM: Samuel and Saul 89
CHAPTER X THE UNITED KINGDOM: The Establishment of
the House of David 97
CHAPTER XI THE UNITED KINGDOM: Solomon the
Magnificent 112

CHAPTER XII   THE DIVIDED KINGDOM: The Division of the
              Kingdom and the Crisis of Elijah   123
CHAPTER XIII   THE DIVIDED KINGDOM: The First Writing
              Prophets   134
CHAPTER XIV   THE REMAINING KINGDOM OF JUDAH:
              Deuteronomy and the Reformation   151
CHAPTER XV   THE REMAINING KINGDOM OF JUDAH: The
              Fall of Jerusalem, and Jeremiah   158

Part Four
The Exile

CHAPTER XVI   EZEKIEL AND SECOND ISAIAH   181

Part Five
The Persian Period

CHAPTER XVII   THE TEMPLE   199
CHAPTER XVIII   THE WALLS AND THE LAW   204
CHAPTER XIX   THE LITERATURE OF THE PERSIAN PERIOD   208

Part Six
The Greek Period

CHAPTER XX   THE MACCABEES AND THE BOOK OF DANIEL   219
CHAPTER XXI   OTHER LITERATURE OF THE GREEK PERIOD   224

Part Seven
Under Rome

CHAPTER XXII   TO THE TIME OF CHRIST   237
CHAPTER XXIII   THE CANON   241
CONCLUSION   246

Appendix

NOTE A   THE NAME OF GOD   247
NOTE B   THE IDEA OF "SPIRIT"   248
NOTE C   FURTHER DISCUSSION OF THE COVENANT   248
NOTE D   JABESH-GILEAD AND THE MEN OF BENJAMIN   249
NOTE E   THE COMPOSITION OF THE BOOK OF ISAIAH   251
NOTE F   THE SO-CALLED "VIRGIN" PASSAGE   253
NOTE G   THE DEAD SEA SCROLLS   254
BIBLIOGRAPHY   258

M A P S

The Near East, Second Millenium B.C.   Front end papers

Relief Map of Palestine   14

Palestine in the Time of the Judges   70

The Persian Empire   Back end papers

11

PART ONE

INTRODUCTION

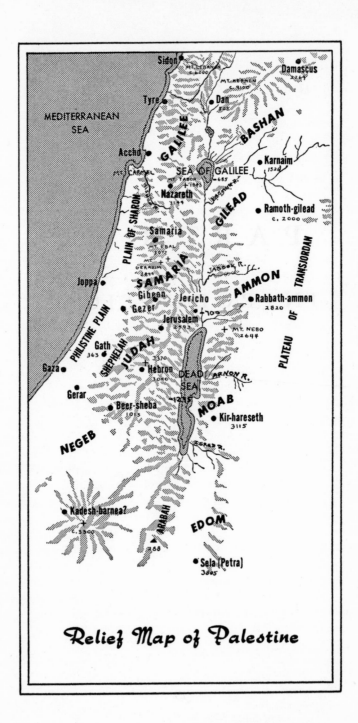

Relief Map of Palestine

CHAPTER I

THE OLD TESTAMENT

Why Are We Interested?

THE CHRISTIAN RELIGION

Jesus was a Jew. The traditions and glories of ancient Israel were part of his heritage. In his early boyhood he was cautioned by the precepts found in the Book of Proverbs. When he learned to read and to write, it was by studying in the synagogue school the "Torah" or "Law"—the first five books of our Old Testament. The simple piety of the Book of Psalms taught him the security to be found in dependence upon his Father in heaven. When, at the age of twelve, he went up with his family to the temple at Jerusalem at the Passover season, he undoubtedly joined with the other pilgrims in chanting the psalms of ascent,[1] each one marking the achievement of a certain landmark along the journey.

From his youth Jesus also knew of the prophets. Probably the rudimentary principles of justice were explained to him and illustrated by the words of Amos. Some of the tragedies in the lives about him were made more understandable by his knowledge of the difficulties of Jeremiah. He was well aware that Malachi had said that Elijah would return to earth before the "day of the LORD," when God's reign in the world would really begin.[2] This knowledge may well have shaped his interpretation of the work of John the Baptist. But of all the prophets, the one who seems most to have influenced his thought was Isaiah, as shown by quotations made from that book, and possibly by the selection of that scroll when he was invited to read in the synagogue.[3]

The apocalyptic writers, who pictured the end of the world by great catastrophes, and the building of a new world, in which God would be supreme and his people the favored ones of the earth, exerted a great influence upon the Jews of Jesus'

---

1. Psalms 120—134, with possibly some others.
2. Malachi 4:5f.
3. Luke 4:16-21.

15

time. Some scholars think this had a determining effect upon
his religion. Certainly he used some of these ideas, as shown
in his picture of the last judgment of Matthew, chapter 25.
However, they were greatly modified in most of his teachings
by his conception of God as a loving Father.

Jesus, then, was a Jew. The Jewish traditions were his
traditions; the Jewish hopes were, at least in part, his hopes;
the Jewish scriptures were his sacred books. This heritage
was the foundation upon which the whole of the Christian
religion was based. To understand Jesus and the church he
founded, it is necessary to begin with the history, the literature,
and the religion of his people.

The Jewish Religion

There are excellent reasons for studying the Jewish religion
entirely aside from its reference to Jesus. God spoke to ancient
Israel, and those who understood and were able to write under
such conditions that their words were preserved have blessed
mankind even to the present. Here we have portrayed the
progress of man's thought about God, from the crudest con-
ceptions to ideals which are still too exalted for us to attain. We
have the picture of his care for his people, and a description
of the religion they developed to show gratitude for that care,
and to assure its continuance. Of all religions practiced before
the Christian Era, it was by a large margin the noblest. We
bear witness to this fact by incorporating its sacred literature
with our own. There are infinite values of a religious nature
which we can learn today from the scriptures of the Jews.

Literature of the World

Not only is the Old Testament of great importance to us in
the field of religion. It has an honored place in the literature
of the world. These Jewish writings take their positions
proudly among the greatest of masterpieces. Not only because
of their own intrinsic worth must they be known: no other
body of literature has exerted so great an impression on the
subsequent writings of any people. Most of the literary accomplishments of occidental writers for the last eighteen

centuries can be fully understood and appreciated only by those having an adequate knowledge of the literature of Israel. Thus, whether we are concerned with literary importance and beauty, or with vital spiritual values, or with the background of the Christian religion, there are genuine rewards available to those who study the records of the chosen people.

What the Old Testament Is

THE VARIOUS BOOKS

The Old Testament is not a book, but a collection of many books. Because it has been in existence in its present form for so many years, it is sometimes difficult for us to realize that it is not one composition with a single purpose, written from a single point of view. In reality it is a library—a collection of nearly all the extant writings of a people. Aside from these biblical records, we have no fragment of writing from the authors of these people until the last couple of centuries before the Christian Era—and comparatively few then.

These books which make up the Old Testament are of many different types, and have many variant aims. Some boast of victorious wars; some complain of the oppression of conquerors. Some are deeply religious; one at least is inclined toward skepticism (Ecclesiastes) and one does not even mention God (Esther). Some are intensely ritualistic, and some condemn ritual. We have law, both civil and constitutional; poetry— some showing the deepest contrition, and some the happy, sensual songs of the wedding feast; history; genealogical tables; curses; ethical teachings; and the most magnificent statements of God's concern for the welfare of man. It is impossible to speak in general terms: each writing has its own purpose and its own worth, and, so far as possible, should be considered in front of its own background.

THE WRITERS

The authors of the Old Testament are legion. No one can guess how many contributed to its pages. The earliest forms were poetry, as they were transmitted in oral form for many years before they were written. Many of these early poems were war songs, at least two of which are attributed to women.

The amazing thing about these authors is their diversity. Not only do we have hundreds of them, coming over a span of perhaps 1,200 years: we have people from all different walks of life. Many chapters were written by dry legalists, who wanted no change in either the ancient canon law or the ritual of the worship of the LORD. To them, what had been, had been ordained by God, and therefore was right, and should not be changed. On the other hand, many chapters were written by some of the greatest preachers of all times. (A prophet was, above all else, a preacher.) They felt that the LORD had spoken to them, and they were compelled to give his message to the people. As this message was frequently critical of things as they were, the prophet was often directly opposed to the priests—or even to other prophets.[4] Some sections were written by shepherds; some by statesmen or kings. Some were written by warriors, men of peace, teachers, hymn writers, short-story writers, philosophers—men of all types and positions of life.

What was the unifying factor which united these heterogeneous authors, and welded their divergent writings into one book? In the first place, it was the connected history of a people—the saga of Israel. With one possible exception (the Book of Job), all their literature may be considered as coming from the one group, traditionally descended from the patriarchs and especially from Jacob or Israel. In the second place, there was eventually the firm conviction that these people were children of destiny, and that their God breathed his word into (inspired) their writings. True, being human, the writers were not capable of receiving and transmitting that inspiration without any change, but they did a marvelous job. No other writers have come close to equaling it, and none ever will. The product of their work is the Old Testament. It contains the religion, the literature, and the history of the chosen people. In our study of them we must begin with the place in which they lived, and the people from whom they had come.

---

4. Jeremiah, chapter 28.

CHAPTER II

THE LAND AND THE PEOPLE

The Land of Palestine

PALESTINE

Palestine is a land of dimensions absurdly small, in proportion to the influence it has exerted upon the history and thought of mankind. Located at the eastern end of the Mediterranean Sea, it extends only a hundred and fifty miles north and south, and its greatest width, which is at the southern end, is less than one hundred miles. And of this small area, a large part is so dry and rocky that it can with difficulty be used for the herding of sheep. Only a very small part could be called fertile ground.

DIVISIONS

The easiest way to picture the land is to divide it in imagination into four strips, running from north to south, each one a little wider at the south than at the north. We must remember, however, that straight, regular lines are not found in geographical boundaries: what we shall have is more of a diagram of the territory than an outline of its various parts. These strips are known as the Maritime Plain; the Central Highlands; the Jordan Valley; and Transjordan.

MARITIME PLAIN

The most westerly of these divisions is the Maritime Plain, overlooking the Mediterranean Sea. At the north is the Plain of Phoenicia, with its two great seaports, Sidon and Tyre. In some places the hills come almost to the sea, and nowhere is it more than ten miles in width. As a consequence, it was not primarily an agricultural region, but was known throughout the ancient world for its trade. The city of Carthage in

19

northern Africa—at one time a rival of Rome itself—was founded by men from Phoenicia.

About one-third of the way down the coast of Palestine Mount Carmel juts out into the Mediterranean Sea, forming a semicircular bay on its northern side. This bay offered a fair anchorage, but was not a completely protected port. That part of the plain directly south of the mountain was called the Plain of Sharon. Rainfall is good, but the scarcity of remains of towns and villages indicates that it was not a very productive area in biblical times. The only seaport in those days was the city of Joppa, which marked the southern end of the territory called "Sharon."

The third section of the Maritime Plain is the Plain of Philistia, which reaches some twenty miles back into the foothills. It is well watered and fertile, except in the southern part, where it slopes off into the desert. The five great cities of the Philistines, who occupied the land during Old Testament times, were Ashdod, Ashkelon, Ekron, Gath and Gaza, of which only Ashkelon was a seaport.

CENTRAL HIGHLANDS

There are five sections of the Central Highlands, though one of them is really not in the highlands at all. The most northern section is the Highland of Galilee. It starts on the southern slope of Mount Lebanon and reaches a line about opposite the southern end of the Sea of Galilee. The county is fairly rugged, though not completely unsuitable for agriculture. The southern part is the more fertile; the northern part is used largely for grazing sheep.

There is a break in these highlands just south of Galilee: a beautiful plain, shaped roughly like an isosceles right triangle, with the hypotenuse reaching from northwest to southeast, just above Mount Carmel. This area is so fertile the Israelites called it "Jezreel," or "Yahweh[1] has sown." The later Greeks, who were the geographers of antiquity, could neither spell nor pronounce this word, so it has come down to us as "Esdraelon," but the Israelites called it the "Valley of Jezreel." There were

---

1. See Appendix, Note A.

a city and a river of the same name.   No other place in Palestine can compare in fertility with this beautiful valley.

The Valley or Plain of Esdraelon comes to an abrupt but
irregular end where the Highland of Samaria begins.   Overlooking the plain from the northwest is Mount Carmel, where
Elijah made the test with the 450 prohets of Baal to see
whether Baal or Yahweh was the true God.   Overlooking
it from the southeast is Mount Gilboa where Saul fought his
final battle against the Philistines.   To the northeast of this
line of hills is the River Kishon, on the banks of which Barak
and Deborah won their great victory over the Canaanites.

The main overland trade route of ancient times for Palestine
came through Damascus, northeast of Palestine, around the
northern side of the Sea of Galilee, and then through the Plain
of Esdraelon.   There are a number of breaks in the hills at
the edge of the Highland of Samaria.   Through each of these
breaks, one of the branches of the trade route continued on to
the south, and, guarding the approach to the plain, there was
a city.   We thus find a line of cities at the dividing line between
Esdraelon and Samaria: Megiddo, Taanach, Ibleam, and,
farther to the east, Beth-shan.   The greatest of these was
Megiddo, the scene of many battles in which attempts were
made to stop invading armies.

The Highland of Samaria is lower in elevation than Galilee.
Though less fertile than Esdraelon, it was capable of supporting many people.   The center of early biblical tradition was
the city of Shechem, almost in the middle of this area.   In the
time of Omri the city of Samaria was built, ten or fifteen miles
northwest of Shechem.   Samaria was the capital, and gave
its name to the entire country.   Halfway between Shechem
and the border of Judah to the south was the city of Bethel,
a sanctuary which became the official religious center for that
part of the Northern Kingdom.

There is no physical transition to mark the dividing line
between the Highland of Samaria and the Highland of Judah.
The old capital was Hebron, near the center of Judah, but
after David had captured Jerusalem, the latter became both
the political and the religious center, not only for Judah, but
for all the territory David ruled.   There were two other cities

to the west and a little north of Jerusalem—Gibeon and Gezer
—which were not conquered by the Israelites before the time
of the monarchy.   When the kingdom was divided the line
between the Northern Kingdom (later called Samaria) and
the Southern, or Judah, was just north of these three strong-
holds.

The western part of the Highland of Judah was called the
"Shephelah" or "Lowlands," as it is the part adjoining the
Plain of Philistia.   It is in some places quite fertile, and is
traversed by five east-and-west valleys, each of which has, at
one time or another, been used by an invading army to attack
the land of Judah from the Coastal Plain.   It was the traditional battleground of the Philistines and Israelites.

The main part of the Highland of Judah, in the center of
the area, was suitable for grazing sheep, and for some agriculture, but east of the watershed, where the land slopes toward
the Dead Sea, is the impossible Wilderness of Judah.   Going
toward the south, the land gets lower in elevation, and drier,
until the desert or "Negeb" is reached.   Here it was possible
to sustain life only at occasional oases, one of the most important of which was Beer-sheba.   This place—"the sacred
well" or "the well of the oath"—was considered the southern
extremity of Palestine.

THE JORDAN VALLEY

Two prehistoric cataclysms combined to make the Jordan
Valley one of the world's most unusual places.   First, a great
crack appeared on the earth's surface, so that the water from
the Red Sea reached far up into Palestine.   Then, ages later,
the land between Palestine and the Red Sea raised sufficiently
to form a watershed.   To the south of the watershed, the arm
of the sea remaining became the Gulf of Akabah: that part
trapped on the northern side of the elevation became the Dead
Sea, with small tributaries flowing into it from all sides except
the west, the Jordan River entering from the north, and no
outlet of any kind except by evaporation.   No wonder it is so
salty!

The Jordan River has four sources, all of which are found on
or near the slopes of Mount Hermon, the highest mountain

in the region. One of these sources is very close to the site of the ancient city of Dan, which was considered the northern extremity of Palestine. A few miles below the joining of these sources, the river flows into a marshy area, part of which merges into a small body of water called Lake Huleh. Ten miles south of this lake the river enters the Sea of Galilee, but in that short distance it drops over 900 feet. As a consequence, the current in many places is extremely swift.

The reason for the sudden drop is the fault in the earth's surface previously mentioned. The level of the Sea of Galilee is nearly 700 feet below the level of the Mediterranean. Yet the great rift continues to a greater depth, so the water flows out of Galilee as fast as it flows in, and continues its course over sixty miles to the south, until it empties into the Dead Sea, nearly 1,300 feet below the level of the Mediterranean. During most of its course, the Jordan twists and turns within the high banks which enclose the valley, yet in many places the current is extremely swift. Travel from one side of the Jordan to the other is difficult, especially in its lower part; not because of the depth of the water, but because of the steep banks and, in some places, because of the turbulence of the water.

There are no tributaries of importance north of the Sea of Galilee. A short distance south of it, the Yarmuk flows in from the east, and two-thirds of the distance from Galilee to the Dead Sea, the Jabbok joins the Jordan from the same direction. Farther to the south, the Arnon empties into the middle of the east side of the Dead Sea, and, near its southern end, the Zered, also from the east. There are no tributaries to the Dead Sea from the west, and the only streams of consequence flowing into the Jordan from that direction are the River Jalud, a short distance below the Yarmuk, and the Wâdī Fara. A wâdī is a stream which, during part of the year, is a bed of dry stones. From Lake Huleh to some distance south of the Sea of Galilee the land close to the Jordan system is quite fertile, and there is reason to believe it was far more productive in biblical times. In many places, however, there is almost a jungle in the immediate area through which the river flows. In much of the lower Jordan, the value of the water as a source of fertility is greatly lessened by the extremely rough terrain immediately adjacent to it, which makes access to it so difficult.

TRANSJORDAN

The northern part of the land beyond the Jordan was called Bashan. Its soil, of volcanic origin, would be quite fertile if there were sufficient rainfall—but there is not. Beyond the immediate valley of the Jordan, therefore, there were practically no cities. The nearest large settlements of ancient times toward the northeast were in the vicinity of Damascus. There were some attempts at settlements even in the forbidding valley of the upper Yarmuk.[2] Nearer the Jordan there was more water, so the area was more thickly populated. It was called Gilead, the location of such cities as Ramoth-gilead, some thirty miles east of the Jordan, which Kings Ahab and Jehoshaphat sought to wrest from the hands of the king of Damascus; and Jabesh-gilead, quite close to the Jordan, which Saul saved from Nahash the Ammonite, thereby presenting himself as the most eligible man for the kingship of Israel.

Farther to the south, there are extensive remains of irrigation projects, indicating that, in the distant past, the land was well populated and well administered. It is difficult to be definite about the boundaries of the various countries, as they changed with the rising and waning of their power, and of the power of Israel. In the early period of the Israelites, i.e., when they were first settling among the Canaanites of Palestine, the country of Edom probably ruled Transjordan south of the River Zered, while Moab occupied the land between the Zered and the Arnon. All the rest of Transjordan was controlled by certain of the tribes of Israel, except a strip running north from Rabbath-ammon about the headwaters of the Jabbok, some distance east of the Jordan. This was the country of Ammon, which at one time reached nearly to the Jordan, when its king besieged Jabesh-gilead.

In recent years, archaeological discoveries have shown us something of the size and power attained by the Kingdom of Moab. At one time it occupied the territory east of the entire

---

2. See Nelson Glueck, *The River Jordan* (Philadelphia: Westminster Press, 1946), p. 118.

Dead Sea, and even opposite the lower part of the Jordan. This was probably about the time of the Israelite judge Ehud, who assassinated Eglon, king of Moab. Later, all this territory was conquered by David.

Adjacent Lands

MESOPOTAMIA

One of the great centers of civilization in biblical and pre-biblical times was Mesopotamia. The Tigris River rises in the mountains west of Lake Van, far to the northeast of Palestine. It flows toward the southeast, and joins the Euphrates River a short distance from the delta of both rivers, at the upper end of the Persian Gulf. About one hundred and fifty miles south of Lake Van on the Tigris was the city of Nineveh, for many years capital of Assyria. Another fifty miles south was Asshur, an earlier capital of the same empire.

The two main sources of the Euphrates are north of the Tigris source, but the river swings far to the west in what is known as the "Great Bend of the Euphrates," which was the site of the Kingdom of the Mitanni. It then turns to the southeast, and runs roughly parallel to the Tigris for many miles, until they unite near their joint delta.

The land about these two great rivers is called the "Land between the Rivers" or "Mesopotamia." It was far more productive in ancient times than it is now, having the advantages of rainfall in most areas, seasonal overflow of the river in others, and, in some places, a fairly intricate system of irrigation canals. Some of the great empires which, one after another, developed in Mesopotamia were the Old Babylonian Empire (roughly, the 19th-16th centuries B.C.) with its capital at Babylon on the lower Euphrates; the Kingdom of Mitanni (15th century); the Assyrian Empire (intermittently, 12th-7th centuries) which for so many years terrified all that part of Asia; the Neo-Babylonian Empire (6th century), responsible for the exile of Israel; and the Persian Empire of Cyrus, Darius, and their successors (6th-3rd centuries B.C.). These mammoth powers must be considered in a study of the history of Israel.

EGYPT

Down the coast from Palestine and around the southeastern corner of the Mediterranean Sea lies Egypt. The fertile triangular delta was called "Lower Egypt," and the narrow ribbon of land from the delta to the first cataract, made fertile by the seasonal overflowing of the Nile, was called "Upper Egypt." For many centuries of antiquity the Egyptians were content to remain pretty much within their own borders, but, at the time the Hebrews were working their way into Palestine, that country was controlled by Egypt. Her grip was slipping, but there were three more times in the history of Israel, before the Romans came, when Egypt ruled the land of the Hebrews. However, the second of these times—the invasion of Shishak I after the death of Solomon—was little more than a plundering expedition. Time after time in the late years of the Hebrew monarchy, Israel counted upon the help of Egypt in revolting against the ruling power of Mesopotamia—but always in vain.

The People of Palestine

THE SEMITES

There are varying opinions as to the place of origin of the Semites. Many scholars think they came first from Arabia. One authority considered the northern part of the Tigris-Euphrates valley their original home. Another thought that they originated in the Sahara region of northern Africa. But whatever the location of their primary origin, all authorities seem agreed that they spent enough time in Arabia for us to consider that the source of their migrations. Probably because of fluctuations in the productivity of the land, great successive waves of these Semites were forced to migrate to other areas in search of food.[3]

THE AMORITES

One of the early series of migrations involved a Semitic people called "Amorites" who settled in many parts of the

---

3. For a condensed discussion see G. A. Barton, *Semitic and Hamitic Origins* (Philadelphia: University of Pennsylvania Press, 1934), pp. 1-11.

Near East. Mingling with the already mixed races of the lower Euphrates basin, they established the Kingdom of Mari and later the early Babylonian Empire with its great king Hammurabi. They probably spread also to the north, and they certainly covered most of Palestine, from the Plain of Esdraelon nearly to the borders of Egypt. In Old Testament references they are usually spoken of as belonging to the hill country, though some passages refer to them as being in the land east of the Jordan. It is probable that, in general, they occupied the Central Highlands, and absorbed some of the non-Semitic people who had been living there. In turn, they were later absorbed by the Hebrews.

THE ARAMEANS

The Arameans were a later migration of Semitic people. Originally nomadic, in some areas they became settled dwellers in the land, and mixed their blood with those who had been their predecessors. There was a great concentration of Arameans in the upper Euphrates valley, where they absorbed what was left of the ancient Hurrians. Later they extended southeast to the Persian Gulf, and in the west clear down to southern Palestine. The Canaanites and Phoenicians of Palestine were largely of Aramean origin, and there was quite a concentration of them northeast of Palestine, in the region around Damascus. They gave this country its name, "Aram," which is usually translated "Syria." The language of Aram, Aramaic, became the language of the Israelites in the late years of the pre-Christian era, though earlier their tongue had been more like that of the hill-country Amorites.

THE HEBREWS

Various records of ancient times speak of groups of "Habiri" or "Apiru," who seem to have been nomadic plunderers. The word may be related to a Hebrew verb which means "to cross over," i.e., to violate boundary lines. Probably people of various races were so described. However, there has been found a great collection of manuscripts called the "Amarna Letters," written by the governors or kings of certain Palestinian cities to their master, Pharoah Akhnaton (Amenophis IV) of Egypt. These letters, a number of which came from the king of Jerusalem, begged for military assistance against the "Apiru" who were plundering the land—probably the Hebrews coming into Palestine about the middle of the 14th century B.C. If the traditions are correct, certain other Hebrew tribes calling themselves "Sons of Israel" or "Israelites," presumably descended from Jacob-Israel, were already in Egypt, whither they had been led by one of Jacob's sons, Joseph. These Israelites, when they later made their exodus from Egypt, drew with them many Semites of different origin—most if not all of the group being serfs or slaves. Under the leadership of Moses, they became a more or less unified group during their wilderness wanderings. Entering Palestine they fought for the land, becoming amalgamated with other Hebrew tribes already there. However, the name "Hebrew" gradually dropped out of use, though it continues to this day to be used of the language of these people. The only Hebrews with whom we are concerned are the Israelites.

THE PHILISTINES

The only purely non-Semitic people in Palestine were the Philistines. They were a highly civilized people who had gone from Crete, scene of the earlier Minoan and Mycenian civilizations, to the eastern section of Lower Egypt. They then had worked their way north along the coast to the Plain of Philistia, arriving in Palestine about the same time as the Israelies. After the two peoples had settled down and had begun to expand, there was a great deal of conflict between them, especially during the early days of the Israelite monarchy. The Philistines gave their name to the land—"Palestine."

PART TWO

THE EARLY DAYS
OF ISRAEL

CHAPTER III

THE

ANCIENT TRADITIONS

Sources

SOURCES

The early narratives of the Old Testament, from the stories of the creation probably through the life of David, are recounted in four great historical records, which have been woven together in a most complicated manner. That is, almost any story in that part of the Bible can be identified as coming from one of these four accounts. On the other hand, there is no word from these accounts to be found any place today *except* in those early books, Genesis through 2 Samuel (but not including the Book of Ruth).

J HISTORY

The oldest of these strands is called the J history, or J code, because it is usually held to have been written in Judah, the Southern Kingdom of the Hebrew people, and because for God it uses the name "Jehovah." The Hebrew word for this is "Yahweh"—translated in the King James and in the Revised Standard Versions of our English Bible as "LORD," with all capital letters.[1]

Most scholars believe this J history was produced about 850 B.C. in or near Jerusalem, by one or more men who collected many poems, stories, and legends of the early days and worked them into a great history. It starts with the creation story in Genesis 2:4b, and shows the place of the Israelitish people against the background of what was considered world history.[2]

---

1. See Appendix, Note A.
2. Many maintain that it is possible to recognize two different elements in the J history, and label them J_1 and J_2. These two elements are so similar that, in a work like this, nothing is to be gained by separating them. The J history will be discussed as though it were a single unified strand.

31

E History

The next strand is called E, because it was almost certainly written in Ephraim, the most important tribe of the Northern Kingdom, and because in the earlier part it prefers the word "Elohim" for God. In its subject matter it does not go earlier than Abraham, the traditional ancestor of the Hebrews. After the introduction of that hero, the E history parallels the J history throughout, though there are many stories which appear in only one of these histories. E was written about 750 B.C., and then, after the fall of the Northern Kingdom in 722 B.C., was combined with J (probably about 700 B.C.).

JE History

This combined record is called the JE history. The original J and E writings were not preserved, after the combination had been effected. There was some editorial work done by the one who combined these narratives, but in a great many instances the two stories, differing slightly one from the other, were left as they had been found, to the confusion of modern readers. A clear example of this is the duplication of stories about Abraham (or Abram) introducing his wife as his sister in the J account (Genesis, chapter 12) and in the E account (Genesis, chapter 20). To make the matter yet more confusing, there is a third story in Gen. 26 which is closely related to the earlier two.

D History

There are two later strands which are also woven into the fabric of these early narratives. The first is the D history, written about 650 B.C., and found in the Book of Deuteronomy (whence its name). About 600 B.C., and again about 550 B.C., a group of "Deuteronomic" editorial writers revised a great deal of JE material in what we now know as the books of Joshua, Judges and 1 and 2 Samuel. Using some other source material, they wrote also 1 and 2 Kings and enlarged the Book of Deuteronomy. As shown in the next paragraph, Joshua had some further revision, but Deuteronomy, Judges, 1 and 2 Samuel and 1 and 2 Kings were left by these Deuteronomic editors practically as we know them today, the first historical books to be completed.

P HISTORY

The final strand is the P or Priestly History, written by a group of priests about 450 B.C. in Babylon, where their fore-fathers had been taken as captives in exile, one and a third centuries earlier. This history was written in dry legalistic language, showing interest in ritualistic matters, laws, and genealogies. It begins with the majestic account of the Creation in the first chapter of Genesis. About 400 B.C., also in Babylon, a writer from this same Priestly group of historians made the final revision of the JE and the first Priestly material. As the six books above had been revised by the editor of the Deuteronomistic school, they were not altered by this final Priestly editor; but Genesis, Exodus, Leviticus, Numbers, and Joshua were given their final revision. These five, with the first six, formed the first historical series, composed of the four great strands, J, E, D, and P, with the work of the editorial writers tying them together. It is easy to see why so many biblical stories appear in two, or sometimes in three, forms when we realize that they came from these different histories, originally independent of each other, but composed largely of the same subject matter, and eventually combined into the same books.[3]

---

3. There is another later series of historical writings: the books of 1 and 2 Chronicles, Ezra, and Nehemiah. Wherever there is a difference in the accounts, it is wise to follow the earlier series as the more accurate record. However, for the period between the close of the Exile in Babylon and the Greek period (538 B.C. to 332 B.C., the time of Persian supremacy) the later series is our only biblical historical writing.

CHAPTER IV

THE

ANCIENT TRADITIONS

Stories of Origins

THEORIES OF ORIGINS

Philosophy was not a forte of the ancient Hebrews. They had difficulty in dealing with abstract ideas, but they did attempt a kind of *a posteriori* or backward reasoning, from effect back to cause, and nowhere is it more in evidence than in their ideas of the origins of nations, tribes, professions, and so forth. For example, there were comparatively few blacksmiths in Israel. Almost every smith had learned his trade from his father, for the age-old guilds of craftsmen treasured their trade secrets, and a son not only made the best apprentice, being completely under his father's control, he was also the one the father most wanted to benefit by his precious knowledge. Since every smith thus seemed to come from a long line of metal-working ancestors, the ancient thinker bridged the gap at one leap, and assumed, very early in the history of mankind, a man named Tubal-Cain, the father of all smiths. If this were true of men of the forge, it must have been equally true of shepherds, musicians—of all professions of mankind (Genesis 4:19-22)—each profession having one man who originated it and passed it on to his descendants.

A parallel line of thought explained the relationships of men and tribes. Watching a family increase from one man and his wives to a complete community—something quite possible within two or three generations, where they had plural marriages and a prolific people—it is easy to see how some thinker pictured an entire nation as descended from one man—who usually was assigned the name of the nation as his own name. Likewise, the relationships of nations or groups one to another were described by the relationships of these original ancestors of the nations. For example, the Israelites thought themselves all descended from Jacob or Israel, and considered themselves racially akin to the people of Edom, descended from Esau or Edom, twin brother of Jacob.   (Genesis 25:19-34; 32:22-28.) Other stories show the old Hebrew conception of the division of mankind into races (Genesis 9:20-27), and eventually trace back to the original couple from whom these writers thought all mankind had descended: Adam, whose name means "ground," and Eve, whose name is akin to the word "life." (Genesis 3:20-21.)

LATE CREATION STORY

The Old Testament opens with one of the stories of creation, but it is the late, or Priestly account, not the early one.   It begins in Genesis 1:1 and continues through the middle of the fourth verse of chapter 2. This is the one place where the tremendous theme makes the dry style of the Priestly writer come alive, to create one of the most sublime chapters ever written.

The orderly account of creation by days indicates a keen methodical mind. It was probably considered the equivalent of a modern "scientific" account—but it is the magnificent picture of God as Creator which is of value to us today. "In the beginning God created the heavens and the earth" is a most comprehensive statement of faith, and it is equalled in religious value by the reiterated idea that, after each day's quota of creation, "God saw that it was good." Truly, to one who believes that God created the world and made it good, the order of events and the details of technique are of relatively small importance, over the elapsed eons of time.

This picture of the beginning of creation probably originated in the time of the overflow of the great river of Babylon—for we believe it was in that country that the account was first given. The mist made everything "without form and void," and, as day came, there was light. This light was not thought of as coming from the sun, as that was not considered as being made until the fourth day. This description of creation is sometimes called "Fiat" creation, for God is pictured as accomplishing it by word of command.

The events portrayed for the next day depended upon the clearing of the atmosphere so that blue sky appeared. "God said 'Let there be a firmament in the midst of the waters, and let it separate the waters from the waters.' " The "firmament" was the great arch of the heavens, which, like an inverted bowl, forced upward a part of the "waters," to keep them there until such time as God should "open the windows of the heavens" and let the rain descend. The events of the third day resulted from the waters receding, so that the dry land appeared, and the river resumed its normal bed. Then followed in orderly procession vegetation, the lights of heaven (to mark the divisions of time), creatures of the sea, birds, land beasts and creeping things, and finally man, both male and female, to have dominion over all else.

It was quite natural to think of God as being shaped like a man. Indeed, there are many today who have difficulty in outgrowing this primitive conception. If, then, the writer thought of man and God being of the same shape, and thought of God as creating man, he must inevitably have thought that he created man in his own image. But there are two ways in which we today can accept this marvelous expression into our own consciousness: God created man capable of choosing between right and wrong; and God, the Creator, made man capable of creating in his turn. Thus, although we cannot intelligently conceive of God as being physical in form (John 4:24 "God is Spirit"), we can think of man made in the spiritual image of God.

And after the labors of the six days, each lasting, as in Jewish reckoning today, from sunset to sunset, God rested on the seventh—the story of the origin of the Sabbath.

EARLY CREATION STORY

About four centuries before the account of creation just described was written, the J writer wrote the account which begins in Genesis 2:4b. To him the beginning of creation— the essence of all that was good, just as in the P account—was a garden, watered prodigally by four great rivers. The third and fourth of these were the Tigris and the Euphrates: we cannot determine which rivers the author had in mind when he described the first two.

The order and entire theme of this story are different from the other. The Lord God (Yahweh, in the Hebrew) made man, later named "Adam," out of the dust of the earth, probably by moistening it to make mud or clay. He then breathed his spirit into him and he became a living being.[1] Perhaps the finest religious idea we can get from this story is the conception that it is the presence of the Spirit of God in a man that gives him life. The Lord then made the garden, and put man in it for a gardener. Because man was lonesome, he then made the animals and birds to keep him company. But, after man had named them all (with Hebrew names, the writer seems to have believed), man was still unhappy. The Lord therefore caused him to fall asleep, and from one of his ribs created a woman for his wife, thus explaining the strong attachment of man to woman—they were once of the same flesh.

ORIGIN OF SIN

Most of the narrative material from this point on part way through the story of the flood is from the J account. The author wanted to show the origins of things, but, since the Lord was good, he did not attribute to him the origin of sin. The story of how it did begin, told in Genesis, chapter 3, is a marvelous accomplishment, for it answers a number of other questions as well. All told, the following explanations are given:

1. How sin came into the world
2. Why man hates a serpent
3. Why a serpent must travel upon its belly
4. Why man must work to earn a living
5. Why woman must suffer in childbirth
6. Why modesty requires the wearing of clothing

The primitive ideas of this writer are clearly revealed in the picture of the Lord coming to the earth to rebuke man and his wife, and also in the apparent fear the Lord had that man might become his equal. There were two trees by which he felt this might have been accomplished. Man had already eaten of

---

1. See Appendix, Note B.

the fruit of the tree of the knowledge of good and evil: if he were to go further, and to eat of the tree of life, he would live forever; so the Lord God drove him out of the garden. This attitude differs from the attitude attributed to Jesus of Nazareth when, for example, he offered "living water" which would well up to eternal life. (John 4:7-15.)

Near the end of this story we have introduced the name of the woman, "Eve," closely related to the word for life. The author portrays all mankind as descended from these two original parents.

Origin of Death

The stage had been set for the idea of death in the story of the Garden of Eden, with Adam and Eve driven out from its utopian precincts because of their sin, and kept from access to the tree of life. Yet here again, in Genesis, chapter 4, the J writer portrayed death as first coming not from the hand of the Lord, but from man. In the background of the story is the struggle between the growers of grain and the keepers of flocks. When the Hebrews came into Palestine after their nomadic pastoral existence under near-desert conditions, they knew nothing of agricultural methods. In their eagerness to learn the new technique of living, they absorbed many of the religious practices of the resident Canaanites, for worship and sacrifice were part of the formula for growing crops. For many centuries there was a struggle between those who adopted the Canaanitish religion, and religious leaders who wanted "to worship the Lord as their fathers had worshiped him in the desert." These reformers also opposed the process of agriculture, which was associated with Canaanitish religion—called the worship of Baal. It was such a reformer who wrote this story of Cain and Abel, with the sacrifice of the flock, which was though acceptable to the Lord, and the sacrifice of the grain, which was not. The very fact that Cain was older than Abel is proof that the writer considered the agricultural life in Palestine to have been of older tenure than the pastoral type.

One of the most vivid bits of writing in all this J history is the description of Cain's deed of violence against his brother and its consequences. The jealousy and sullen anger of the older man, after his sacrifice had been rejected and his brother's had been accepted, was followed by murder, and then, in answer to the LORD's question about his brother, the eternal query: "Am I my brother's keeper?"

When a man was slain in ancient Israel, and his blood was spilled upon the ground, they thought that the ground cried out for vengeance against the killer, and there was a curse both upon him and upon the near-of-kin of the slain man, until vengeance had been exacted. Instead of being a source of violence, this "blood feud" was really a deterrent, for responsible men kept their kinsmen from starting serious and costly quarrels. Forgetting that there was, according to his story, no one except Cain's father or mother to execute vengeance on Cain, the author described him as being terrified at his helpless situation. He pictured the LORD putting the "mark of Cain" upon him for his protection, saying that if anyone should slay Cain, vengeance would be taken upon him sevenfold. It may be that this story was suggested because there was a tribe named Cain which was so ferocious in its vengeance that it exacted not one life, but seven lives for one, and any person who saw the mark of the tribe on the forehead of a man was duly warned to make no trouble. (Genesis 4:1-16.)

ORIGIN OF PROFESSIONS

As already suggested, the Israelites thought that every profession could be traced back to one man, the common ancestor of all practicing that profession, who had first developed it. In Genesis, chapter 4, after the writer has ignored the fact that, according to his account, there were no women from whom Cain could have chosen his wife, he describes several of Cain's descendants who originated professions: Jabal, "the father of those who dwell in tents and have cattle"; Jubal, "the father of all those who play the lyre and pipe"; and Tubal-cain, "the forger of all instruments of bronze and iron."

Far older than the J history in which it has been incorporated is the song attributed to Lamech, the father of Tubal-cain. This song possibly represents the song of triumph uttered when the first Israelitish smith made his first sword:

> Lamech said to his wives:
> "Adah and Zillah, hear my voice;
>   you wives of Lamech, hearken to what I say:
> I have slain a man for wounding me,
>   a young man for striking me.
> If Cain is avenged sevenfold,
>   truly Lamech seventy-sevenfold."
> —Genesis 4:23-24

Many scholars believe these are the oldest words in the Old Testament.

THE FLOOD

In one sense the flood story does not belong with stories of origins. Yet the story of the division of mankind into races comes directly after the flood story, and concerns Noah. It is probably for this reason that the whole account was placed where it is.

Many different civilizations have stories of floods in their early traditions, but the Israelitish account seems to be based upon the traditions of Babylon. The best record we have is the story of the traveler-philosopher named Gilgamesh, who, in the course of his journeys, encountered a relative named Ut-napishtim, who had become immortal. When asked how he had achieved immortality, Ut-napishtim (the Babylonian counterpart of Noah) told a story very similar to the biblical flood story, explaining that immortality for himself and his wife was his reward. In many respects this story is extremely crude: there were many gods, rather than one; when the deluge started, the gods crouched in terror against the walls, like a group of dogs; and when the flood was over, and Ut-napishtim offered a sacrifice, they hovered above it like flies, because of its smell. Yet there are many items which show its relationship to the Ishraelitish account, such as the construction of the ark, the embarking of the animals, and the sending forth of the birds to see if the water had gone down. This record came from the library of the Assyrian king Asshurbanipal, in the seventh century B.C., but it had been copied from other records made many centuries earlier.

The Old Testament story of the flood extends from the middle of the sixth to the middle of the ninth chapters of Genesis, and both the J and the P writers are included in it. It was the peculiar genius of the writers of Israel that they could take the crude, polytheistic accounts of other peoples and rewrite them with the spiritual ideals these Old Testament stories show. Here there could be no quarrel among the gods, for there was only one God; the reason for the deluge was the sin of man, which was such a terrible disappointment to God; Noah was directed to build the ark because he had found favor in the eyes of God, and God wanted to save something from the debacle of mankind; and the bow of the covenant, the rainbow, terminated the story—the agreement of God that there would never again be such a curse.

ORIGIN OF RACES

Immediately following the flood story is the picture of the origin of what the J writer thought were the three races of mankind, the Semitic, Hamitic, and Japhetic, coming from the three sons of Noah: Shem, Ham, and Japheth. A very ancient poem—in existence before the J history, but included in it by the J writer—is found in Genesis 9:25-27. It explains why the Canaanitish people were servants of the Semitic and Japhetic people, by relating the story of Noah (here pictured as the first vinegrower) becoming drunk, after which one son, Ham, looked upon his nakedness. In order to reconcile the older poem, where the curse was upon Canaan, with the other account, which thought of Shem, Ham, and Japheth as the sons of Noah and, therefore, the only other men in the world, Canaan is pictured as having been the son of Ham.

ORIGIN OF LANGUAGES

It is quite evident that the J writer, who was responsible for the preservation of these origin stories, thought that the original language of mankind had been Hebrew. As late as the eleventh chapter of Genesis he stated that there was only one language in the whole earth; but in the story of creation Adam, who had a Hebrew name, had given all the animals their permanent names (Gen. 2:19f), ostensibly in Hebrew. To explain the appearance of different tongues, he told the story of the Tower of Babel in the first nine verses of Genesis, chapter 11.

The main part of Babylonia, in which the city of Babylon was located, was a flat lowland. The inhabitants thus did not have hills or "high places" on which they could erect their altars, close to the gods they assumed to be dwelling in the sky. They therefore built huge towers, or ziggurats in connection with their temples, putting their altars on top—probably the origin of our modern church steeples. The foundations of some of these towers are still in existence. It is easy to imagine that, some time in the distant past, Israelitish slaves were forced to work on such a structure, which, since it was being erected for a foreign god, would have been thought of as an attempted threat to the supremacy of the LORD of the Israelites. When an incompetent overseer, in panic because he was behind in his quota of work, began to speak rapidly to those who knew only a few words of his language, and to depend upon the lash rather than upon patient explanation, the confusion grew, and the work was hindered rather than accelerated. The arrival of new slaves of different languages compounded the turmoil, and, when some crisis prevented the completion of the project, the explanation that the LORD had confounded their language was eagerly accepted. The word "Babel" is the Hebrew word for "Babylon." It is here associated with the word "balal," which means "to cause confusion."

CHAPTER V

THE

ANCIENT TRADITIONS

The Patriarchs

It is important to remember that the Hebrews were originally a number of related tribes, operating more or less independently. A large part of what we know of their early days—especially their relationship to other peoples—must be gleaned from the ancient traditions of their forefathers or patriarchs. Of these, Abraham was thought of as the originator of the Hebrews, just as Adam was considered the one who began the human race.

ABRAHAM, GENESIS 11:26—25:11

The word "Abraham" appears in very ancient archaeological records, so there certainly was at least one man of that name. However, many of the actions and descriptions ascribed to that man must be considered as really referring to the Hebrews as a whole. The same is true of other early characters.

The Hebrews probably were a mixture of different peoples who had come from the lower and the upper Euphrates. Thus we have the story that Abraham's father started with him from Ur, in lower Babylonia, and traveled as far as Haran in Upper Babylonia (Genesis 11:31), whence Abraham later started a second migration. A shortage of pasture seems to have forced some of these Hebrew tribes to find food and fodder in Egypt— just as happened later in the Joseph story, and probably other times as well—so we have the story of Abraham's trip to the court of Pharaoh, where both men found themselves in love with Abraham's wife. (Genesis, chapter 12.)

The people of Moab and Ammon were thought of as closely related to each other, but distantly related and decidedly inferior to the Hebrews. We thus have the disgusting story of

Lot, Abraham's nephew, and his two unmarried daughters, resulting in the birth of Moab and Ben-Ammi—and the origin of the peoples of Moab and Ammon—who were both first cousins and brothers of each other, and grandnephews and great-grandnephews of Abraham, or the Hebrew people. (Genesis 19:30-38.) The traditional relationship of the Hebrews, descended from Abraham and Isaac, the son of his legal wife, to the Ishmaelites, is portrayed by the story of the birth of Ishmael to Hagar, Abraham's concubine. (Genesis, chapter 16.)

Isaac and Jacob were of course also forefathers, but Abraham was the first, hence, in the Hebrew mind, the greatest. He was the one who in their traditions had led the migration from the upper Euphrates to Palestine; the one who made the covenant of circumcision with God, whereby every Hebrew male was identified; the one whom God blessed with the promise that he should be the father of a multitude, and his seed should be given the land of Canaan for an everlasting possession. (Genesis, chapters 15 and 17.)

ISAAC, GENESIS 21:1—28:5; 35:27-29

The story of Isaac is overshadowed by the stories of his father and his son, Abraham and Jacob, with which it naturally is merged. Later generations emphasized the concern of God by describing an unusual birth story, occurring by the special dispensation of God, long after Sarah the wife of Abraham had passed the age of bearing children. The same technique was used to show God's concern in the birth of Jacob (Genesis 25:21f) and Joseph (Genesis 30:22) and many other of the great characters in the Old Testament.

The best-loved story of Isaac is the account of Abraham's willingness to offer him as a sacrifice to God. It is possible that in the dim past of the Hebrew people, it had been the custom to offer in such a manner the first-born male of each family, just as the first-born of the flock was sacrificed. (Exodus 13:1-2, 11-15; 22:29-30.) There is no proof that this human sacrifice was universally or even generally practiced during the times of biblical record, though the story of Jephthah in Judges, chapters 11 and 12 shows that it was not unknown. Also, the fact that the story was inserted to prove to the people that God did not demand such sacrifices is an indication that at least occasionally they were made. But the pathos of the great man of God, ready to give up the son for whom he had yearned so many years, and the poignancy of Isaac's question: "where is the lamb for a burnt offering?" make an indelible impression upon the reader. (Genesis 22:1-19.)

The Hebrew pride of race, which crops up time and again in the biblical narrative, is shown when Abraham sent back to his Aramean kinsman for a wife for his son Isaac, who was to be the one from whom the Hebrew line of descent was recorded (Genesis, chapter 24), just as Isaac later sent his son Jacob to the same place for the same purpose. (Genesis 28:1-3.) On arriving at his destination, the servant used a typical test to determine which was the correct girl for his master's son. He left the choice to God, asking that he would cause the proper maiden to offer water both to him and to his camels. By this gracious act, God was expected to reveal his choice. This process of interpreting the will of God by chance happenings was recorded over and over again in the Hebrew scriptures.

JACOB, GENESIS 25:19—35:29; 48;49

The story of Jacob also presents the relationship of the Hebrews to their neighbors in narrative form. Possibly the most insisent enemy of these people was the country of Edom. Bitterness existed from the earliest days. Edom would not let Moses lead the Israelites through their land on their way into Palestine (Numbers 20:14-21); the whole of the Book of Obadiah is a denunciation of Edom. Edom, or Esau, was portrayed as the twin brother of Jacob, whose other name was Israel. True to their national hatred, the historian depicts the traditional originators of the nations struggling before their birth in their mother's womb. The Edomites were in the land of Palestine before the Israelites—hence the first-born of the twins was Esau-Edom. But then how can it be explained why Israel was greater than Edom? By the story of Esau returning hungry from the chase, and selling his birthright to his younger brother for the pottage he was cooking. (Genesis 25:29-34.) There is also another completely independent story explaining the same thing. When Isaac was so old he could no longer see, he sent the older son, the hunter, to get venison for a stew, that he might eat it and then give him his blessing. During his absence, Jacob-Israel, with the help of their mother, presented their father with a stew made from a kid from their flocks. Fearing detection, he wore his brother's garments, and fastened the skins from the kids upon his hands and neck, for Esau-Edom was a hairy man. Feeble Isaac was uncertain about the voice, but the skins persuaded him to give Jacob the blessing, giving us an expression for deceit: "The hands of Esau." (Genesis, chapter 27.)

The Hebrews had an unusual delight in clever dealing, and took great pleasure in stories of their ancestors outwitting the ancestors of other peoples. Sometimes they even disregarded the truth, as when they told of Jacob lying to his father and claiming to be Esau. Most of the story of Jacob is along this vein. When his mother sent him to her homeland to get an Aramean wife, her brother Laban made him work seven years as a dowry for his daughter Rachel, whom Jacob loved, and then passed off her older sister Leah, keeping her identity hidden until the day after the marriage; Jacob then had to work another seven years to get the bride he wanted. When they were about to separate their flocks, they agreed that Jacob would take the spotted goats and black lambs, and Laban the others, and Laban again cheated by separating the spotted animals ahead of time, and sending them under his sons to a distant pasture. According to the story, however, Jacob came out on top by peeling part of the bark from fresh-cut branches and placing them before the sturdier females at the mating period, thus causing the better animals to give birth to spotted young—a process which has no biological backing, but which greatly appealed to the readers. (Genesis 29—31.)

This contest of cleverness continued when Jacob's family finally separated, and Rachel stole her father's household gods. When in his pursuit he overtook them, she put them in the saddle of a camel in her tent, and sat upon them, so he could

not find them. Here Rachel received the credit for the cleverness, for we are told that Jacob knew nothing of it. There is
also a wonderful slap at the foreign gods which had been stolen,
in the idea that a woman could sit upon them without injury
to herself. This delight in the cleverness of their forebears
continues through all their early literature. In fact, they were
so pleased with sharp dealing that they preserved the record
when the Hebrews were the butt of the joke, as in the story
of the men of Gibeon. (Joshua 9:3-27.)

A number of the sacred places of Palestine are associated
with incidents in the traditional life of Jacob. For example,
there was one ford which had probably been sacred centuries
before the time of the Hebrews. Possibly the rippling of the
water over stones had suggested the voice of a spirit, and then,
later, some unknown hero had tried to cross in high water and,
struggling against the pull of the current, had fallen, injuring
his hip. Years after the Hebrews, entering the land, had
adopted the sacred spot as their own, the story became associated with Jacob, the spirit became either God or his messenger, and the name "the face of God" or "Peniel." This is
one of the passages which gives the explanation for the double
name, "Jacob," and "Israel—the one who strives with God."
(Genesis 32:22-32.) Another sacred place, later associated with
Jacob, was the spot where he was said to have slept with his
head on a stone, dreaming of a ramp leading up to God. Upon
awakening, he poured oil upon it, and called it the "temple of
God," or "Bethel." It was for many centuries one of the great
religious centers of these people. (Genesis 28:10-22.) A third
well-known shrine was the pile of stones called "Mizpah,"
where Jacob and Laban settled finally their family quarrel.
(Genesis 31:43-55.)

To the Israelites, the most important feature of the story of
Jacob was the listing of the names of his sons. These Hebrews
were in their early history a group of nomadic tribes, each one
closely integrated within itself, each occupying a more or less
friendly relationship with each of the others. Just as we have
seen that the attitude of these people toward neighboring
countries—e.g., Moab, Ammon, Edom—was explained by

stories about the men who were the traditional ancestors of these countries, so we can determine the relationship of one of the Hebrew tribes to another by the stories told about the men who were supposed to have been their originators.

About a dozen of these Hebrew tribes were so closely related to each other, they assumed that the men who, according to their ideas, were the progenitors of the tribes must have been brothers. Hence the theory that Jacob or Israel had twelve sons, from each of whom was descended a tribe bearing his name. The name by which they most commonly called themselves was "Sons of Israel" or Israelites, from one of the names of Jacob-Israel. These tribes of Israel are sometimes divided for convenience into three groups: a. the "Rachel" tribes— Benjamin, the son of Rachel the beloved wife of Jacob, and Ephraim and Manasseh, sons of Joseph, and hence grandsons of Rachel; b. the "Leah" tribes—those sons of the unloved but legitimate wife Leah; and c. the "Concubine" tribes—the sons of the two concubines. It is easy to see that a large part of this history was preserved in the Rachel tribes, because they claim that their traditional ancestress was the "beloved" wife. The Concubine tribes were the ones which dwelt in the extreme north of Palestine, and hence were considered barely within the group of Israelites.

Centuries after the boundary lines of these tribes had become fixed, an editor collected a number of poetic descriptions of the personalities and locations of the individual tribes, and presented them as though Jacob, the father of the men who originated the tribes, had looked ahead through the years and predicted to his sons what the fate of each would be. This assembled poem—parts of which could not have been written until after David's dynasty had become thoroughly established on the throne—is called "The Blessing of Jacob." (Genesis, chapter 49.)

These tribes of Israel, who considered themselves all descended from the traditional twelve sons of Jacob or Israel, are the ones who became unified during the later years of the Judges, sufficiently to form the Kingdom of Israel, and produced the religion and literature which have so greatly blessed mankind.

JOSEPH, GENESIS, chapters 37; 39—48; 50

The story of Joseph is one of the most beloved of all stories. There are occasional places where there is a little confusion, due to the combination of two different stories—as in the early part where both Judah and the Midianites are pictured as selling Joseph to the Ishmaelites (Genesis 37:25-28), and all through the story where Reuben and Judah are not clearly separated. But, on the whole, the narrative runs in a straightforward manner.

Joseph, the first-born of the beloved wife Rachel, was greatly favored by his father Jacob, and was apparently quite ready to take full advantage of this position. Two of the dreams attributed to him in the early part of the story seem to have convinced him that not only his brothers, but even his father and mother were to bow down before him—the dreams of the sheaves of wheat and of the sun, moon, and stars. (Genesis 37:5-11.) This is a most unusual idea among Israelites.

Angered by this, his brothers were about to kill him, when Reuben (or perhaps Judah) intervened, and he was cast into a pit. Later they sold him as a slave to a band of nomad Ishmaelites, stained his long-sleeved robe—an envied gift of his father—in the blood of a goat, and took it home with them as an indication that he had been slain by wild beasts.

The second part of the story places him in the home of Potiphar, captain of the guard of Pharaoh, where, as elsewhere in the story, the LORD blessed with success everything he did, so that all household matters were left in his charge. During the absence of Potiphar, his wife persistently made advances to Joseph, which he just as persistently resisted, until her fondness turned to hatred and she accused him of the very thing he had refused to do.

Unjustly thrown into prison, Joseph interpreted the dreams of two fellow prisoners, and two years later one of them, by then restored to his position as Pharaoh's cupbearer, recalled Joseph's accuracy, and recommended him as an interpreter of dreams to Pharaoh. The two dreams for which he was summoned were the seven fat cattle eaten by the seven lean ones, and the seven good ears of grain eaten by the seven poor ones. When

Joseph's interpretation convinced Pharaoh that there would be seven years of plenty followed by seven of famine, he was appointed premier of the country, with power to administer the food program. Once again the blessing of the LORD was thought to have been upon Joseph, who handled the exchange of food from the storehouses with such sharpness that, before the end of the famine, he had bought for food all the land of the Egyptian landowners, and secured it for the throne, selling an entire nation into serfdom.

At the zenith of Joseph's power, the famine in Palestine forced Jacob to send his sons—all except Benjamin—to Egypt for food. All the drama of the wronged brother Joseph, now in the seat of power but unrecognized, is present here. First he accused them of being spies, understanding their conversation when they did not think it possible. Then he retained one as hostage and sent the others back to their father, their sacks filled with grain and their money hidden in it, with orders to return bringing their youngest brother, of whom they had told him. When the pressure of hunger finally overcame Jacob's reluctance to part with Benjamin, they returned again with their original purchase money, additional funds for the new grain, and extra gifts. Once again there is some confusion in the narrative as to whether Judah or Reuben was personally responsible for Benjamin's safe return.

This time there was a banquet for the visiting sons of Israel, and Joseph with difficulty concealed his emotions. When the time for departure arrived, the sacks were again filled, and once more the money was hidden in them, but this time Joseph's divining cup was also placed in the sack of Benjamin. The departing Israelites were overtaken and searched by Joseph's men, who returned them to Joseph. He said they were all free to go back to Palestine except Benjamin, in whose bag the cup had been found; he was to be Joseph's slave. When Judah described his father and the probable results of his bereavement of Benjamin, the only remaining son of his favorite wife Rachel, Joseph could no longer contain his emotion and revealed himself to his brothers. Jacob and all his possessions were brought to Egypt, and the entire family, with the approval of Pharaoh, settled in that part of the country east of Lower

Egypt called Goshen, where they remained until the time of the Exodus.

Although the socio-economic ideals of this story would not be acceptable today, the sturdy integrity of the hero, coupled with his forgiving nature; the magnificent speech of Judah (Genesis 44:18-34); the portrayal of the overlying care of God; and the wonderfully vivid development of the personalities and plot make it one of the great stories of the literature of the world.

THE TIME OF THE PATRIARCHS

The four great literary personalities described above dominate the Book of Genesis, from the story of the flood in the eleventh chapter to the close of the book. They give us neither exact history, nor, in a true sense, biography; but they do show us much about the early days of Israel. The stories of Abram-Abraham tell of the two sources of the Hebrew tribes; the early migration into Palestine; the seminomadic type of living; the general tendency to locate in the hilly central section of the country. (Genesis, chapter 13.) Though most of the story of Isaac is included in the accounts of his father and sons, he does figure very largely in the illuminating story of his father's willingness to sacrifice him, possibly a landmark in the transition of the religion of the Hebrew people. The stories of Jacob-Israel tell us more of the relationship of these people to neighboring tribes, identify many of the sacred places, show us some of the characteristics greatly admired, and draw more definitely the lines of the tribes thought of as belonging to the group with whom we are concerned—those who considered themselves as descended from the sons of Jacob or Israel. The Joseph story presents the first co-ordinated literary effort, in which an over-all plot organizes the incidents into a connected whole. There certainly were Joseph tribes—possibly originally one Joseph tribe which split into the Ephraim and Manasseh tribes. The story also forms a connecting link to explain how the Israelites got into Egypt. It sets the stage for a new movement and a new actor—one of the greatest in the melodrama of mankind.

CHAPTER VI

THE

ANCIENT TRADITIONS

Moses and the Exodus

INTRODUCTION TO MOSES, EXODUS, chapters 1—2

As when the great peak of a mountain range first appears, rising out of the mist—partly with sharp delineation, partly with shadowy outline—so the figure of Moses appears in the history of Israel. In Egypt a new king had arisen "who did not know Joseph," and as a result, one of the earliest accounts of Hebrew persecution is given. The destruction of the newly born boys was, according to the story, because of the Egyptian fear of a strong group of unassimilated foreigners in their midst. The beloved story of Moses in the bulrushes particularly pleased the sense of humor of the Israelites: the daughter of Pharaoh paying Moses' mother for nursing her own child, and his education at the court of Pharaoh in preparation for his later efforts to free his people from their Egyptian bondage. Moses' intense nationalism is portrayed in the story of his murder of the Egyptian who was oppressing an Israelite, with the consequent necessity that he leave the country.

MOSES AND THE LORD, EXODUS, chapters 3—6

There are some who think the sojourn of Moses with Jethro in the land of Midian was the most important single incident in the history of Israel. The account is confusing, because of repetition due to the different sources. For example, there are three different names for Moses' father-in-law: "Jethro," Exodus 3:1; "Reuel," Exodus 2:18; and "Hobab," Judges 4:11, though in one of the two places in which Hobab appears, Reuel is called the father of Hobab. (Numbers 10:29.) The

52

particular name used is of little consequence, but it is important to remember that:

   a. Jethro was a *priest* in the land of Midian
   b. Moses accepted Jethro's counsel, even after becoming the recognized leader of Israel (Exodus 18: 13-27)
   c. It was while Moses was away from his own people, working for Jethro, that he had his great vision of God, and was persuaded that the LORD would help him lead the Israelites from Egypt (Exodus, chapter 3)

The story of this vision of Moses is that he was tending sheep on the mountain of God, here called "Horeb," but frequently, as in Exodus, chapter 19, "Sinai." Attracted by the sight of a burning bush which showed no sign of being consumed, Moses turned to investigate, and heard the voice of God, which commissioned him to liberate the Israelites in Egypt, and told him his name.

THE NAME OF THE LORD, EXODUS, chapter 3; 6:1-4

When Moses asked what his reply should be if the Israelites inquired as to the name of the God of their fathers (Exodus 3:13-15), he was told to tell them: "I AM WHO I AM (or WHAT I WILL BE) . . . The LORD, the God of your fathers . . . this is my name for ever. . . ." In the Hebrew, the word translated LORD is YHWH,[1] probably originally pronounced Yahweh. It is a personal name for a particular god, the God of the Israelites —just as Zeus is a personal name for a particular Greek god. There is another Hebrew word, "Elohim" (closely related to "El"), which is often used for the God of Israel (for example, in the E history). It may also refer to one or more gods of other peoples. It is not a *name* for any god, and is always translated "god," though sometimes in the plural form.

In Exodus 6:2, Moses is told: "I appeared to Abraham, to Isaac, and to Jacob, as God Almighty, but by my name the LORD [Yahweh] I did not make myself known to them." Moses, while under the jurisdiction of his father-in-law Jethro, a priest

---

1. See Appendix, Note A.

of Midian, thus had a vision of a God which was so startling
and new that he felt he could not even be identified by the
same name his ancestors had used for God; i.e., that he was a
completely different God, whose name was "Yahweh" or "the
LORD." It was this new God, introduced to Moses by Jethro,
who persuaded him to return to Egypt, and, by his help, to seek
to free the Israelites from their bondage.

THE PLAGUES AND THE EXODUS, EXODUS, chapters 5, 7—14

The magnificent narrative of the release of the Israelites from
the bondage of Egypt has been beautifully embroidered by the
traditions of many later generations. It starts with the record
of a great man who was not afraid to stand before a monarch
and to demand the freedom of his people. The magic which
adorns the story is typical of Oriental tradition—changing a
rod into a serpent, and back again into a rod. The power to
accomplish this was possessed equally by Aaron, brother of
Moses, and by the magicians of Pharaoh, except that, true to
the nationalistic pride of the narrator, Aaron's rod devoured
the rods of the Egyptian magicians. Similarly, the first plague
of blood in the Nile (possibly some unusual organic growth
occurring at low water) was accredited to the Egyptian magicians (Exodus 7:22) as well as to Moses.[2]

It is easy to believe that, over a period of many years, each
of the plagues actually occurred to the Egyptians, and the
stories eventually became associated with the Hebrew account
of the Exodus. For example, the natural enemies of the tad-
poles may have had one bad year, which threw the biological
balance out of kilter so that there were many more frogs than
usual—some of them even entering the houses and becoming
nuisances there. Likewise, one year the gnats may have been
unusually bad; one year there was a disease of the cattle, etc.
Looking back over the records, the Hebrew narrators readily
believed that these plagues had been sent by this new God,
Yahweh, who had brought them out of Egypt.

Even the terrible epidemic which killed so many Egyptian
children (the first-born, as the prospective heads of families,

---

2. See also Exodus 8:7.

would have been more deeply mourned, so attention would have been focused upon them) may have missed the Israelites, for they were probably in Goshen, east of the Delta of Lower Egypt, and not in the valley of the Nile. The traditions of that night, with the sacrifice of the lamb, the sprinkling of its blood on the lintels and doorposts of the Israelitish houses so that the LORD might identify them, and the death of the Egyptian first-born, resulted in the great annual feast of the Passover, observed by Jews to this day.

Shortly after leaving Egypt, the Hebrews were pursued by the army of Pharaoh, and found themselves caught in a cul-de-sac at the edge of the Sea of Reeds (sometimes incorrectly identified with the Red Sea). The original account describes their deliverance as the result of a strong east wind, which the LORD caused to blow all night, driving the water back so they could cross. A later writer so enlarged this that the waters formed a wall on the right hand and on the left, which is the picture most people have retained to the present time. The destruction of the following Egyptian army was celebrated by two great poems: the earlier one, quite possibly composed by Miriam, the sister of Moses, is found in Exodus 15:21; the later one, which also incorporates the short two lines of Miriam's song, quite clearly is to be dated at least two centuries later, after the Israelites had overcome the people of Philistia, Edom, and Moab. (Exodus 15:1-18.)

THE COVENANT OF SINAI, EXODUS, chapters 19—20

The great desire of Moses, after the Exodus, seems to have been to make secure and permanent the relationship of the Israelites with the LORD, Yahweh. The period of testing was over. The LORD had indeed freed Israel and delivered the people from bondage. Now the welfare of the group required that the bond be made permanent. The people as a whole seem to have held this attitude also, but they were not made of as stern stuff as their leader. They were not an united people, and they had just been released from slavery. When food was lacking, they longed for "the fleshpots of Egypt" (Exodus 16:3), and grumbled frequently. Nevertheless, they followed their leader to Mount Sinai (Horeb), where the LORD had promised that Moses would serve him. (Exodus 3:12.)

Jeremiah tells us (Jeremiah 34:18ff) that when a covenant was made ("cut" is the word used), the sacrificial animal was divided into two parts. Those cutting the covenant then made their agreement, after which they walked between the severed parts of the animal, which were offered as a burnt offering. This was supposed to make the agreement irrevocable. This was almost certainly the procedure at the time of the great covenant between the LORD Yahweh and the people of Israel at Mount Sinai. The Israelites, either in mass or as represented by their leaders Moses and Aaron, walked between the divided parts of the animal, while the LORD, possibly represented by the ark of the covenant[3] as carried by the priests, signified his agreement to the pact.

The important feature is the fact that this was a contract entered upon with free will by both parties Israel and the LORD. In the first place, the LORD had chosen Israel when, from the burning bush on Mount Sinai, he had agreed to lead the people from bondage in Egypt. Having proved his power and his concern by accomplishing that deed, he was now willing to covenant with them that he would be their God and protect them. Israel's contract was to worship him alone and to obey his law. If the Israelites failed in this agreement, they might lose the protection of their powerful God—hence the constant self-examination to make certain their obedience. Of all the people of antiquity there were none who were so conscious of right and wrong as were these Israelites. It is no wonder that, even to this day, they consider themselves the people of a covenant. One of the greatest contributions to mankind is the so-called Ethical Decalogue associated with this covenant:

"I am the LORD your God . . .
"You shall have no other gods before me.
"You shall not make yourself a graven image . . .
"You shall not take the name of the LORD your God
    in vain . . .
"Remember the sabbath day to keep it holy . . .

---

3. See below, page 58; see also Genesis 15:12-21.

"Honor your father and your mother . . .
"You shall not kill.
"You shall not commit adultery.
"You shall not steal.
"You shall not bear false witness . . .
"You shall not covet . . ."[4]

THE TABERNACLE AND THE ARK, EXODUS, chapters 25—31;
35—40

The latter part of the Book of Exodus contains an elaborate description of the tabernacle, or tent of meeting, and its furnishings. Probably the years intervening between the time of Moses and the writing of the account tended to add glamor to the specifications. Certain it is, however, that there was some form of portable sanctuary used by the Israelites before they were able to erect a permanent place of worship at Shiloh, and it seems to have been a tent.

The most important of the furnishings was the ark. This is not to be confused with the ark of Noah, which is a translation of a different Hebrew word meaning "ship." This word, in the Hebrew, means "chest." It is described in detail in Exodus, chapter 25, beginning with the tenth verse. Made of acacia wood and overlaid with gold, it was supposed to contain the tables of stone or the "testimony" of the LORD. It was frequently called the "ark of the testimony," and occasionally (e.g., Numbers 10:33) the "ark of the covenant." It was quite in keeping with the customs of ancient nations that a contract with a god should have been engraved on stone and preserved at a sanctuary.[5]

On top of the ark were the cherubim which guarded the "mercy seat." They were winged bulls, possibly with the faces of men, and were another evidence of the influence of ancient Mesopotamia upon the Israelitish people. The top of the ark was the mercy seat, where the LORD was to meet with the people, or at least with Moses. (Exodus 25:22.) In other words, the ark was the visible symbol of the presence of the

4. For a further discussion of the covenant in ancient Israel, see Appendix, Note C.
5. George E. Mendenhall, *Law and Covenant in Israel and the Ancient Near East* (Pittsburgh: Biblical Colloquium, 1955), pp. 38f. See also Deuteronomy 10:1-5.

Lord. When they went into battle they carried the ark with them, and Moses said:

"Arise, O Lord, and let thy enemies be scattered; and let them that hate thee flee before thee."

On its return, he said:

"Return, O Lord, to the ten thousand thousands of Israel."
—Numbers 10:35f.

These two phrases are among the very early compositions of Israel. It is probable that this mysterious chest, so sacred that even the priests dared not touch it except with long poles, struck fear to the hearts of the enemies, and greatly aided Israel in battle—at least until they encountered the Philistines, who promptly captured the ark. (1 Samuel 4f.)

We are not certain as to the time the ark was constructed. If it was finished at the time the covenant between the Lord and Israel was "cut" on Mount Sinai, it was probably carried between the separated parts of the sacrifice to symbolize the Lord's participation in the agreement. If it had not been completed by that time, probably some other symbol of the presence of the Lord was used—possibly something which would produce the smoke and fire so often associated with his appearance. (Exodus 40:38.)

TRADITIONS OF THE WILDERNESS, EXODUS, chapters 16—18; NUMBERS, chapters 11—14; 16; 17; 21—24

The tremendous figure of Moses is the personality about whom practically all of the Israelite traditions of the wilderness wanderings gathered. As would be expected, in their transmission (for centuries by word of mouth) they have been enlarged to show the miraculous powers which were thought bestowed by the Lord upon his great servant.

In the Book of Exodus, the incidents which stand out and have become part of world literature, between the crossing of the Sea of Reeds and the Covenant on Sinai, are the following:

a. The giving by the Lord of manna, for bread, and of quails for meat for the Israelites in the wilderness.

Only sufficient manna for one day could be gathered at a time, except on the day before the sabbath, when a double portion could be collected without spoilage. (Exodus, chapter 16, repeated in Numbers, chapter 11.)

b. Moses striking the rock to produce water. (Exodus 17:1-7, repeated in Numbers 20:1-13. It is from this passage in Numbers that the idea is derived that Moses was guilty of presumption in ordering the water in his own name, rather than in the name of the LORD, and therefore was not permitted to enter the Promised Land.)

c. The war with Amalek (Exodus 17:8-16), where Joshua did the fighting and Moses, on the hilltop, held his rod in his raised hand, so that Israel would prevail. When weariness overtook him, Aaron and Hur held his hands up until sundown, and the people of Amalek were annihilated, giving origin to the expression "uphold the hands of Moses."

d. The advice of Jethro, father-in-law of Moses (Exodus, chapter 18), in accordance with which Moses organized the Israelites in groups of a thousand each, with each thousand subdivided into hundreds and again into tens, each with a ruler or arbiter, so that Moses' burdens would be carried by subordinates, and only the decisions they were incapable of rendering would be referred to him. Those he could not settle would be referred to the LORD. His ready acceptance of this suggestion shows the extent to which he was influenced by this priest of Midian, who had at an earlier date helped introduce him to the LORD, Yahweh.

Well-known traditions from the wilderness account in the Book of Numbers are as follows:

a. The insubordination of Miriam and Aaron to their brother Moses, and the consequent punishment of

Miriam by the temporary affliction of leprosy.
(Numbers, chapter 12.)

b. The sending of the spies into the land of Canaan—
one from each tribe—only two of whom, Joshua and
Caleb, brought back the report that, with the LORD's
help, the Israelites could conquer the land. (Numbers, chapters 13—14.) Because the people urged
that these two be stoned, the LORD decreed that no
adults except Joshua and Caleb should live to enter
Canaan.

c. The insubordination of Korah, Dathan, and Abiram (Numbers, chapter 16; 26:9-11), resulting in
the burial alive of the three men and their families, and the destruction by fire of 250 followers of
Korah. The mingling of two separate accounts here
makes the record quite confusing. When the congregation of Israel murmured again against Moses because of his harsh measures, 14,700 more were stricken
by the plague.

d. To show which tribe would have religious leadership, the LORD directed that one leader from each
tribe should put his name upon his rod, and place it in
the tent of meeting, to see which one the LORD would
cause to bud. The next day the rod of Aaron had not
only sprouted buds, but was bearing ripe almonds, thus
indicating that the LORD had chosen his tribe, Levi, to
minister to him. It was ordered that "Aaron's rod
budded" should be placed as a perpetual memorial in
the tabernacle *before* the ark of the testimony, that
there should be no more murmuring against the tribe
of Levi (Numbers, chapter 17), not, as in the New
Testament, *within* the ark of the testimony. (Hebrews 9:4.)

e. Another time, when the Israelites complained about
the leadership of Moses—and, behind Moses, the leadership of the LORD—we are told that fiery serpents
were sent to bite the people so that many of them died.

When they appealed to Moses and he prayed to the LORD, he was told to make a fiery serpent and to put it on a pole. If anyone who had been bitten looked upon this bronze serpent made by Moses, his life was saved. It is probable that we have here a record of some prehistoric serpent worship, adopted possibly from Egypt in the distant past, but with the record made over to conform to the worship of the LORD, which was in effect at the time the present account was written. (Numbers 21:4-9.)

f. A group of ancient poems about the military success of Israel is found in the blessing or curse of Balaam in Numbers, chapters 22—24. Balak, king of Moab, feared the Israelites, and arranged what he considered the most certain means to protect his people from them—he hired a man, Balaam, who had a reputation for being able to pronounce a curse which would be effective. The part of the story best known is the argument of Balaam with his ass, which could see what Balaam could not see: the angel of the LORD sent to tell Balaam not to curse any whom God did not want cursed. The important feature of the story is the idea that Balaam, following the will of the LORD, pronounced a blessing on Israel (that is, a curse upon the enemies of Israel, most important of which was Moab), although he had been paid to do the opposite, and, once the curse or blessing had been pronounced, nothing could change it. This passage is made up of a number of parts, the poems of blessing probably being much older than the story of Balaam, which was woven about them. The incident is narrated before the story of the commissioning of Joshua (Numbers 27:15-23), but the name of Moses is not mentioned by Balaam, in connection with it.

THE MAN BEHIND THE TRADITIONS

Coming out of the distant past, the story of Moses was, as we have said, embroidered by incidents of magic and supernatural accounts, to illustrate the power the LORD was supposed to have conferred upon his servant. Far more difficult to separate than the actual occurrences and the accounts of them, however, are the laws given by Moses and the laws attributed to him. There is no question but what Moses is one of the great lawgivers of history, but eventually it became the custom to attribute almost any body of laws of unknown origin to this man of God. Both the D and the P histories mentioned above add great blocks of legal material—the former found largely in the Book of Deuteronomy, the latter principally in Exodus, Leviticus, and Numbers. In fact, there are still many people who believe that all of the first five books of the Bible—Genesis, Exodus, Leviticus, Numbers, and Deuteronomy—were written by Moses himself. What then shall we accept of these sometimes difficult and often conflicting accounts?

It is not necessary to think that Moses, in the thirteenth century B.C., gave massive bodies of legislation, suitable for a settled agricultural community, to a group of nomadic herdsmen, in order for us to accept him as one who brought important laws of God to a people who were to bless mankind. Neither is it necessary to hold that Moses, by the power of God, caused the earth to open and to swallow the families of Korah, Dathan, and Abiram who challenged his authority, and fire to consume the 250 who were party to the conspiracy, in order to see in this stalwart hero one of the great leaders of all time.

Here was a man who, serving as a shepherd for a priest of Midian (his father-in-law Jethro), received a vision of God so startlingly different from anything he or his people Israel had ever known, that he thought of him as being different even in name. Probably under the counsel of Jethro he was convinced that the new God could deliver his people from Egypt. With unbelievable courage he faced the authorities and led his people to freedom. When they were free of pursuit, he conducted them to the place where he had first seen the LORD in a burning bush, and there engineered a covenant, binding his people by laws which bound the individual tribes to each other, as well as to the LORD. With military skill, the power of patience, almost unparalleled religious genius and a dogged persistence, he led these frequently unworthy people through one hardship after another till at last he could see the Promised Land he was not permitted to enter—turning the leadership over to another great leader. Over the hills and down through the centuries reverberates that mighty voice, telling mankind what was revealed to him on the holy mountain: "I am the Lord thy God. . . ."

CHAPTER VII

THE SETTLEMENT OF

PALESTINE

The Story According to Joshua

THE BOOK OF JOSHUA

All four of the great narrative strands we have discussed are found mingled in the Book of Joshua. The first twelve chapters, consisting largely of stories of the conquest of Canaan, are probably a result of the JE combination, with a rather thorough rewriting by the Deuteronomic editors. One of the principal characteristics of these revisers, which shows up in all the rest of the first historical series—Judges, 1 and 2 Samuel, 1 and 2 Kings, but most markedly in Judges—is a tendency to moralize about history. When the Israelites were victorious, it was because the LORD had given them the victory, and he had done so because they had been obedient to him. When they were defeated in battle, it was because of their sin, usually the worshiping of false gods.

Chapters 13—24, containing chiefly the acount of the division of Palestine among the various tribes of Israel, are ascribed by most people to the Priestly writer, who was always concerned with such matters as genealogies and boundary lines.[1]

JOSHUA AND JUDGES

Although they both deal with the settlement of Canaan, and seem to have some of the same general source materials, the Books of Joshua and Judges have markedly different viewpoints as to what transpired. Joshua describes an invasion of the land by the united Israelites, under the leadership of the one man, in a campaign which was completely successful within a relatively short time, and resulted in the annihilation of most of the in-

---

1. Following a German scholar, Martin Noth, there are now some who believe this latter part of Joshua, as well as the first part, is chiefly the work of the Deuteronomic writer.

habitants and the division of the land among the tribes. The Book of Judges, on the other hand, depicts the experiences of individual tribes or of small groups of tribes—sometimes quite successful; sometimes completely unsuccessful. Also, there is less of continuity in the narrative. The account seems to be a series of separate stories tied together by the Deuteronomic (moralistic) editor. Most likely we shall be correct in assuming that Joshua describes phases of the initial impact of these terrible fighters, while Judges portrays the "mopping-up" process, which continued over many years.

CROSSING THE JORDAN, JOSHUA, chapters 3—4

It is probable that a number of the tribes of Israel were already in Palestine before the events pictured in the early part of the Book of Joshua, but their traditions hold otherwise. They relate that the group of tribes seeking to enter Palestine traveled far to the south, around the boundary of Edom (Numbers 21:4), and north again on the east side of the Dead Sea and the Jordan River. At their request, Moses gave to the tribes of Gad and Reuben, and to one-half the tribe of Manasseh, land on the east of Jordan, the recently conquered territory of Kings Og and Sihon, with the understanding that they would help the other Israelites conquer the territory to the west. (Numbers, chapter 32.) There, at Mount Nebo, Moses before his death was permitted to look across the Jordan to the Promised Land, after which Joshua assumed command. (Deuteronomy, chapter 34.)

There was apparently some stoppage of the flow of the Jordan just at the time the Israelites were about to cross from the east to the west side. Possibly it was accomplished by an earthquake. It may even be that the walls of Jericho were destroyed by the same catastrophe, or one related to it. Whatever the cause, the credit was given to the LORD in both instances. Two different stories describe the erection of a monument of stones to memorialize the crossing, one placing it in the bed of the river, the other at Gilgal, the first camping place after the crossing. It is frequently said that the actual history of the Hebrew people or Israelites begins with the crossing of the Jordan River.

THE FALL OF JERICHO, JOSHUA, chapters 2, 6

The first important city confronting the Israelites as they crossed the Jordan was Jericho. In accordance with the custom, Joshua had sent spies on ahead while the main body was still on the east side of the river. Finding refuge—and probably information—at the home of Rahab the harlot, they discovered that she was terrified at the military prowess and ferocity of the Israelites, giving credit, of course, to their God. The destruction of Sihon and Og was particularly mentioned. Very likely the rest of the city shared her fear. Making a deal with the spies, she hid them on her roof when the king's officers searched for them, and they agreed that she and her family would be saved if the city was captured.

Although Rahab is listed in the great chapter on heroes of the faith (Hebrews, Chapter 11), there is little in the story to command our admiration for her: her profession, her willingness to trade the safety of her city for her own safety, even her care for her own family was a selfish concern, for a family was a unit, and the salvation or destruction of one member meant the salvation or destruction of all, as we shall see a little later in the story of Achan.

Archaeological investigations show the complete destruction of Jericho by fire, though it is as yet difficult to pinpoint the exact date. The use of the figure seven—one trip around the city each day for six days, then seven trips on the seventh day— was in accordance with Semitic superstition, and probably had a terrifying effect upon the people of Jericho, as well as a reassuring result for the Israelites. Seven appears as a sacred number innumerable times throughout the Bible: e.g., seven days for creation; seven clean animals in the ark; seven years of famine in the Joseph story; the Sabbath on the seventh day; the seven lamps on the lamp-stand of Zechariah; and almost all of the latter part of the Book of Revelation.

After the burning of the city the contents were "devoted," or destroyed in the name of the LORD. Rahab and her family were saved according to the agreement, vessels of bronze and iron and all silver and gold were presumably put into the treasury of the LORD, and everything else, including men, women and children, was destroyed.

FALL OF AI, JOSHUA, chapters 7—8

The next city in the line of march was Ai. The men sent to spy out the city reported that all the Israelites were not needed to effect its capture. Consequently, a part of the men attacked Ai in a spirit of overconfidence, and were thoroughly defeated, about thirty-six being slain.

The Israelites had some method of casting lots, called "inquiring of the LORD." One interesting account of this process is the description later of Saul trying to find whether guilt was upon his house or upon the people of Israel:

> Therefore Saul said, "O LORD God of Israel, why hast thou not answered thy servant this day? If this guilt is in me or in Jonathan my son, O LORD, God of Israel, give Urim; but if this guilt is in thy people Israel, give Thummim." And Jonathan and Saul were taken, but the people escaped. (1 Samuel 14:41.)

There are still many people today who feel that they can determine the will of the LORD by the use of chance—the opening of the Bible to a chance reference, for example.

When Joshua inquired of the LORD after the defeat by the men of Ai, he was told the Israelites had stolen some of the "devoted things" from the city. Then came the elimination process, where the guilt was finally assigned to Achan, and he and his family were stoned to death. By that means, the guilt was removed from Israel, and probably every member of the congregation was expected to throw a stone so that all would have a hand in the cleansing of the people. The solidarity of the family—the guilt of the father requiring the punishment of all—is well illustrated by this incident. It is quite possible that, had the lot fallen on a man other than Achan, the same kind of stolen material would have been found buried within his tent. The Israelites may even have recognized this, and figured that, by the casting of lots, the LORD had designated the particular man he wanted punished.

After the sin had been removed from Israel, the entire army was taken for the second attack, and a clever ambush prepared, so that the city was captured without difficulty and burned. The Israelites were permitted to keep plunder from Ai.

THE COVENANT WITH GIBEON, JOSHUA, chapters 9—10

The fear of the Israelites spread among the neighboring cities, and persuaded the men of Gibeon to seek safety in intrigue rather than in battle. Wearing worn-out clothes and carrying moldy provisions, they rode their asses into the Israelite camp at Gilgal and claimed to be emissaries from a distant but very strong country, with authority to make a covenant with the Israelites. Only after the covenant had been effected did Joshua find that their city was only a few miles from Ai—and by that time it was too late. There are two interesting examples of "face-saving" in the story. To protect the prestige of the God of Israel, we are told that the treaty was made without bringing the matter before him. Also, a later writer points out that, in spite of the treaty, the Gibeonites became slaves of the Israelites. Whether or not it involved servitude, this irrevocable covenant protected the Gibeonites for many years. After it had eventually been broken by King Saul, the penalty was the death of seven of his sons, although this was not exacted until after the death of the king. (2 Samuel 21:1-14.)

After the treaty had been concluded, five Amorite kings, led by the king of Jerusalem, attacked Gibeon. In response to a plea for help, Joshua brought his army by a forced march from the camp at Gilgal, and, with the aid of a great hailstorm, won a tremendous victory. Sometime after the battle, but still in very ancient times, an exultant poet wrote, in figurative language, of Joshua's plea for more time to destroy the enemy:

"Sun, stand thou still at Gibeon,
and thou Moon in the valley of Aijalon."
And the sun stood still, and the moon stayed
until the nation took vengeance on their enemies.
Is this not written in the Book of Jashar?
—Joshua 10:12f.

This poem was incorporated in an ancient book of poems called "The Book of Jashar" (Jashar means "the Upright") from which it was copied into the Book of Joshua. Some later writer interpreted it without imagination, and solemnly asserted that there never was another day like that, for the sun did not hurry to go down for a whole day. Later, the five enemy kings were captured and hanged.

DIVISION OF THE LAND, JOSHUA, chapters 13—24

After the destruction of the coalition against Gibeon, there follow two and a half chapters about other conquests of Joshua, including the statement (Joshua 11:16-23) that the whole land was taken, except for some of the cities of the Philistines. The final twelve chapters give in some detail the assignment of territory to the individual tribes of Israel. These chapters were written after the tribes had occupied those specific areas for many years.

THE SANCTUARY AT SHILOH

Throughout the Books of Joshua, Judges, and 1 Samuel there are intermittent references to Shiloh, where the tabernacle was set up after the wilderness and the land was divided among the tribes (Joshua, chapters 18-22), and where the virgins of Jabesh-Gilead were awarded to the tribe of Benjamin. (Jude, chapter 21.) The historical importance of the city is reflected in the fact that two centuries later, it was to Shiloh that Jeroboam (I), because of anxiety for his son, sent his wife to the prophet Abijah, after the division of the monarchy, and long after the destruction of the city. Apparently Abijah continued to live near the ruins of the old sanctuary. (1 Kings 14:1-3.)

The presence of this holy place throughout those critical formative years must have done much to hold together the independent tribes, and to weld them together until Samuel— educated at Shiloh—was able to bring them to the monarchy.

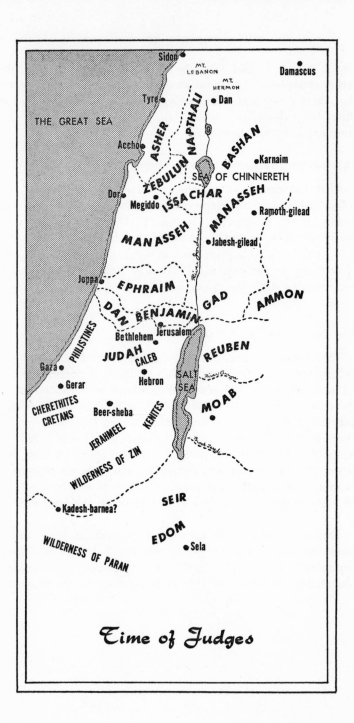

Time of Judges

CHAPTER VIII

THE SETTLEMENT OF

PALESTINE

The Story According to Judges

THE DEUTERONOMIC PHILOSOPHY OF HISTORY

The Deuteronomic editors marked every bit of history they edited with a strong moralistic flavor, but nowhere is it quite so evident as in the Book of Judges. We have here a series of stories of the old tribal heroes who participated in the settlement of Palestine; almost all of them from the JE narrative, and many of them, e.g., the story of Gideon, containing two or more stories woven together. As a skilled gem cutter shapes and polishes precious stones so that, though varying in size, they harmonize, and makes them into a beautiful necklace, so the editor took these stories of various heroes and trimmed them to suit his philosophy by rewriting each according to the pattern given in Judges 2:11-23. The people of Israel sinned against the LORD by worshiping false gods; the LORD therefore sold them into the power of their enemies; eventually he raised a judge who saved them (here follows the original hero story) and the land had peace for 20, 40, or 80 years, depending upon the importance ascribed by the editor to the judge.

But there are three stories in the book which do not fit this framework. The account of Samson is a collection of stories about the great strong man—stories which demanded a constantly hostile enemy, rather than a period of peace—and the stories of Micah and the Danites and of the Levite's concubine deal not with foreign nations, but with intertribal affairs. There is a brief reference to the Levite's concubine in Note D in the Appendix. The other stories will be treated in this chapter.

THE SHOPHET

One of the most interesting words in the Hebrew language is the verb *shaphat,* which means, fundamentally, "to put in

71

the right relationship with." When a man stole a sheep, the restoration of the right relationship involved the returning of the sheep and some penalty. When a wandering tribe invaded an Israelite group, the right relationship demanded that it be driven out, and, if any plunder could be annexed, that helped. If a great nation was the aggressor, it was considered a maladjustment on a larger scale. The active participle, *shophet,* refers to the one who restored this right relationship.[1] It will be seen at once that the most important function of a *shophet* was that he should be a military leader. The Israelites were the chosen people of the LORD. Any land they possessed, they felt had been given them by him. (Judges 11:21-24.) Therefore, if the Ammonites took the land away from them, it called for a *shophet* to restore the correct relationship: i.e., to drive out and to defeat the Ammonites—in this case, Jephthah. To be sure, there were undoubtedly many civil cases brought before the *shophet,* after he had been established by his military prowess. Sometimes his wisdom may have reached far beyond his tribal boundaries, as seems to have been the case with Deborah. (Judges 4:4ff.) It was the LORD who raised up the *shophet* to deliver the people. (Judges 2:16.) The *shophet* was completely in the control of the LORD: "But the Spirit of the LORD took possession of Gideon"—literally, "clothed itself with Gideon." (Judges 6:34a.) Naturally, then, a divinely inspired leader would normally have been retained as ruler or sheik of the group after his military success. We thus have three functions of a *shophet:* a military leader; an administrator; and one who settled disputes—but the fundamental idea was one of putting things in their right relationship. It is too comprehensive a concept to be included under the one word "Judge," by which it is invariably translated, but it is doubtful if a better single word can be found. This is why we tend to be confused when we read of the "judges" of Israel and find principally the record of military exploits.

These judges differ greatly in stature from the first, Othniel, to the last, Samuel, who helped in the final step to the mon-

---

1. For the basic meaning of the root of this verb, see my article about another of its participles, *mishpat, Journal of Biblical Literature,* LXI, Part II (1942), pp. 105-110.

archy.   Some are of insufficient importance for us to name them.

EHUD, THE BENJAMINITE, JUDGES 3:12-30

Recent excavations have shown us that at about the time of Ehud, one of the early judges, the country of Moab reached a peak of power.   It may even be that Eglon the Fat, the king assassinated by Ehud, was one of Moab's greatest rulers.   The Moabites had pressed across the Jordan from the east, and were exacting tribute of the Israelites when Ehud conceived and carried out his plan.   First he made a dagger, measured to order for a fat man.   We are told that it was a cubit in length, and that, when used, it was none too long, for the fat came clear up to the handle.   Since Ehud was left-handed (possibly had a defective right hand) he strapped his weapon on his right thigh, where he could more readily draw it, and where it would be less likely to attract attention.

After the tribute had been delivered, Ehud accompanied the Israelite bearers away from the (temporary) royal residence —possibly as far as the boundary lines of the Moabitish conquest—and then returned.   Claiming to have a personal message from the LORD, he was granted a private audience with the king, no weapon being visible.   The Hebrew humor is again evident when the "message" was delivered.   While the servants awaited the termination of the audience, Ehud, his bloody deed accomplished, escaped and rallied the Israelites. Striking quickly against the demoralized Moabites, they seized the fords over the Jordan and annihilated all the oppressors trapped on Israelite soil.   "And the land had rest for eighty years."   Ehud was considered a great judge.

DEBORAH THE JUDGE, JUDGES, chapters 4, 5

A great step toward the co-operation and eventual unification of the tribes of Israel is portrayed in the accounts of the victory by Deborah over the Canaanites in the plain of Esdraelon.   The southwestern edge of the plain, fortified by several Canaanitish cities located just where the trade routes emerged from the hills, had long been a trouble spot for the Israelites.

Maneuvering their iron-bound chariots on the level ground, the Canaanites so terrified the light-armed (sometimes almost un-armed) soldiers that the idea spread that "the LORD was a God of the hills only, not of the plains." Deborah persuaded the reluctant general, Barak, to attempt another battle against the Canaanites. Also, she had sufficient intelligence to select the perfect time for attack—just as a devastating storm was about to break. As the water rolled down the mountains, it created a flash flood in the River Kishon which flows at the edge of the Plain of Esdraelon. When the river overflowed its banks, the iron-bound chariots of Sisera became mired in the mud. It is easy to imagine how the agile Israelites attacked them from the rear and drove the panic-stricken Canaanites into the river itself. The fleeing Sisera sought refuge in the tent of a friend, Heber the Kenite, who unfortunately was not at home. Heber's wife, Jael, offered Sisera food, and then struck him with a maul and drove a tent peg through his head. Except that a few fleeing Canaanites escaped—possibly because the people of a small village, Meroz, did not stand fast—the victory of the forces of Deborah and Barak was complete.

RESULTS OF THE BATTLE

When Israel had settled in Palestine, there were four areas of concentration: north, central, and south on the west side of the Jordan, and the east side of the Jordan. The tribe of Judah, with perhaps a remnant of Simeon and some others, had located in the south, in the Highland of Judah, between the Dead Sea and the Philistines, who were along that part of the Mediterranean Sea. They were so far removed from the northern tribes that, when the Song of Deborah blessed certain tribes for having participated in the battle and criticized others for nonparticipation, the people of Judah were not even mentioned. No one had expected them to take part. A line of strongly fortified hostile cities, including Jerusalem, Gibeon, and Gezer, prevented easy intercommunication between Judah and the central tribes, so that Judah flourished by itself. These cities were not in Israelite hands until the time of the United Kingdom.

A similar line of fortified cities on the edge of the Plain of Esdraelon was broken in power by this great battle of Deborah. Coming early in the settlement of the Israelites, it enabled an intimate contact between the central tribes and the tribes to the north. Thus the one great victory made possible the development of a unified people in the central and northern parts of Palestine, including in the group those tribes east of the Jordan. So from the time of Deborah on there were two points of concentration of the Hebrew tribes: the south, or Judah, and all the rest, usually spoken of as the north. Only for a short time during the United Kingdom was this division healed. Immediately after the death of Solomon the land was again divided.

THE SONG OF DEBORAH

The oldest of the great poems of Israel is the Song of Deborah. Scholars are generally agreed that, if it was not written by Deborah, it at least came from a contemporary. The tribe of Dan migrated at an early date from a location between Judah and Philistia to a site on the slope of the inland Mount Hermon. Since the Song of Deborah criticises Dan because he "abode with the ships," and there are no ships on Mount Hermon, it seems to date the poem earlier than the migration of the tribe. There are other reasons for this early dating.[2]

The intensity of emotions, the brilliance of the figures:
"From heaven fought the stars,
    from their courses they fought against Sisera."
The orderly division into stanzas, the skillful use of parallelism to build up to a crescendo—all stamp this as the work of a literary genius. The chance references to tribes and nations are of inestimable historical value, and the narrative and descriptive qualities seize upon the attention of the reader and will not be denied.

The final picture is of the mother of Sisera. In those days the position of a queen mother was a semiofficial one. A king

---

2. George Foot Moore: *Judges* ("International Critical Commentary," New York: Charles Scribner's Sons, 1895), p. 155, thinks the Danites were in northern Palestine by this time. In any case, too much emphasis should not be placed upon the reference to ships, as the original location of the Danites seems not to have been directly on the seacoast.

could have many wives, and many daughters—but only one mother. She was the one who had cared for him, instructed him, fought for him through the intrigue of the harem, pushed him into the notice of the king ahead of all his half brothers, and probably helped to engineer the final coup which brought him to the crown. Here, then, we have the pathetic picture of the queen mother, worrying about the delay of her son in returning from battle, but being reassured by her ladies in waiting that it was only the greatness of the plunder which was holding him back. Meanwhile he lay in the open field, prey for the birds and the dogs, slain by the hand of a woman.

A much later prose account of the story of Deborah is found in Judges, chapter 4. It refers to Jabin as the king of the Canaanites, and Sisera as his general. It also mentions a smaller number of tribes as participating in the battle.

GIDEON—JERUBBAAL, JUDGES, chapters 6—8

One of the most confusing stories of the Book of Judges is that of Gideon. When there are two different names for a man, with one part of the narrative ascribed to one name, another part to the other name, and a short explanation inserted to explain the difference in names, it is certain that there is a mixture (conflation) of two accounts. Here we have stories about Gideon and about Jerubbaal, with a great many discrepancies between them.

One account brings Gideon into the story as the first worshiper of the LORD to take overt action against Baal worship. The morning after he had destroyed the altar of Baal and had offered a young bullock to the LORD, the men of the town demanded that his father produce Gideon for them, that they might kill him. With a cleverness not lost to those who heard the story, the father pointed out that they sought to deprive Baal of the pleasure of executing his own vengeance. "If he is a god, let him contend for himself." Won by his logic, they spared Gideon and his name became "Jerubbaal," or "Let Baal contend." One wonders if, twelve centuries later, this story may not have been the source of the argument of the great Jewish scholar Gamaliel, who advised against persecuting

Christians, saying that, if they were not of God, their move-ment would perish; but if they were of God, it would be un-fortunate to be found opposing him. (Acts 5:33-40.)

There are many other points where it is evident that we have two, or even three, stories confused. Thus we have the impres-sion that Gideon started his career, not because of the incident of the altar to Baal, but because the Midianite nomads were destroying Israelite crops. Also, there is the idea that he came into active life to avenge the slaying of his brothers. One ac-count gives the sign that the LORD was with him because, in the morning, the fleece was wet and the ground around it dry; the other because the fleece was dry and the ground around it was wet. The explanation was that he was not satisfied with one test, and asked corroboration by a second. The three dif-ferent figures for the men in Gideon's army are another indica-tion of three different accounts (32,000; 10,000; and 300) although here also there is a story seeking to reconcile the dif-ferences: a. those who desired to do so were permitted to re-turn home and b. the final number was selected by the chance manner in which they drank at the river.

Perhaps the most important divergence, though, is in the question of whether or not Gideon was a king. When offered the crown, he vehemently refused it, yet he certainly acted like a king in meting out punishment to the two cities which refused to help him, and one of his sons was named "Abimelech," which means "my father is king."

It is difficult to separate these various strands, and, for our purpose, unnecessary. It is probable here that we have a leader of the tribe of Manasseh who took overt action against the worship of Baal; who achieved distinction by carrying out under difficulties the requirement of a blood feud; who was recognized as a judge or *shophet* far beyond the boundaries of his own tribe; who with a surprise night attack successfully op-posed the earliest invasion of Palestine by camel-riding nomads of which there is record[3]; and who probably came closer to being a king over Israel than any other man before Saul.

3. W. F. Albright: "The Biblical Period" from *The Jews, Their History, Culture and Religion*, ed. Louis Finkelstein (New York: Harper and Brothers, 1949), p. 21.

ABIMELECH AND JOTHAM, JUDGES, chapter 9

One of the many sons of Gideon (seventy we are told, although that is not an accurate figure—merely an indication of a great number) was Abimelech, born to a concubine of the great man who lived in the city of Shechem. When he offered himself to his mother's city to be their king, the citizens were disposed to accept him, and gave him sufficient money to hire a band of cutthroats. They killed all the other sons of Gideon except one, Jotham. Apparently these Shechemites had some idea of the son of a judge succeeding his father, although there is no earlier record of this. Abimelech was then made king of Shechem.

Unable to exact vengeance by force, Jotham delivered his fable of the trees. Seeking a king to rule over them, the trees first asked the olive tree, but it was too busy producing oil. Next the fig tree refused because it was too busy growing figs, and the vine because it was producing wine. When they finally asked the worthless bramble, it accepted, but there was a reference to the danger of fire—probably a danger well known to the men of Shechem. So the people of Shechem had chosen a worthless man to rule over them, and thereby incurred the danger that the city might also be destroyed by the fire kindled about Abimelech. Upon delivering this fable from the security of Mount Gerizim, Jotham quickly departed and went into hiding. This "Fable of the Trees" is quite ancient, and has no exact counterpart in biblical literature.

JEPHTHAH, JUDGES 11:1—12:7

Jephthah was the son of a harlot. With this as an excuse, his half brothers drove him from his home that they might not be required to divide the inheritance from their father into one more share—though in Judges 11:7 Jephthah accused the elders of Gilead, rather than his family, of the action. In any case, he was deprived of hope of inheritance and of the protection a family could have given him. There was no one to carry on a blood feud in his behalf, so he could have been slain by anyone with impunity. He therefore did what was probably done by many others under those circumstances—joined a band of men assembled for mutual protection, and soon became their leader. Not many years later, David, a fugitive from Saul, organized such a band, whose roster eventually became a list of the most honored men of the kingdom.

When the Ammonites began attacking the people of Gilead there were many regrets over the action taken against Jephthah, for his small group had achieved a reputation as fighters. Jephthah was invited to come back with them to fight against the Ammonites. Only after an agreement that, if he could overcome the enemy, he would be the leader of the Gileadites, did he agree to return.

Before hostilities commenced, Jephthah argued with the Ammonites that the Lord had given Israel the land they were occupying, three hundred years before, and no one had objected. Since the Ammonites kept the land Chemosh their God had given them, would they not expect the Israelites to keep the land the Lord their God had given them? It does not look like a promising effort to avoid conflict, and it did not succeed. In fact, there is some indication that the entire palaver was introduced by a much later writer.

When the fighting began, Jephthah sought to win the help of the Lord by his vow that, if he conquered the Ammonites, he would offer as a sacrifice the one who came from his home to meet him on his return. On his triumphant return his virgin daughter, an only child, came with timbrels and a dance to welcome him. When the heartbroken father explained the vow, she insisted that it be fulfilled, but requested an interval of two months in which she and her maidens should wander in the hills and "bewail her virginity." After that period, the vow was accomplished.

The men of Ephraim, jealous because of the military success of Jephthah, or disappointed because they did not share in the spoils, took him to task for not having included them in his expedition. Ephraim was the tribe which had made a similar complaint to Gideon (Judges 8: 1—4), although by diplomacy he had been able to smooth their ruffled feelings. This Jephthah was unable to do.

The men of Ephraim had to learn the hard way from Jephthah. After the battle, which resulted in a great victory for

Gilead (although the figure given of 42,000 Ephraimites slain is out of all proportion), the Gileadites seized the fords of the Jordan River. When the Ephraimite stragglers sought to cross on the way home, each was asked to pronounce the word "Shibboleth." As men of that tribe could not pronounce "sh," the answer was "Sibboleth," which in each case proved to be the last mistake that Ephraimite ever made. From this incident the word "Shibboleth" has come to be a synonym for "password."

As the fossil of a sea-creature in a broken bit of limestone can reveal many variant items of information about some past geologic age, so this one story of Jephthah opens a window on the religious practices of ancient Israel. First, there was the recognition of Chemosh, god of the Ammonites,[4] as a god with power similar to, if not equal to, the power of the LORD: "Will you not possess what Chemosh your god gives you to possess?" (Judges 11:24.) Then there was the idea of striking a bargain with the LORD: "If thou wilt give the Ammonites into my hand . . ." (Judges 11:30), an idea of religion which has not yet completely disappeared from our thinking. There was unquestioned human sacrifice: "Who did with her according to his vow." (Judges 11:39.) This was probably not a universal custom at that time, but the sacrifice was made to the LORD, and there certainly is no hint of criticism of Jephthah. Quite the contrary, in fact. Then, since there are three references to the virginity of the daughter, it is possible that the idea of virgin sacrifice was present in at least one of the accounts of the story. Then there is the very common idea of determining the will of the LORD by chance: "Whoever comes forth from the doors of my house to meet me." (Judges 11:31.) In other words, the LORD would select the one he wanted for the sacrifice, and would show his choice by causing that one to be the first to greet Jephthah. Finally, we know that a period of organistic weeping by women was a part of ancient Babylonian worship, sometimes practiced in Palestine. (Ezekiah 8:14.)

4. Actually, Chemosh was the god, not of the Ammonites, but of the Moabites. Either we have here people worshiping gods of other countries, or a confusion of two accounts, one picturing Jephthah fighting the Ammonites, the other fighting the Moabites. Either is possible.

Quite possibly the two months spent in the mountains by the daughter of Jephthah and her companions (Judges 11:38) had reference to this practice.

The deliverance by Jephthah was probably an important milestone in the journey toward the United Kingdom, but the record indicates only six years as the interval between his victory and his death.

SAMSON, JUDGES, chapters 13—16

Near the borderline between the tribe of Judah and the tribe of Dan, in the days before the Danites migrated to northern Palestine, there lived a devout man named Manoah. His wife had borne no children before a messenger from the LORD appeared and told her she was to have a son (Samson). The story is typical of the stories of semimiraculous birth told by many peoples—especially the Hebrews—about those heroes who were so glamorous it seemed the only way they could be explained was by some special dispensation of the LORD, e.g., Isaac, Samuel. In this case, the son was to be dedicated to the LORD throughout his life as a Nazirite.

The Nazirites were people who ostentatiously opposed the agricultural religion of the Canaanites, demanding the austere worship of the LORD as it had been carried on in the nomadic days of the wilderness. They insisted upon abstention from all products of the grape, because it was a symbol of agriculture, and was used—most likely in the form of wine—in the ritual. The Nazirite vow included letting the hair grow, and avoidance of touching a dead body, as well as refraining from the fruit of the grape. (Numbers 6.) At least at one time it was possible to take a temporary Nazirite vow, but Samson's obligation was for life. Indeed, his mother was not allowed to touch wine even before his birth.

The credentials of the messenger of the LORD who came to advise Manoah about the prospective birth of Samson and the Nazirite regulations, included the ignition of a sacrifice by heavenly fire. Except that, in the case of Gideon's messenger, the offering was more in the nature of a picnic lunch (Judges 6:19-24), the incidents are quite similar. Each culminated in the disappearance of the messenger concerned. There are in the Old Testament other vivid pictures of the igniting of sacrifices by heavenly fire.[5]

Nearly every country devotes at least a small section of its literature to stories of the strength of some of its great heroes. The Greeks had the semidivine Hercules, and the legendary Achilles; the Persians had Rustam and Sohrab. Our own country in the lighter vein admires Paul Bunyan and a half-dozen lesser heroes; in a slightly more serious mood we have a collection of stories of strength, as well as of other laudable characteristics, which have been attracted by the gleaming personality of Lincoln. The Hebrews had their Samson. It is easy to imagine a group of shepherds protecting their flocks through the night, and whiling away the dark hours with stories of the strong man of Dan, who constituted a one-man army against the hated Philistines.

Of course the stories grew in the telling. For instance, it is quite difficult to imagine Samson rooting up the gate posts and the gates of the city of Gaza and carrying them up to the hill before Hebron, when all the time his enemies were waiting for him at the gate of Gaza. It is also quite likely that some unattached stories of strength became affixed to the personality of Samson. But there is no question but what there was such a man of legendary power, and that at times he proved most embarrassing to the Philistines. It is possible that some illness, with an attendant high fever, caused at the same time a loss of hair and a loss of strength, both of which eventually returned to him. Naturally, since the strength was the gift of the LORD, its loss must have been considered to be because of a violation of the requirements of the LORD. If such an example of cause and effect was not indicated in the original story, it is certain that the Deuteronomic editor would not have missed such an opportunity for a moral.

The vivid stories of Samson are part of the heritage of the Judeo-Christian tradition. Our literature would be greatly impoverished did we not have the accounts of the lion slain by his

5. See, e.g., 1 Kings 18:20-40.

bare hands; the riddle about the honey:

> "Out of the eater came something to eat
> Out of the strong came something sweet"
> —Judges 14:14;

the story of the foxes with their tails tied together running with attached firebrands through the Philistine wheat fields; the multitude slain with the jawbone of an ass; the treachery of Delilah; the brawny hulk of a slave blindly turning the mill; the final destruction of the temple and those in it, including himself. Samson gave us no great moral values. The Israelites were serving the Philistines when he started public life: they were serving the Philistines when he finished it. But he left some wonderful stories which will last forever.

MICAH AND THE DANITES, JUDGES, chapters 17—18

Except that it comes from the same period and is included in the same book, the story of Micah (not to be confused with the prophet Micah some four or five centuries later) and the Danites has nothing to do with the stories of the judges. However, it is a very illuminating account of those days.

Micah stole a large sum of silver from his own mother. She roundly cursed the thief before she found him to be her own son. One of the two main themes of the story was a demonstration of the conviction that, once pronounced, a curse cannot be recalled. Probably terrified by the curse, Micah confessed the crime, and his mother desperately tried to transform the curse into a blessing—frequently the obverse side of a curse. The silver was dedicated to the LORD, and a sacred image was constructed of part of it, though there is some confusion as to whether the image was an "ephod" or a graven or molten image. Once again we have different accounts combined.

At first it seemed that the mother was successful in transforming the curse into a blessing, for a young Levite in the vicinity agreed to serve as his priest. Apparently at the time of the story a Levite was already considered better fitted than any other to function in that capacity. But soon the blow fell. Five spies of the Danites, looking, because of pressure from the Philistines, for a new location for the tribe of Dan, passed near the home of

Micah and recognized the voice of the young Levite serving as his priest. They asked the Levite about their journey, and he told them it had the blessing of the LORD. Later, with 600 fighting men from the old territory of Samson, they returned to Micah's home, seized the silver image, persuaded the priest to switch his allegiance, and convinced Micah that it would be most unwise to attempt by force to regain his property. Proceeding to the slope of Mount Hermon, where their spies had previously discovered Laish, a peaceful, undefended Sidonian city, the Danites captured it, destroyed all its inhabitants, renamed it "Dan," and installed their recently acquired silver image as its main object of worship, supervised by the Levite. The second, and main, theme of the story is the account of how Dan, later one of the two principal sanctuaries of the Northern Kingdom, originally became a center of worship.

THE RELIGION OF CANAAN AND ISRAEL

In our day we have a tendency to separate religion from our daily experiences, at least to the extent that we do not think of the hand of God manipulating all the events of our normal lives. This was decidedly not the case in the time of the judges, either with the Canaanites or the Israelites. If rain came, and it was usually very welcome in Palestine, it was because God had sent it. If there was a famine or pestilence, it was because of God, and the Israelites usually considered it a punishment for sin.

The Canaanite inhabitants of Palestine were a very cultured people. We are only now beginning to appreciate them. When a Canaanite city was destroyed by the Israelites and rebuilt for Israelite occupancy, it was built on a far less elaborate scale. But religion and morals were on a much lower plane than those of the invading Israelites. The Canaanites being agriculturists, their religion was largely an attempt to secure better crops, and took the form known as a "fertility cult." The legend of the marriage and death of their god, and the birth of the new god, were enacted by the king and queen, or their representatives, and sometimes by the people generally, with emphasis upon the sexual part of the story. This was the function of the sacred prostitutes—both male and female. In no other part of the world have there been recovered so many religious statues of the naked fertility goddess. There were of course other gods of the Canaanites, but it was largely to this feature of their religion that the religious leaders of Israel objected so strongly.

When those Israelites who treasured the record of the Exodus from Egypt entered Palestine, they were officially worshipers of the one God, the LORD (Yahweh). There is no Palestinian record of any goddess ever being associated with his name. The religion was austere, based upon the covenant, and sometimes extremely cruel, as when whole cities were "devoted" or sacrificed to the LORD. But there was no sexualism in it. And it was intolerant of other gods. "You shall have no other gods before me." (Exodus 20:3.) Nevertheless, there was a terrific struggle before this ideal was accomplished.

When the Israelite tribes entered Canaan, they wanted to grow grain. Inquiring of the people already settled upon the land, who in most cases were by that time either their masters or their servants, depending upon the success of Israelitish arms, they were told that approved agricultural methods involved the worship of the god Baal. How else could they grow crops? The LORD (Yahweh) was a god of the desert, where farming was not carried on. The Israelite tribes which had been in Palestine before this new wave of invasion under Joshua were using the Canaanite technique. No one opposed it except the conservative leaders who based all religion upon their gratitude for their marvelous salvation when they had come out of Egypt, and the solemn covenant subsequently made at Sinai. It was religion as taught by Moses versus religion as taught by the Canaanites, who had already learned to live in settled communities and to grow crops.

Of course we do not have a complete picture—only the record of scattered incidents. But the worship of Baal by the early Israelites was certainly much more prevalent than the stories would indicate. There is no account of opposition to it before Gideon, but the appearance of "Baal" compounded into the names of worshipers of the LORD, e.g., Gideon himself (Judges 6:32), is an indication of the prevalence of Baal worship by Israelites.

As late as the time of Ezekiel (592 B.C.) we find mention of the women of Jerusalem "weeping for Tammuz" (Ezekiel 8:14), a reference to a fertility cult similar to, if not associated with, Baal worship; and all through the records down to that time we have accounts of the struggles of the various reformers. Eventually the worship of the "'Baals and the Ashtaroth" was stamped out; and the sexualism, though in the early days it may have been attractive to the Israelites, was completely eradicated from their religious practices. The sexualism was never called part of the worship of the LORD, but one impression of the agricultural religion *did* register: eventually agricultural feasts and sacrifices became an important part of the worship of Israel, and remain that to this day.

PART THREE

THE MONARCHIES

CHAPTER IX

THE UNITED KINGDOM

Samuel and Saul

THE BANDS OF PROPHETS

The bands of prophets played an interesting part in the story of the coronation of Saul. These groups were not much like the great writing prophets—Isaiah, Jeremiah, Ezekiel, and such leaders—but they did have an important place among the early Israelites. The word for prophet, "nabi," is related to the word "to rave." In the Old Testament, a person who was unbalanced mentally was thought to be possessed by the spirit of the LORD, just as in the New Testament such a one was thought to be possessed by demons, e.g., the man of the Gerasenes, Luke 8:26-33. In no other way could they explain his irrational actions. This does not mean, of course, that the actions and words of all prophets were irrational, but it does mean that the spirit of the LORD controlled the prophet. Even in the case of the late great prophets, when the prophet spoke he pronounced the word of God.

The bands of prophets were groups of emotional men who, by means of musical instruments and ecstatic dances, roused themselves to so high a pitch they were considered controlled by the spirit of the LORD. They had a strong effect sometimes upon the political activity of the people. Samuel and Saul were associated with prophets of this type at the time of Saul's coronation. Indeed, we are quite certain that Saul was unbalanced mentally, which fact, interpreted as his possession by the spirit of the LORD, may possibly be the reason he was chosen king. We are told that Saul stripped off his clothes and prophesied before Samuel and "lay naked all that day and all that night." (1 Samuel 19:20-24.) When he killed his yoke of

89

oxen—certainly a desperate action, although a justified one— we are told that "the spirit of God came mightily upon Saul." (1 Samuel 11:61.) We do not have any record of similar eccentric actions by Samuel, but we are told that he was called a "seer," and a later insertion explains that that was but another name for a prophet. (1 Samuel 9:9.) Also, Samuel knew just where the band of prophets would be met by Saul, and that they would prophesy, and Saul would prophesy with them—so that a saying arose in Israel "Is Saul also among the prophets?" (1 Samuel 10:5-13.) What more likely explanation than that Samuel was their leader, and had told them what to do?

The Old Story of Saul's Coronation, 1 Samuel 9:1— 10:16; chapter 11

The original story of the anointing of Saul begins with Samuel the seer (or prophet) serving also as a judge in a rather limited area in Ephraim. Seeking lost asses belonging to his father, Saul and a servant approached the city of Samuel, who apparently was unknown to Saul. The servant suggested asking him about the lost animals, and indicated that the coin he happened to be carrying in his pocket would be adequate recompense for the service. When he saw him, Samuel hailed Saul as the one chosen by the LORD to be king, offered him the portion of honor at a feast, and, sending the servant on ahead on the next day, privately anointed Saul to be King of Israel. He then advised him that he would meet three groups of men: the first group telling him the asses had been found, the second giving him a gift of bread, and the third group, appearing on the hill of God where there was a garrison (perhaps the word means military commander) of the Philistines, played musical instruments and "prophesied." Apparently these prophetic bands were so active stirring up resistance to their overlords, it was necessary for the Philistines to keep a military detachment on the hill where they operated. Saul then for a time returned to private life.

This old story of Saul reaches its climax in the raising of the siege of Jabesh-gilead. Nahash the Ammonite had invested the Israelitish city, and, when asked upon what terms a surrender would be accepted, demanded the right eye of every man in the city. In his overconfidence he permitted the people to send messengers to all Israel requesting help, for he was certain none would come. But the word came to Saul—already anointed by Samuel in private, and accepted by the prophetic band. In a startlingly dramatic act he slaughtered his oxen, sent bits of bloody beef throughout the countryside, and pronounced a curse on any who did not come to the aid of him and Samuel against Nahash.[1] In an unbelievably short time an army was assembled, the Ammonites defeated and scattered, and the hero Saul was made King of Israel.

And indeed, Israel needed a king! The pressure of the Ammonites was far less than that of the Philistines, whose five kings were now learning to co-operate one with another. They had already driven the people of the Israelite tribe of Dan from their original area near Judah, where Samson had held forth, into the extreme northern part of Palestine. Later, at a crucial point in one battle, the Israelites took their great talisman, the sacred ark of the covenant, symbolizing the presence of the LORD himself, into the fight. The Philistines promptly captured it and bore it as a trophy to the temple of their god Dagon, introducing a delightful series of stories about the power of the ark. (1 Samuel, chapters 4—6.) The first morning after the installation found the god Dagon on his face before the ark. Replaced on his pedestal by the Philistines, he was found the next morning in the same attitude, but with his wrists and neck broken. Then an epidemic hit the Philistine cities, and the ark was transported from city to city, subduing by disease the people the Israelites had been unable to conquer in war. Since the Philistines, when they finally sent the ark home, included votive offerings of golden images of mice and ulcers, the most likely conjecture is that the disease was something like the bubonic plague, identified by ulcers, and transmitted by the fleas which accompany rats.

When word of the capture of the ark by the Philistines, and the death of his two sons who had accompanied it, was brought back to Eli, the aged priest and judge at Shiloh, he fell off his bench and broke his neck. His daughter-in-law died in child-

1. See Appendix, Note D.

birth, hastened by the bad news, but, just before her death, named her new son Ichabod, "The glory is departed." It must have been at about this time that the Philistines captured Shiloh and destroyed there the great unifying force of the Israelites, the sanctuary—an event whose horror was so great that it was still a vivid sermon illustration for Jeremiah 500 years later—"therefore I will do to the house that is called by my name, and in which you trust, and to the place which I gave to you and to your fathers, as I did to Shiloh." (Jeremiah 7:14.) Eli had served as priest and judge many years at Shiloh, and Samuel had been educated there, but when he was described as judging Israel, Samuel was pictured as on a yearly circuit of Bethel, Gilgal, Mizpah and Ramah—but not Shiloh. (1 Samuel 7:15f.)

Israel needed a king to rally the people and to lead them in battle, and Samuel gave them Saul—not a completely satisfactory solution, but one which met the immediate need. Not before the time of David would it be fully realized how much a king could do for his people.

THE LATE STORY OF SAUL'S CORONATION, 1 SAMUEL, chapters 1—3; 7—8; 10:17-25; chapter 12

The late story of the coronation of Saul was written after the people had become greatly disillusioned with the monarchy. Only a casual glance at 1 Samuel, chapter 8 is necessary to see how unhappy the people were with their taxes and forced labor, all of which were blamed upon the kingship. Naturally they looked back to the good old days before Saul, and wondered why the LORD had ever given them so evil an institution as the monarchy. Clearly, he must have done so against his own better judgment, because of the insistence of the people. And the more they thought of Samuel, the more he increased in stature and approached perfection.

Consequently, we have the idealized picture of this man who was truly great in his own right. Beginning with a semimiraculous story of his birth, after his mother had given up hope of bearing a son, we find that "all Israel from Dan to Beersheba knew that Samuel was established as a prophet of the LORD."

(1 Samuel 3:20.)   This encompassed the whole of Palestine, much as our expression "from New York to San Francisco" covers all of the United States.   It is quite a different picture from that given in the old story (1 Samuel 7:15f), which portrays Samuel serving as a judge all the days of his life, and making an annual circuit of the cities Bethel, Gilgal, Mizpah, and Ramah, all of them probably located within a radius of fifteen miles.   In the late story we are told that, when Samuel offered the sacrifice at Mizpah and called upon the name of the LORD, the Philistines were so thoroughly defeated that they never again during his lifetime entered the territory of Israel, and all captured Israelitish lands were restored (1 Samuel 7:3-14), which is certainly not the picture given elsewhere in 1 Samuel.

According to this story, the people demanded a king; the LORD told Samuel that he himself was the one who was being rejected, not Samuel, but agreed to their request.   Saul was chosen by lot (indicating that, if there was to be a king, Saul was the LORD's choice), and the monarchy was established.

THE RULE OF SAUL, 1 SAMUEL, chapters 13—15

The most brilliant exploit of Israelitish arms during the reign of Saul was the attack on the Philistines made by Jonathan, son of Saul, and his armorbearer.   After the military situation had reached a stalemate, these two decided to make an attack by themselves.   First they agreed that the first challenge by the enemy would tell them whether or not the LORD would be with them in their desperate venture.   Then they charged across the ravine which separated the two forces.   Having decided by this means that the LORD favored their exploit, they attacked, and the very boldness of their action brought it success.   When the first of the enemy rushed back to their camp, they created a panic.   Israelites who had been forced to labor for the Philistines grabbed weapons as they were dropped (one reason for the previous success of the Philistines was that the Israelites lacked blacksmiths to make weapons for them) and joined in the fray, multiplying the confusion till the Philistines could not distinguish between friend and foe.

Encouraged by the progress of the battle, Saul pronounced a curse against anyone who ate food before evening.   Not knowing of this, Jonathan ate some honey, strengthened by which he was better able to fight, but, when Saul asked God whether he should go on after the Philistines, he was unable to get what he considered an answer. He therefore ordered the casting of lots—the clearest example of it we have in the Old Testament —to see where lay the guilt which prevented a message from God. The lot fell first upon the house of Saul rather than the rest of Israel, and then upon Jonathan rather than Saul, and Jonathan admitted eating the honey. Saul therefore ordered the death of his son, who was responsible for the entire victory. It is an interesting step in the development of democratic action to note that the people overrode the command of Saul and saved Jonathan's life.

Although Samuel had made Saul king, he had never completely relinquished his own authority. There are two stories of how he finally announced to Saul that he was rejected from the kingship. According to one, Saul could not delay making the sacrifices necessary for starting a battle, until Samuel should arrive. He therefore made the sacrifice himself. At this moment Samuel appeared, in a towering rage because Saul had usurped his privilege, and told him he was no longer to be king. The other story tells of Samuel's command that Saul should completely destroy the Amalekites and their animals. When Saul saved their king, Agag, and the best of their cattle, claiming, when Samuel questioned him, that he was saving the sheep and oxen for sacrifice to the LORD, we have for the second time the statement that Saul has been rejected from his position. It is against this background that we have the statement, attributed to Samuel:

> "Behold, to obey is better than sacrifice,
> and to hearken than the fat of rams."
> —1 Samuel 15:22b

Eventually the Philistines, possibly worried because of some degree of unity among the Israelites, formed a firm coalition of their various cities and moved to wipe out the threat of these people. Just before the great and decisive battle, we have a pathetic picture of the king of Israel. His armies probably had the advantage of position, being drawn up on Mount Gilboa.

Certainly he had no other advantage: numbers, weapons, morale were with the Philistines. If only he had not been rejected by the LORD! He tried to inquire the LORD's will by lot, but was unsuccessful. Then we come to an idea difficult to understand. Since Samuel was the one who had rejected him, only Samuel could restore him to the LORD's favor. But Samuel was dead. Seeking out a medium at the town of Endor, he promised her protection if she would bring him Samuel. She probably recognized Saul by his height (1 Samuel 10:23), and claimed that she saw someone who resembled Samuel. The word to Saul was that his fears of the Philistines were well grounded, for the LORD had rejected him—something anyone could have told him. She gave him food, and then he went on—probably the next day—to the battle. (1 Samuel, chapter 28.)

Saul's attack was a hopeless venture. We know he had previously ordered Jonathan killed, and had driven David from his kingdom. How many other of his great generals had been similarly treated we can only guess. At least Jonathan still stood by his father, for he and two brothers died in the battle. Saul, mortally wounded, ordered his armorbearer to slay him, lest he be captured alive by the Philistines and tortured in front of his own people. This his servant feared to do, so Saul fell upon his own sword and perished. (1 Samuel, chapter 31.) There is another account that an Amalekite killed him at his own request. (2 Samuel, chapter 1.) When the news was given David, he composed what may well be his greatest poem, the "Elegy over Saul"—

> "Thy glory, O Israel, is slain upon thy high places!
> How are the mighty fallen!
> Tell it not in Gath . . ."
>
> —2 Samuel 1:17-27

This poem was included in a very early collection of Israelite songs, *The Book of Jashar* (or *The Book of the Upright*), from which it was copied into our Book of 2 Samuel.

When the Philistines found the body of Saul, they cut off his head, put his armor in the temple of Ashtaroth, and nailed his body to the wall of Bethshan. The men of Jabesh-gilead, whose eyes had been saved for them by Saul just before his coronation, now repaid the debt by stealing the body at night, burning it in their own city, and giving a decent burial to the bones.

So ends the story of the first king of Israel. The accounts of his contacts with David will be included under the story of the second king.

CHAPTER X

THE UNITED KINGDOM

The Establishment of the House of David

DAVID AT THE COURT OF SAUL, 1 SAMUEL, chapters 16—20

The story of David is somewhat confusing, because the different sources are intermingled. Also, it is of course necessary to go back in the narrative some time before the death of Saul, for in many incidents of David's life, Saul was one of the participants.

As Samuel had anointed Saul to be king over Israel, so we are told he anointed David. One of the best-known stories of David's youth is the account of how Samuel, directed by the LORD, went to the house of Jesse and cast lots over each of Jesse's sons. After calling in the youngest, David, from the field, he was chosen and anointed, probably in strict secrecy, to be king in place of Saul.

The emotional instability of Saul which may have had something to do with his selection as king, was also responsible for fits of deep depression. As these probably made him extremely difficult to get along with—and he was the king—his servants suggested that David, who had a reputation for being a man of valor and a clever musician, be brought to the court to soothe the king in his violent fits of temper. The king acquiesced and for a while, according to the account, David was very popular with him.

It may seem queer at first that Samuel, an Ephraimite, should have selected David as a king when he was a man of Judah, and that David should have been popular with Saul, who was from Benjamin. Traditionally, the tribe of Judah was not particularly friendly with either of the other two. However, it must be remembered that Saul, on the command of Samuel, had dealt a terrific blow against the Amalekites (the time when he failed to kill their cattle and king), and the Amalekites were bitter enemies of Judah, as we shall soon see in the story of David. The intensity of friendship among various Israelitish tribes must have been subject to great variations.

A completely different account of David's introduction to Saul's court is found in the well-known story of David and Goliath, in which the shepherd boy, bringing provisions to his brothers, heard and accepted the challenge of the giant, and, refusing the armor and weapons of his king, stunned him with a stone from his sling and beheaded him with his own sword. We are told elsewhere (2 Samuel 21:19) that Elhanan, another man from Bethlehem, the home town of David, killed Goliath. It may be that David did slay a Philistine champion, and a later editor inserted the name of Goliath. We are told that at Nob (1 Samuel 22:9f) David was given the sword of Goliath, which may well be responsible for the insertion of his name here.

However happy Saul may at first have been with David, his jealous nature would not permit an enduring friendship, especially when the girls of the city were chanting:

"Saul has slain his thousands,
and David his ten thousands"
—1 Samuel 18:7

At this point we see the development of one of the most beautiful friendships in world literature. David and Jonathan, the son of Saul, made a covenant with each other, Jonathan giving him his robe and weapons. But the jealousy of the king suggested a plan for ridding him of his popular young officer. He offered him in marriage his daughter Michal, who loved him—the only dowry demanded being proof of the death of one hundred of Saul's enemies, the Philistines.[1] Instead of being killed in the undertaking David slew 200 of them, so Saul was forced to give him his daughter as a bride. At night messengers from the king came to the house for David, but Michal had let him down through

---

1. We are also told that David was offered an older daughter of Saul, and then she was given to another man—possibly another version of the same account.

a window, put a ritual image in his bed, covered it, and told the messengers her husband was sick. Not until after Saul had told them to bring David upon his bed that he might kill him did they discover the deception. David escaped, and Saul gave Michal as a wife to another man—presumably for a somewhat more substantial dowry.

Sometime later David, because of Saul's anger, hesitated to present himself at court on a feast day, as required by protocol. Jonathan arranged a code with him whereby, after attempting to intercede for David with his father, he would advise him if flight was necessary. When Saul tried to kill his own son, Jonathan went with bow and arrow to the appointed place in the field and called, in the hearing of David, to direct his squire to go farther away to find the arrow he was seeking. This elaborate technique for showing David that he should leave the court was proved quite unnecessary when Jonathan fell on David's neck as he bade him farewell.

DAVID AS AN EXILE, 1 SAMUEL, chapters 21—27; 29; 30

David's experiences as an exile from the court of Saul provided a most important source of training for David the king. He learned the strategy of guerrilla warfare; he became thoroughly acquainted with the foothills of Judah, a battleground through many years; he learned to command men and to deserve the respect of Israel.

The first account given is the description of his experience at Nob. Ahimelech the priest was in charge of a group of priests, possibly as their instructor. David, plagued by the perpetual problem of a leader, that of finding food for his men, presented himself as an officer of Saul on a secret mission, and asked for provisions. Probably the claim of a secret mission was to explain the fact that David was unarmed, which suggests that this incident follows soon after his escape from the messengers of Saul by the assistance of Michal. Upon the solemn assurance that the men were not ceremonially unclean, Ahimelech gave him some of the sacred bread which had been displayed before the LORD—the only food he had—and added the sword of Goliath, which had been deposited there at the sanctuary.

When Saul upbraided some of his men for helping David, Doeg the Edomite claimed that he had seen David at Nob, receiving food from Ahimelech. Saul summoned Ahimelech and the other priests before him, but they claimed ignorance of any disagreement between Saul and David. The king ordered all of them killed, but his servants were afraid to kill the priests of the Lord. However, Doeg, at Saul's command killed them all except Abiathar, a son of Ahimelech, who escaped to David's band and became his priest, and probably later his high priest. Doeg was from the country of Edom, a bitter perpetual enemy of the tribe of Judah, which accounts for his hostility against David the Judahite. That also may be the reason why he was not afraid to kill the priests of the Lord, the God of Israel. He belonged to a different nation. This action of Saul against the priests is in keeping with the gradual deterioration of the king after his rejection by Samuel.

There follow two stories of David and Saul so similar that it is likely they are the same story told by different narrators: the cave at Engedi, where Saul, pursuing David, blundered into a cave where David was already hiding, and would have lost his life had it not been for the young man's hesitancy to kill the Lord's anointed; and the camp at Ziph, when David found the king asleep and again spared him. In the former story David cut off a piece of Saul's robe to prove he could have killed him; in the latter one, he took his spear and water bottle. In each, Saul was deeply repentant, and sought a reconciliation —at least at the moment of his embarrassment. The second story gives a sidelight on the conception of the Lord. David complained that, because he had been driven from Israel, he had been compelled to worship other gods. It was long after this before Israel thought of the Lord as God of all the earth.

The story of David at Paran is based upon his old difficulty of providing adequate food for his men—here estimated as about 600 in number. He asked Nabal, a wealthy landholder, for food in payment for the protection given Nabal's shepherds by his men. We shall never know whether this was an excuse to demand provisions or a legitimate claim for services rendered, but Nabal—the name means "fool"—bluntly refused anything. In his anger, David started with his fighting men, swearing to kill all males in Nabal's establishment, but someone carried the story to Nabal's wife, Abigail. Hastily she prepared as much food as could be transported, and set out to intercept David and to dissuade him from his purpose. She was completely successful, and when shortly after her husband died from what looks very much like a cerebral hemorrhage, she became a faithful wife of the future king.

Finally the problem of securing food for his followers without alienating the countryside became too great, so David sought service with Achish, king of the Philistine city of Gath. He gave David the city of Ziklag for his home (probably after David had captured it from some of Achish's enemies), and he became a trusted follower. His technique was more effective than commendable. He would lead his band of 600 valiant fighting men against one of the cities of the land—possibly the Amalekites, who were hostile to the people of Judah. Having captured it, David's band would sack it, and kill all the inhabitants, so that no word would get back to Achish. Then David would divide the spoil, giving part to the elders of some city of Judah (in at least one case), part to Achish, and the rest to his own men, and telling Achish that he had destroyed one of the cities of Judah, or an ally of Judah. Thus his master was persuaded that David was perpetually widening the breach between himself and his own people, whereas he was really preparing the way to go back to them should occasion arise—as it did.

Finally the Philistines reorganized their forces perparatory to destroying once and for all, the power of Saul. Achish was quite proud of his band of Israelites at the mobilization of forces, but the other kings of Philistia refused to accept them. Perhaps some of them had been present at the battle of Micmash, when the Israelitish servants in the Philistine army had seized weapons from fallen contestants and demoralized their masters. David and his band were dismissed in peace, and returned to Ziklag long before they were expected, only to find that a detachment of Amalekites had turned the tables, and captured and sacked the city. By quick action they overtook them and recovered their wives and possessions, plus all the other plunder the marauding expedition had accumulated. Thus

David by one decision of the Philistine kings was saved the
necessity of either fighting against the Philistines on the side of
Saul—which probably would have resulted in his death—or
fighting against Israel—which would have made it forever impossible for him to be their king—and was at the same time
enabled to return and to rescue the people of his own little city
of Ziklag.

EARLY DAYS OF DAVID'S RULE, 2 SAMUEL, chapters 1—10

After the death of Saul in the battle of Mount Gilboa, David
inquired of the Lord whether or not he should go up to the
cities of Judah, and the lot fell in such a way as to indicate that
he should go.   He went to Hebron, and there the elders
crowned him king of Judah.   Before he had finally left Ziklag,
he had caused the execution of the Amalekite who claimed to
have killed Saul, and had composed the magnificent elegy over
Saul and Jonathan.   (2 Samuel, chapter 1.)   Also, shortly
after his coronation, he commended the men of Jabesh-gilead
who had given decent burial to the body of Saul.   But from
that time on, the relationship between Israel, the North, and
Judah, the South, was for a while not so friendly.   Ishbaal,
the weak son of Saul, succeeded to the rulership of the North,
bolstered by the power of Abner, a relative (possibly uncle) of
Saul who had been his commander-in-chief.   During an en-
gagement with some of the men of David, he was pursued by
Asahel, a younger brother of David's great general, Joab.   He
probably had no great fear of Asahel, but he did not want to
start a blood-feud with his brother.   However, Asahel, intoxi-
cated by the idea that he had put Ishbaal's general to flight,
would not be dissuaded from the pursuit, and, since he was fleet
of foot, Abner had no recourse save to thrust behind him with
his spear, killing his adversary, and starting the feud with Joab.

Some time after this, Ishbaal accused his general of taking as
his wife a woman who had been a concubine of Saul.   Among
the ancient Hebrews, as with most other Orientals, it was the
custom for a new king to inherit the entire harem of the preceding ruler, with the exception of course of his own mother,
who became the queen mother.   Since Abner was a relative of
Saul, the accusation that he had taken Saul's wife was equiva-

lent to charging him with conspiring to seize the throne. Abner was quite indignant but there is a real possibility that the claim of Ishbaal was justified. As a result of this disagreement, Abner sought to default to Ishbaal's mortal enemy, David. David, however, demanded that, if Abner came under his banner, he should bring with him Michal, his former wife, who was the daughter of Saul and therefore a strong support to any claim David might make to the throne of Israel (the North). Abner brought her, with her pathetic second husband following and bewailing his grief until he was sent back home. David welcomed Abner to his forces, but, after David had sent him back to organize men in the North in his behalf, Joab returned from a marauding expedition and was told what had happened. Without David's knowledge he summoned Abner to return, and, speaking to him in private, killed him—thus terminating the feud which had begun with the death of Joab's brother, Asahel.

This action put David in an embarrassing position. How could he expect men of consequence to desert Ishbaal and to serve the king of Judah when the first and foremost of them had met immediate death? To proclaim his innocence, David mourned and fasted all the day; ordered his followers to mourn; and composed an elegy for Abner. His sorrow seems to have been accepted as a token of good faith. Shortly after this, Ishbaal, with no one of ability to protect him, was murdered. David executed the murderers, who came to him expecting a reward. He had no desire to promote the idea that anyone could with impunity murder an anointed king: he held that office himself. Shortly after this the people of the North accepted the inevitable and crowned David king.

David had considerable trouble with the Philistines before he finally overcame them as a threat to Israel. It is most likely that this trouble broke out shortly after he had been crowned king of the united country. He had been a vassal of the Philistine king Achish before the death of Saul, and probably continued paying tribute. If the Philistines were able to destroy Saul and his army, they probably demanded tribute from his successor, Ishbaal—and he had little recourse but to pay it. But when David had united the kingdoms under his compelling personality, the Israelites once again became a threat to the Philistines. However, there now was a better man than Saul in charge.

One incident, which might not appeal to men of the present day, is characteristic of the hold David had on the imagination and affection of his men. Fighting against the Philistines (2 Samuel 23:13-17), he longed for a drink of water from the well at Bethlehem, which he had undoubtedly known as a boy. Three of his mighty men broke through the Philistine lines, then at Bethlehem, and brought water to him. Overcome by the heroism of the men, he claimed unworthiness for such a gift, and poured it out on the ground as a sacrifice to the LORD, even as the Israelites in the time of Moses had poured out water, their most precious possession in the desert, unto the LORD. Such spontaneous actions made him one of the great leaders of all time.

Early in his reign David captured from the Jebusites the city of Jerusalem which was to be his great capital, and called it the "City of David." The text in the Hebrew is not clear, but it is likely that, after the inhabitants had taunted the Israelites with the statement that the blind and the lame would be able to defend it, some of David's men (the account in 1 Chronicles 11:6 mentions Joab as the first) entered by a secret passageway used for carrying water and opened the gates. (2 Samuel 5: 6-9.) The city was an ideal one for the capital of the newly united kingdom: it was easily defended; almost centrally located; and David could not be accused of favoritism either to his old friends in Judah or to his new supporters in Israel, the North, for it had not previously belonged to either. Soon after, he made it the religious capital as well, by bringing in the ark of God.

For some time after the Philistines had been so glad to get rid of the ark, it had remained in a private home in Judah. David went with a great crowd to bring it to Jerusalem, but, when one of the oxen drawing the cart stumbled, a man named Uzzah put his hand on the ark to steady it, and fell down dead, quite possibly the result of a heart attack after the exertion, or the realization that he had touched so sacred and dangerous an object. After an interval of three months, a second procession was formed, and this one brought the ark into Jerusalem. David marched in the procession and "danced before the LORD with all his might," wearing a somewhat scanty garment called a linen ephod. He was quite happy about his accomplishment until he reached home and found that his wife Michal had been watching him in disdain from the palace window. There followed a family argument of classic proportions, the sad outcome of which was that she never bore David a child.

Having made Jerusalem the center of religious life, the king wanted to build a great temple for the LORD, but something interfered. We have a late addition to the narrative in the form of a speech by the prophet Nathan, explaining that the LORD did not want David to build a house for him. Not until the time of Solomon was it erected.

The brilliance of David as a military commander, and, above all, his genius for instilling loyalty in his followers, enabled him to conquer one nation after another of the people about him. He came at a time when both Egypt to the southwest and Assyria to the northeast were weak, which helped make his expansion possible. Among the nations annexed by David were Syria, with its capital Damascus; Edom, the long-time enemy of Judah, Moab, traditionally the home of David's great-grandmother, Ruth; and Ammon, whose king Nahash had been the bitter enemy of Saul.[2] It is a bit embarrassing to the reputation of David to note that, in the beginning of the story of the subjection of Ammon, Saul's enemy was called by David his own close friend, and it was only when the son of Ammon accused David's ambassadors of being spies, shaved off half the beard of each, and sent them back home with their garments cut off at the waist that the guise of friendship was dropped. (2 Samuel, chapter 10.)

David wished to show favor to someone of the house of Saul, and found Meribaal (Mephibosheth),[3] the lame son of his friend Jonathan, still alive. (2 Samuel, chapter 9.) David gave him servants who had previously served Saul, and a per-

---

2. See also Appendix, Note D.
3. Meribaal, as in 1 Chlronicles 8:34, was the original name—changed to Mephibosheth to avoid writing Baal. See Henry Preserved Smith, *A Critical and Exegetical Commentary on the Books of Samuel ICC* ("International Critical Commentary"; New York: Charles Scribner's Sons, 1909), p. 285.

manent place at his table. This was without any danger to
David, since Jonathan's son, though of the house of Saul, was
lame, and, because of this infirmity, could never have become
king.

THE SIN OF DAVID, 2 SAMUEL, chapters 11—12

In spite of the admiration the author had for the king of
Israel, we have a marvelous straightforward account of his
great sin, told with complete candor. Fortunately the subject
was great enough to be recognized as a hero because of his
other actions, even though this most discreditable incident is
the best-known story in his life.

There is an implied criticism in the opening words: "In the
spring of the year, the time when kings go forth to battle."
David was at home, though his army was in the field. He saw
the beautiful Bathsheba, wife of Uriah the Hittite, bathing herself, and ordered her brought to the palace. Some time later,
when she found she was to bear a child and told David, he
ordered her husband brought back from the front lines, and,
after inquiring of him about military affairs, told him to go to
his own home, sending a present after him, and hoping the
husband would bear the responsibility for the child when it
was born. There was both a religious and a military restriction
against any man of the army living with his wife when the
army was on active duty. Either out of regard for this custom,
or because Uriah had received some inkling of what had transpired, he refused to go to his home, but remained in the one
place where a soldier could be on active duty and could be seen
by all—on guard at the door of the king's house. When this
plan failed, David sent him back to battle, bearing his own
death warrant: a letter to Joab ordering that Uriah be placed
in the forefront of the hardest fighting, and that those with him
should draw back, leaving him to be killed. This plan worked.
After Bathsheba had finished her period of mourning for her
husband, she was again brought to the palace, and became
David's wife.

The most beautiful parable in the Old Testament is here attributed to the prophet Nathan: the story of the rich man who
took the single lamb owned by his poor neighbor, which had

been raised as a pet in his home, and killed it for a feast for a wayfarer, rather than sacrifice one of his own large flock. When the innate decency of David roused his anger so that he shouted to Nathan that the man was worthy of death and should restore the lamb fourfold, the prophet leveled his finger at him and said, "You are the man." It is often easy, after a series of events has transpired, to trace a relationship of cause and effect from the first to the last of them. It is particularly easy to do this in the series of misfortunes which dogged David's later life, blaming each on the one which preceded it, and thus accrediting the whole list to this sin of David. This is expressed in the words of the LORD attributed (later) to Nathan:

"Now therefore the sword shall never depart from your house, because you have despised me, and have taken the wife of Uriah the Hittite to be your wife." (2 Samuel 12:10.)

He also is pictured as predicting the death of the child, which in due time occurred.

RESULTS OF DAVID'S SIN, 2 SAMUEL, chapters 13—20

The first step in this unhappy series of causes and effects was the unbridled license of David's son Amnon, brought up in the unwholesome atmosphere of the harem. Falling in love with his half sister Tamar, he listened to the advice of an evil cousin, and, feigning illness, asked that Tamar should come to his house to prepare food for him. When they were alone, he failed to seduce her, so took her by force. The custom of the time would have permitted him to marry her, but this he refused to do. After David's great sin, it was most embarrassing for the father to punish his son for this action—so he did nothing. But Tamar's full brother, Absalom, felt that the responsibility of avenging his sister fell upon his shoulders. Also, the breach between David and Absalom began when David shirked his responsibility.

Biding his time, Absalom after two years invited all David's sons to a sheep-shearing festival, and, when Amnon was under the influence of wine, caused his servants to kill him. Absalom fled from the country, remaining abroad for three years, and

David, becoming reconciled to the loss of Amnon, began to grieve for the son who had killed him. Joab, intimately aware of the king's moods, instructed a clever woman to appear before him with an imaginary case for his judgment. She claimed that she was a widow, and one of her two sons in a quarrel had struck and killed the other. Her late husband's family demanded the death of her remaining son, presumably that they might receive the inheritance, thus leaving no descendant to preserve the family name. In those days, when the belief in a life after death had not yet arisen, the desire for children to perpetuate a family was very great. David granted her request for the life of her son, whereupon she accused him of inconsistency in granting forgiveness to a stranger while his own son was in exile. The wise old king recognized the hand of Joab in the incident, but permitted Absalom to return to Jerusalem— although not to his presence. After another two years, Absalom called Joab to him—setting fire to his grain field to make certain that he would come. This time Joab himself interceded with the king, Absalom was allowed to come and bow before David, and his father kissed him. But the bitter resentment still smouldered in Absalom's heart.

As soon as Absalom had the free run of Jerusalem, he began to undermine the prestige of his father, getting a chariot and horses, with footmen to run before him. He also accosted those who came to appear before David for judgment, telling each that his cause was just, and that a good arbiter like Absalom would assuredly decide in his favor. After four years of this undercover work, when he had his agents selected and instructed, he went to Hebron, former capital of Judah, under the pretense of making sacrifices, and the revolt came to a head. David and his household fled from Jerusalem, leaving ten of his concubines in charge of the palace.

It is interesting to note how the characters of the various actors in this drama were revealed by the disaster which had overtaken the king. Ittai, an officer of the mercenary soldiers who had recently come from Gath to serve David, was told that he was at liberty to return, but he responded with words which will be quoted forever:

"As the LORD lives, and as my lord the king lives, wherever my lord the king shall be, whether for death or for life, there also will your servant be." (2 Samuel 15:21.)

Ahithophel, David's counselor, served Absalom as one of the intellectual leaders of the conspiracy. He seems to have been the grandfather of Bathsheba (2 Samuel 11:3; 23:34) with whom David had committed adultery, and whom he later married. It may be that on this account Ahithophel nourished a grudge against the king. Hushai, another of David's counselors, took exactly the opposite course. He risked his life by going to Absalom as a counselor, passing the word from the inner council to the two priests, Zadok and Abiathar, who forwarded it to David, and was even able to persuade Absalom to disregard the wise counsel of Ahithophel, and to give David time to collect his followers before he was forced into battle. Because his advice had been spurned, Ahithophel killed himself.

Meribaal (Mephibosheth), the grandson of Saul whom David had befriended, had a servant Ziba, who brought quantities of food to the exiled monarch, and told him his master was in Jerusalem, rejoicing because he expected to be reinstated in the kingdom of Absalom. David promptly gave Ziba all the property which had belonged to Meribaal. (2 Samuel 16:1-4.) However later, when Meribaal came to David dirty and unkept because he had mourned long over the king's misfortune, and accused Ziba of lying about him, David gave up trying to find the guilty one and divided the land of the house of Saul between them. Of the two, it would seem that Meribaal was more likely telling the truth—being lame he could never have aspired to the kingship, and it is difficult to see how he could have hoped his position would have been improved under Absalom. (2 Samuel 19:24-30.) Another man of the house of Saul, Shimei, threw stones at David and his servants and cursed him. Joab's brother begged for permission to kill Shimei, but David said the LORD was punishing him for his sins, and spared him.

But the crowning insult was perpetrated by Absalom, David's son, who publicly took as his own wives the concubines his father had left, thereby proclaiming in an irrevocable manner that David was deposed and he, Absalom, was now king in his place.

By the time Absalom finally moved to attack David, the crafty old warrior was ready. Because his lieutenants would not let him endanger himself in battle, the troops were divided among three competent generals, who received from the king their parting injunction: "Deal gently for my sake with the young man Absalom." A great victory was won by David's troops, and Absalom, riding under a tree, caught his head in its branches and hung suspended in the air. Joab, disregarding the orders of David, killed him. When news of the victory was brought to the king, his first question was about the welfare of his son, and after he had been told, he gave the shortest and most poignant of the three elegies ascribed to him:

"O my son Absalom, my son, my son Absalom! Would I had died instead of you, O Absalom, my son, my son!" (2 Samuel 18:33b.)

When Joab drove his darts through the heart of Absalom, he removed the gravest danger to the peace of the kingdom, but there were still disturbing factors which had been set in motion by David's ambitious and unscrupulous son. David's grief was so great, he neglected to show proper appreciation to those who had saved his throne for him, until after Joab had rebuked him to his face. Partly because of the coldness which had grown up between him and his general, partly in an attempt to win back his own tribe of Judah, which had supported Absalom, David removed Joab from his position and replaced him by another Judahite, Amasa. It was a poor bit of statesmanship. An adventurer from the north named Sheba sought to capitalize upon the unrest of the kingdom, and led a new insurrection, giving out the battle cry which shows the deep-seated disaffection which had probably existed in the north from the very beginning of David's reign, and which was not settled until Jeroboam finally broke the bonds of the United Kingdom:

> "We have no portion in David,
> and we have no inheritance in the son of Jesse;
> every man to his tents, O Israel!"
> —2 Samuel 20:1b

David's tribe of Judah was at this time loyal to him, but his
new general lacked the aggressiveness of the former one. When
he delayed too long, David ordered the brother of Joab to take
up the pursuit of Sheba. Joab himself joined the chase and,
when he encountered Amasa, the man who had supplanted him
as general, he promptly killed him. Continuing the pursuit of
Sheba, Joab took complete control, chased the rebel until he
took refuge in a city in the extreme northern part of the kingdom, and started a siege of the city. He agreed to raise the
siege if the people would deliver up Sheba, and eventually settled for his head, which was tossed over the wall to him.

It is possible to trace a thread of cause and effect through all
these misfortunes. Because David committed his great sin with
Bathsheba, he was hesitant about punishing his son Amnon for
his sin against his half sister Tamar. Because of this, Absalom
killed Amnon, and opened the breach between himself and
David. This resulted in the division of the kingdom at the
time of Absalom's revolt, and ill will between David and his
most loyal follower Joab, and the subsequent but ill-fated
revolt of Sheba. The weak ties between the north and south
were severely strained—after the death of Solomon they were
permanently severed—and the revolt and death of Absalom
deprived the kingdom of a logical heir to the throne, so that
ultimately there was more bloodshed before Solomon felt his
position was secure. All these can be suggested as possible results of David's sin, backing up the statement attributed to
Nathan, that the sword would not depart from David's house.

CHAPTER XI

THE UNITED KINGDOM

Solomon the Magnificent

THE SUCCESSOR TO DAVID, 1 KINGS, chapters 1—2

King David was an old man. Since he was no longer able to keep warm, no matter how many clothes were piled upon his bed, the men of his court sought to find a beautiful young woman to become his wife. They brought him a girl named Abishag the Shunammite, whose duty it was to sleep with the old man and to keep him warm. She bore him no children.

It may be that the choice of Abishag as David's last wife was really a test to determine whether or not he was still able to father children. Some religions of the ancient Orient required fertility of the king and queen to insure fertility of the fields, the flocks, and the citizens of the country. It is not difficult to imagine the action described in 1 Kings 1:1-4 as the cause of which verses 5-10 was the result, where, after we are told that the king did not beget any children, the action of Adonijah toward claiming the kingship was described.

Whatever the reasoning, it was time for a successor to David to be chosen, but as yet there was no established rule of procedure. Saul, the first king of Israel, had been succeeded by his son Ishbaal for a short time, but only in the northern part of the kingdom. In reality, David was the second king, and his only relationship to Saul was that of son-in-law. The fourth son of David was Adonijah, but at least two of the three sons older than he were dead by the time David approached senility. Whether the other was still alive or not, we do not know. Eager to lose no opportunity, Adonijah prepared a retinue for himself, and arranged a great sacrificial feast, apparently expecting to be crowned king. He must have had many qualifications for rulership, for he was supported by two of the great men of the kingdom: Abiathar, who had been David's priest since his days as an outlaw from Saul's court, and Joab, the great general who, though impulsive and brutal when necessity had arisen, had been more loyal to David's wel- fare than had David himself.

When word of this feast was brought by Nathan to Bath- sheba, she realized that she had to act quickly. Her one op- portunity to become queen mother[1] was at hand. She per- suaded the feeble king that he had promised her to put their son Solomon—many years younger than Adonijah—upon the throne when he could no longer occupy it. By the king's order, Nathan and a priest, Zadok, anointed Solomon and introduced him to the people as king. Then Solomon followed a typical oriental procedure in making himself secure upon the throne. Much of the blame was placed upon the orders of David, but we must remember that we have the report of only one side of a palace coup. It is difficult to imagine David ordering the death of his old comrade-in-arms Joab, as Solomon says he did. But Joab had supported Adonijah for the throne, so he had to die. Even though he fled to the sacred altar of the LORD, where by all the laws of Israel he should have been safe, he was struck down by the express order of Solomon (claiming that David had required it) and the command of the army turned over to his executioner.

Abiathar, the old chaplain of David, had also supported Adonijah, but Solomon wanted no part in the death of a priest of the LORD. He knew that Saul had slain many of them, in- cluding the father of Abiathar, and the latter part of Saul's reign had been anything but happy. So Abiathar was exiled to his home in Anathoth. Shimei, the man who had cursed David at the time of Absalom's rebellion, was not mixed up with Adonijah's abortive attempt for the throne, but his association with the house of Saul made him a dangerous man. He was therefore ordered to remain in Jerusalem (the exact opposite to the fate of Abiathar). However, when some of his runaway slaves were captured in the city of Gath, he went there to claim them, and paid with his life.

---

1. It may be, however, that the plan to crown Solomon was at least as much the work of Nathan as of Bathsheba.

But it is in the excuse for the execution of Adonijah that our
credulity is stretched to the maximum. We are told that Solomon at first spared his life, but later Adonijah asked Bathsheba
to intercede with her son, so that he would grant him permission
to marry Abishag. It is difficult to believe that Adonijah, who
had just been pardoned for seeking the crown, would run the
risk of asking for marriage to the former king's last wife—the
equivalent, as Solomon pointed out, of again claiming the kingship. But even that would be more credible than to believe that
he would ask, of all people, Bathsheba, who had started the
campaign against him, and had only at that time achieved what
must have been for many years her ambition, the position of
queen mother. Whether we can believe Solomon's explanation
or not, Adonijah did not live out the day. That the writer of
the account realized something of the purpose of Solomon in
removing all these men who might have caused him trouble is
evident from the conclusion of the section in the latter part of
the last verse of chapter two: "So the kingdom was established
in the hand of Solomon."

THE GLORIES OF SOLOMON, 1 KINGS, chapters 3—7

Nearly 1,000 years after the time of Solomon, when Jesus
wanted to emphasize the beauty of the natural lilies, he said:
"Consider the lilies of the field, how they grow; they neither
toil nor spin; yet I tell you, even Solomon in all his glory was
not arrayed like one of these." (Matthew 6:28f.) Throughout all time, Solomon has been considered the standard of glory
and, as we shall shortly see, of wisdom. His greatest claim to
glory is based upon the erection of the temple, a task he had
inherited from his father. With the co-operation of Hiram,
king of the city of Tyre, he erected the splendid structure over
a period of seven years. We are told the sound of iron was not
heard in the temple area, all the fitting of parts was done elsewhere—very likely because there still may have been a taboo
against the innovation of iron tools on so sacred a structure.
It is interesting to note, though, that his own palace required
nearly twice as long for its completion. A number of other
great buildings were erected by Solomon, the first real builder
of Israelitish history. It was partly by his building program

that he bankrupted his kingdom, for all except the commonest of labor had to be imported, and Israel produced very little of the necessary building materials.

Solomon was noted for at least two international alliances: one with Egypt and one with Tyre. The former, sealed by the marriage of the Israelite king to the daughter of the pharaoh, was made in the interest of international security. If the pharaoh in question was the last one of the 21st Dynasty, the security did not last long, for that dynasty was soon overthrown by the invading Libyans. If, however, the alliance was made with the first of these Libyan rulers, Sheshonk (or Shishak) I, it likely was made with the provision that a son of the marriage of Solomon and the Egyptian princess would succeed him upon the throne of Israel. Since, eventually, Solomon's successor was Rehoboam, son of an Ammonite princess (1 Kings 14:21), this may have been the reason for the subsequent enmity of Pharaoh Shishak, who invaded Jerusalem shortly after the death of Solomon and plundered the temple and city.

The alliance with Tyre provided Israel with luxury goods and ships. It is doubtful that the trade carried on through this Phoenician city was of great financial benefit to Israel. The products of Solomon's land were the staples by which men lived —wool, grain, wine, olive oil, and so forth. Whatever was brought in in exchange, the balance was decidedly against Israel. In spite of Solomon's efforts to increase taxes, even sending forced labor out of the country, it was necessary for him to cede cities in the area of Galilee to square accounts with Hiram, King of Tyre. (1 Kings 5:10-18; 9:10-14.) Even though we read of Solomon's merchant fleet (1 Kings 9:26-28), the ships were undoubtedly built by Hiram's craftsmen and manned by his sailors. Nevertheless, one thing may be said in favor of Solomon's commercial enterprises. Recent excavations south of the Dead Sea have uncovered extensive iron works originally developed by this interesting king. He must have been intelligently progressive in at least one very important section of his country's economy.

The delightful story of the Queen of Sheba has done much to enhance the reputation of Solomon as a glorious monarch. (1 Kings 10:1-13.) Having made a long journey to see for herself the wonders of his kingdom and examples of his wisdom, she professed that they far surpassed any report of them she had received. Today the ruling house of Ethiopia claims direct lineal descent from an otherwise unrecorded matrimonial alliance between Solomon and this queen—hence Haile Selassie's proud title "Lion of the Tribe of Judah."

THE FOLLIES OF SOLOMON, 1 KINGS 4:20-28; 7:1-12; 10:14-29, chapter 11

There are several areas in which the actions of Solomon are not characteristic of one of the world's great wise men. For one, we have the record of his extravagance. Perhaps later writers, seeking to extol his magnificence, enlarged too greatly upon the way he spent. Certainly the record is entirely out of proportion to the simple country kingdom which never boasted of even a provincial capital until well on in the reign of Solomon's father. Nevertheless, he spent what he had inherited, taxed the people to the point of rebellion, and then had to give away cities to his creditor to balance his accounts. And certainly the excessive taxation was not the act of a wise man. All the northern part of the kingdom—ten and a half tribes, which had never thought of itself as thoroughly integrated with Solomon's tribe, Judah—attempted to revolt and immediately after Solomon's death made a second and successful attempt.

It did not take Solomon long to lose other large segments of his empire. Though he did maintain a tenuous hold on his own Israelitish tribes, he soon lost both the Kingdom of Damascus and the Kingdom of Edom, which his father had subdued. A later moralistic editor explained the loss of this territory as a punishment of the LORD because Solomon had worshiped foreign gods—probably a just accusation.

REPUTATION FOR WISDOM, 1 KINGS, chapter 3; 4:29-34

More than any other incident, the story of Solomon's dream at the sanctuary of Gibeon is responsible for his fame as a wise man, yet it is a singularly unsubstantial basis for such a reputation. He claimed that, in a dream, the LORD offered to grant a wish, and when Solomon requested wisdom for governing his country, the LORD was so pleased, he also granted him long life and great wealth. People of ancient days thought of dreams as the direct manifestations of the future, as revealed by the LORD, but today we are more likely to question the validity of so complimentary a dream when it could have been repeated only by the one who was complimented. Likewise, the accuracy of the prediction is open to question. Though he was supposed to be rich, he ran his kingdom out of funds, and though he was supposed to administer it wisely, he lost a large part of it through inadequate defense, and alienated three-quarters of the original Israelitish territory.

However, there were two ways in which, according to the ideas of his time, Solomon qualified as a wise man. He knew the names of trees, plants, animals, birds, and fish, and he "uttered" (not necessarily originated) 3,000 proverbs. Knowledge of a wise saying to the ancient Oriental was wisdom, for it was supposed to be a guide in time of decision. It is largely from this passage (1 Kings 4:32) that we get the expression repeatedly used to designate certain of the passages in the Book of Proverbs as "the proverbs of Solomon," which, in turn, is responsible for the belief of many people that Solomon was the author of a large part of that book.

One other well-known story which is associated with Solomon's reputation for wisdom is the account of his decision regarding the two harlots, both of whom claimed to be the mother of the same infant. By threatening to cut the child in two, Solomon was thought to have discovered as being the true mother the one who refused to let the child be harmed.

RULERS OF THE UNITED KINGDOM

Because the weakling son of Saul, Ishbaal, ruled only a short time, and then over only part of the kingdom, we may speak of three rulers of the United Kingdom during the century of its existence. Saul, chosen by Samuel, united the tribes of Israel and made possible the kingdom. Selected possibly because his mental instability marked him as being under the spirit of the LORD, that same characteristic probably resulted in his undoing. Samuel, who had never completely relinquished his authority, rejected Saul in the name of the LORD.   Unable adequately to rally his forces, Saul failed and perished in the battle of Mount Gilboa against the united Philistines.

Samuel's next choice (made some time before the death of Saul) was David, whose personality supplied what Saul had lacked. Combining the wise choice of lieutenants with personal competence as a fighter, courage, and the ability to appeal to his followers, David put the kingdom on a solid basis and expanded the boundaries to their greatest extent.

The third ruler, Solomon, presided over a transition as great in proportion as the Industrial Revolution. He introduced industry, and a complete governmental reorganization, and sought to make Jerusalem a great world capital. Possibly, if he had had the rugged military establishment of his father David, he might have been able to postpone the evil day. But he was baffled by four things:

a. His funds were inadequate for his ambitions.

b. Egypt increased in power, and began to meddle in Israelite affairs, offering protection to Jeroboam, who had revolted in Israel, and to Hadad the Edomite, who also revolted against Solomon.

c. An adventurer seized the throne of Damascus, and successfully resisted Solomon in the northeast. A little later the rising power of Assyria posed an even greater threat.

d. Solomon was unable to still the discontent in the northern part of his own kingdom.

RELIGION IN THE UNITED KINGDOM

The religion of Israel during the period of the United Kingdom was primarily the worship of the LORD (Yahweh), but there were many crudities in the technique. When David was driven from Israel by Saul, he complained that he was forced to worship other gods (1 Samuel 26:19) i.e., the power of the LORD ended with the boundary lines of Israel. And, of course, when Uzzah dropped dead after he had tried to save the sacred ark from falling (2 Samuel 6:6f), it was interpreted as a manifestation of the wrath of the LORD, because his taboo had been violated.

There were a number of sacred places for the worship of the LORD, but David, by bringing in the ark, effectively raised Jerusalem to the place of pre-eminence which in the period of the Judges had been occupied by Shiloh, until its destruction by the Philistines. Solomon made the position of Jerusalem secure by building the temple, and something over 300 years later, it became the *only* accredited sanctuary for the worship of the LORD.

Two men who were called prophets of the LORD took active parts in the political life of the period, though not to the same extent as Samuel had. The record shows Nathan as having been an important factor in the selection of Solomon as the successor to David (1 Kings, chapter 1), and Ahijah, who, like Samuel, came from the religious sanctuary of Shiloh, felt that it was the LORD's desire that the kingdom of Solomon should be divided, and designated Jeroboam as the man to accomplish it, by tearing his new cloak into twelve pieces, giving him ten of them. (1 Kings 11:26-40.)

Although the worship of the LORD was the official religion of the kingdom, it is very likely that the worship of Baal continued side by side with it. Probably some of the sacrifices became agricultural, rather than animal, and there were almost certainly sacred prostitutes in the land, dedicated to the Baal form of worship. We find no record of official opposition to Baal worship by any king before the great-grandson of Solomon, Asa, who drove the cult prostitutes out of the land. (1 Kings 15:9-15.) But, as mentioned above, we are told that Solomon worshiped many foreign gods.

The glorious temple of Solomon did much to unify both the people and the religion, and the ritual practices of the temple undoubtedly began to crystallize during his reign.

LITERATURE WRITTEN BEFORE THE DIVISION OF THE KINGDOM

There were no writings of any great length completed before the division of the kingdom after the death of Solomon, only a few of them covering more than one chapter each of our present Old Testament. The earliest were short poems, frequently of only two, three or four lines each. One such was the Song of Lamech (Genesis 4:23-24):

> Lamech said to his wives:
> "Adah and Zillah, hear my voice;
>   you wives of Lamech, hearken to what I say:
> I have slain a man for wounding me,
>   a young man for striking me.
> If Cain is avenged sevenfold,
>   truly Lamech seventy-seven fold."

Some think this is a song of triumph uttered when the first blacksmith of Israel succeeded in making his first sword. It may be the oldest passage in the Bible. Another old bit of poetry is the Song of Miriam, assigned (perhaps accurately) to the sister of Moses when the Egyptians pursuing Israel were drowned at the Sea of Reeds (Exodus 15:21):

> And Miriam sang to them:
> "Sing to the LORD, for he has triumphed gloriously;
> the horse and his rider he has thrown into the sea"

In addition to many short poems of a warlike nature, there are some indicating interest in peaceful pursuits, such as the "Song of the Well" (Numbers 21:17f):

> Then Israel sang this song:
> "Spring up, O well—Sing to it!—
> the well which the princes dug,
> which the nobles of the people delved,
> with the scepter and with their staves."

Of somewhat greater length is Jotham's "Fable of the Trees" (Judges 9:7-15), which shows his disappointment because the men of Shechem had made his blood-thirsty half brother Abimelech their king—a man no more fitted to rule than the brambles of the forest. One of the greatest of these early poems is the "Song of Deborah" (Judges, chapter 5) which describes the great battle of the River Kishon and the death of Sisera.

Some of the early poems were collected into two books, "The Book of the Wars of the LORD" (see Numbers 21:14) and "The Book of the Upright (Jashar)." (See Joshua 10:12f and David's beautiful lament over Saul and Jonathan, 2 Samuel 1:17-27.) No one knows how many of the other early poems may have been copied from these or similar books into the narrative books of our Old Testament as were the three examples just given. Of course, the two books—"The Book of the Wars of the Lord" and "The Book of Jashar" have long since crumbled into dust. It is only because of these quotations that we know anything of them at all.

One popular type of early writing was that produced when a man wrote a poem describing a group of people living in his day, and then ascribed its authorship to some great hero of the past. A clear example of this is the "Blessing of Jacob" in Genesis, chapter 49. This series of descriptions of the various tribes of Israel was attributed to Jacob, the traditional father of the men who were the originators of those tribes, as though he had called his sons together and predicted what would happen to the descendants of each. The various poems were probably not written by the same author, but all are many centuries after the time of Jacob. For example, the blessing given Judah, which says "The scepter shall not depart from Judah" would seem not to have been written before the time of David, the first man of the tribe of Judah to sit upon the throne of Israel. There are other writings of this type, e.g., "The Blessing of Noah" (Genesis 9:25-27) and "The Oracles of Balaam." (Numbers 23f.)

One very important section of material written before the division of the kingdom is the so-called "Covenant Code," Exodus 20:23—23:33. This little body of law, though it includes many of the injunctions of the Ten Commandments, is particularly interested in civil legislation. It seems to have come from the period of early settling in Palestine, after the wilderness wandering, and a short time before the monarchy.[2] Also written by this time were many of the stories of Samuel, Saul, and David, and the individual stories of the Judges, all of these to be later edited and incorporated in more extensive books.

2. See Appendix, Note C.

There were many other fragments of the types named in this section which were in written form before the division of the kingdom, e.g., many short poems of various sorts, and many stories of warlike incidents—but there were no books written as we have them today. A century after this time there was a single great epic history developed which we call the "J history." It included many of these individual bits we have described here, and later was interwoven with other somewhat similar histories to form some of the great historical books of the Old Testament as we know them.

CHAPTER XII

THE DIVIDED KINGDOM

The Division of the Kingdom and the Crisis of Elijah

REASONS FOR THE DIVISION, 1 KINGS 12:1-20

The kingdom of Solomon did not last until his son had been seated upon the throne. Jeroboam, former master of forced labor under Solomon, had sought refuge in Egypt after his unsuccessful attempt to divide the kingdom. As soon as he had learned of Solomon's death, he returned to the northern part of the realm and, with the solid backing of the people, demanded that Rehoboam, son of Solomon, lighten the burden of their taxes. Against the advice of his mature counselors, Rehoboam refused, so the people of the north rallied with the same war cry as had been used by Sheba in his revolt against David:

"What portion have we in David?
We have no inheritance in the son of Jesse.
To your tents, O Israel!
Look now to your own house, David."
—1 Kings 12:16

Rehoboam countered by sending his current master of forced labor against them, but they promptly stoned him to death, and drove Rehoboam back to Jerusalem. From that time the kingdom was divided. When the Israelites had originally settled in Palestine, they were located in four areas, but after the time of Deborah they were consolidated into two. All the northern tribes formed a more or less homogeneous group: the one southern tribe of Judah, which had always been pretty much by itself, formed the major part of the other section. The dividing line between the two kingdoms followed roughly this cleavage plane between the two groups of tribes. Part of the small tribe of Benjamin stayed with the south and soon lost its identity: the other part of Benjamin cast its lot with the northern tribes. Since there were now ten and a half tribes of Israel in the north, that kingdom assumed the name of "Israel," while the south was called "Judah." From the time of the division, therefore, until the destruction of the Northern Kingdom, the name "Israel" refers to the north. It was also sometimes referred to by the name of the ruling dynasty, as "the House of Omri," or by the name of its capital (after it had been constructed) "Samaria." Since the principal tribe of the north, in which the city of Samaria was located, was Ephraim, that name is also sometimes used to indicate the entire country. After the fall of the northern kingdom in 722 B.C., the term "Israel" refers to the only tribe of Israel left—Judah, or the southern kingdom.

We may accept as the principal reasons for the division of the kingdom:

a. This original settling of the land in two separate groups.
b. The excessive taxation of Solomon.
c. The folly of Rehoboam when he first came to the throne.
d. The feeling of the northern tribes that the south was favored. The ruling dynasty was from Judah so favoritism was expected. Although Jerusalem had originally belonged to neither group, it was soon known as the "City of David," and, as the capital, received a major share of the new buildings. And, since the taxation was pretty much on a basis of ability to pay, and the northern tribes had the more fertile area, they probably paid more and at least thought they received less.

RELATIVE ADVANTAGES

When the kingdom was first divided, there were certain advantages possessed by Judah, and certain others peculiar to Israel. For Judah we find:

a. Unity. The small part of Benjamin which united with the south did not disturb the dominance of the large cohesive tribe of Judah. There was no room for intertribal jealousies. Though we believe there were some other groups which previously had united with Judah—possibly the tribe of Simeon and some others—they had become thoroughly amalgamated, in contradistinction to the many tribes of the north.

b. Occupation. There was only one great occupation in the south—the herding of sheep. This promoted the integration of the people.

c. Wealth. At least at the time of the division, most of the wealth was in the south—the main buildings, the treasures, many of the wealthy families. This advantage was largely removed shortly after by the sacking of Jerusalem by Pharaoh Sheshonk I.

d. Trade. The trade routes went through the north, but largely by-passed Judah. This made trading more difficult, but gave some added protection against invasion. The Southern Kingdom endured a century and a third after the Northern Kingdom had been destroyed.

e. Line of David. The dynasty of David belonged to the south. Frequently the kings left much to be desired in character, but the tradition of the Davidic line was strong. When a king died, one of his sons was expected to succeed him, whereas there frequently was a period of near-anarchy in the north after a king had died and before a new king could be anointed. There were only six years from the time of David to the fall of Jerusalem when there was not someone of his line on the throne of the south.

There were also a number of advantages possessed by the Northern Kingdom:

a. The territory of the north was far more extensive than that of the south.

b. Not only was it more extensive; it was much more fertile. The Plain of Esdraelon, garden spot of Palestine, was located in the kingdom of Israel.

c. The north was richer in manpower.

d. Though the presence of the trade routes created a military weakness, it also gave a decided economic and cultural advantage.

RULERS IN JUDAH, 1 KINGS 14:21—15:24; chapter 22

There were no great rulers in Judah in the hundred years after Solomon. The only way in which Rehoboam, the son of

Solomon, distinguished himself was by losing the major part of his kingdom.   His grandson Asa at least achieved a reputation through part of his reign as a worshiper of the LORD, for he was the first king to take an active stand against the worship of Baal. He went so far as to depose his own mother from her position as queen mother because of her Baal worship.   When Asa was pressed by Baasha, ruler of the north, he persuaded the king of Damascus to switch sides and to support Judah rather than the Northern Kingdom.   He probably succeeded only in stirring up a three-cornered fight among these small kingdoms.   He was not very successful against Baasha, for we are told there was war between them all their days.   (1 Kings 15:32.)

The son of Asa, Jehoshaphat, had a reputation untarnished as a worshiper of the LORD, but he very likely was little more than a vassal of King Ahab of the north, at least for the part of his reign we know best.   Showing a very evident reluctance to go to war as an ally of Ahab to recover for him the city of Ramoth-gilead, Jehoshaphat asked for the opinions of the prophets.   After 400 had predicted success, he asked if there were any more, but when the final one predicted failure, the expedition started anyway, so Jehoshaphat went along.   And then, just before the battle was begun, Ahab disguised himself, and Jehoshaphat donned his royal robes to serve as a decoy for the protection of Ahab.   (1 Kings, chapter 22.)   If this was friendship it was carrying it pretty far.   However, it was Ahab, not Jehoshaphat, who was killed.   Later Jehoshaphat married his son to Athaliah, the daughter of Ahab.   It probably looked at the time like a brilliant marriage, but eventually it proved disastrous to Judah.

RULERS IN ISRAEL—JEROBOAM, 1 KINGS, chapters 12; 14

During this same hundred-year period, there were three important rulers in the northern kingdom, of whom the first was Jeroboam, the man who split the kingdom.   He must have been a remarkable man, for he rallied the northern tribes behind him the second time, when Solomon had just died, in spite of the dismal fiasco of his first attempt.   One of the first things he had to do was to provide places of worship for his people.   From the time of the judges, when the Danites robbed Micah of his silver image, the city of Dan in the extreme north of Palestine had been an Israelite sanctuary. Even older than Dan was the sanctuary at Bethel, in the tribe of Ephraim, where the patriarch Jacob had seen his vision of God. Since it was unthinkable that the people of the north, or Israel, should have gone over into a hostile country, Judah, to worship in the temple of Solomon in Jerusalem, Jeroboam established these ancient sanctuaries of Dan and Bethel as the official places of worship for his kingdom. It was probably necessary to appoint a number of additional priests, to take care of the new activity there.

From time immemorial there had been contact with the worship of bulls in the religion of Israel. In the time of Moses, Aaron had instituted the worship of the golden calf. There were images of bulls under the great basin in Solomon's temple. Usually the worship of bulls was considered by the later ages as associated with Baal worship. Jeroboam was said to have set up golden calves at his sanctuaries for the people to worship.

The writers who finally put the books of 1 and 2 Kings in their present shape were called the "Deuteronomic editors." They wrote some 350 years after Jeroboam came to the throne, and interpreted all history as the moralistic expression of the LORD's pleasure or displeasure at the actions of men. By the time they wrote, there were no priests except Levites. Also, there was a rigid rule that the LORD could be worshiped in only one place, the temple at Jerusalem, a law which was promulgated in 621 B.C. We must therefore realize that, instead of having an unbiased account of the actions of Jeroboam, we are reading a judgment of the man written by authors who:

a. criticized him because, in opposition to a custom established much later, he ordained priests who were not Levites;
b. condemned him for establishing—or re-establishing—sanctuaries other than Jerusalem, in contradistinction to laws given three hundred years after his action; and
c. looked at the division of the kingdom from the viewpoint of the south, Judah, which felt that the great empire of Solomon had been ruined by his actions.

For these reasons the Deuteronomic editors considered Jeroboam wholly evil, and characterized any subsequent king of Israel of whom they disapproved as one who "walked in all the way of Jeroboam the son of Nebat, and in the sins which he made Israel to sin." (1 Kings 16:26.) Jeroboam ruled twenty-two years, during all of which time—as during all of the first fifty years of the kingdom—there was war between the north and the south.

In the first fifty years after the division of the kingdom there were five kings of the north, three of whom died violent deaths. Then came Omri, who, though he reigned only about a decade, was so powerful he has been called the "David of the North." Long after the death of the last king of his dynasty (the fourth in the Kingdom of Israel, according to the account, although one of them lasted only seven days) the records of the great Assyrian empire spoke of Israel as "the Land of the House of Omri." He greatly expanded the boundaries of the land, and conquered at least part of Moab. The "Moabite Stone," one of the important monuments we have from Palestine, tells how, long after the death of Omri who had conquered Moab, the Israelites were driven out of the land. Omri made many treaties, one of which, with Phoenicia, was sealed by the marriage of Omri's son Ahab to Jezebel, daughter of the king of Tyre, either during Omri's reign or after Ahab had come to the throne. One other accomplishment was the building of a new capital for the kingdom on land bought from a man named "Shemer," hence its name, "Samaria." It proved an admirable site for a great city. But the net summary of his deeds, as given in 1 Kings, is that he did more evil than all who were before him, walking in the way of Jeroboam, the son of Nebat. (1 Kings 16:25f.)

AHAB, JEZEBEL, AND ELIJAH, 1 KINGS 16:29—22:53

Ahab, son of Omri, ruled for two decades and, from a political viewpoint, was probably a pretty good king. Officially he was a worshiper of the LORD, because at least two of his children bore names of which "Yahweh" was a part: Ahaziah and Athaliah, as indicated by the "iah" on the ends of the names. But as part of a political alliance with the Phoenician kingdom of Tyre, he married Jezebel, daughter of Ethbaal the king. Before he had achieved the throne of Tyre, Ethbaal had been a priest of Baal, and apparently had thoroughly indoctrinated his daughter Jezebel with that religion. She went to Israel with all the zeal of a dedicated missionary, and promptly became the driving force behind this religion in her husband's country.

While there were occasionally strict enthusiasts who demanded only one or the other religion, there seems to have been a good deal of tolerance on the part of most people. Many worshiped both religions, though perhaps not at the same time. In his great test on Mount Carmel, Elijah said:

> "How long will you go limping with two different opinions? If the LORD is God, follow him, but if Baal, then follow him."—1 Kings 18:21

It was Ahab's misfortune to be caught between two such enthusiasts, neither of whom could be satisfied by halfway measures. He received warm approval from Jezebel for erecting an altar and a temple to Baal, but when a disastrous drought hit the land, Elijah indicated that it was a punishment from the LORD because of the worship of Baal.[1] Jezebel destroyed the prophets of the LORD (1 Kings 18:3f), and as soon as he was able, Elijah reciprocated by destroying the prophets of Baal, 450 of them. (1 Kings 18:40.)

In spite of the evil she did, one can scarcely avoid a grudging admiration for some of the qualities of this domineering queen. Years after this event, when she knew the brutal general Jehu would soon arrive to kill her, she had her maidens paint her eyes and dress her hair, and then, instead of begging for her life, taunted him with being an assassin. She was thrown from the window and a troop of cavalry rode over her, the dogs (scavengers) finishing what the hoofs of the horses had left. But while she lived, she lived like a queen. It may be that the dressing of the hair was part of a death ritual.

Ahab overcame Damascus and, in spite of previous indemnities suffered at the hands of its king, granted lenient terms and

---

1. The account in 1 Kings 17:1-7; 18:2, is presented as a prediction before the drought, which was described as ending only after Elijah's destruction of the prophets of Baal on Mount Carmel.

paved the way for a later alliance against the great common enemy, Assyria. This forgiving spirit was bitterly criticized by a prophet. (1 Kings 20:30-43.) Though the prophet was not Elijah, he probably represented his attitude.

The main point of conflict between Elijah and Ahab was Ahab's sponsorship of Baal worship, but one other issue arose. Ahab coveted a piece of land used as a vineyard by a man named Naboth. He offered to buy it, but since it had belonged to Naboth's ancestors, there were religious restrictions against its being sold. Jezebel, seeing her husband's frustration, arranged to have false witnesses testify that Naboth had cursed both God and the king. After he had been convicted and stoned to death, his property was forfeited to Ahab. Elijah then brought his hostility against Ahab into the open, and told him that, because of his action, in the place where the blood of Naboth had been shed, dogs would lick the blood of Ahab. Later, in the battle to seize Ramoth-gilead, a chance shot with a bow and arrow severed an artery and Ahab bled to death. When his chariot was washed, dogs lapped up the bloody water, in fulfillment of Elijah's prediction.

THE GREAT TEST, 1 KINGS, chapter 18

The great peak in the story of Elijah is the test on Mount Carmel, the mountain which, midway along the coastline of Palestine, juts out into the Mediterranean Sea. Having summoned the multitude, Elijah challenged the prophets of Baal to have their god ignite a sacrifice. All day they made the attempt, using the oriental methods of crying aloud, gashing themselves with swords, and so forth, but to no avail. When Elijah took up the task of appealing to the LORD, we are told that, although much water had been poured over his sacrifice, fire came down from heaven and demolished it, even drying up the water from a ditch around the altar. Elijah then killed the prophets of Baal. Whatever it was that happened that fateful day on Mount Carmel, it persuaded the people that the LORD (Yahweh) was God.

The imperious queen did not let this injury go unnoticed. She swore that Elijah would die within twenty-four hours. Separated from his enthusiastic followers, Elijah experienced a great reaction to his moment of exaltation. His soliloquy given at this time is the basis for the great aria in Mendelssohn's oratorio *Elijah*, "It is enough—O Lord now take away my life." Elijah traveled, we are told, forty days and forty nights to Horeb (Sinai) the Mount of God, where he found the LORD—not in the wind, nor the earthquake, nor the fire, but in the still small voice—and was ordered to anoint new kings over Damascus and Israel, and Elisha, his servant, to be prophet in his place.

THE STORIES OF ELIJAH AND ELISHA

Just as stories of strength were attracted to the great personality of Samson and stories of impossible age were affixed to the names of the patriarchs before the flood, so stories of the miraculous exhibition of God's concern developed in connection with Elijah and Elisha. The cruse of oil and jar of meal that did not fail, and the child brought back to life (1 Kings 17: 8-24); the igniting of the sacrifice by fire from heaven (1 Kings 18:36-40); the destruction by fire of the companies of soldiers sent to arrest Elijah (2 Kings, chapter 1); the dividing of the Jordan by the mantle; the chariot of fire; the forty-two boys torn by the bears because they called Elisha a baldhead (2 Kings, chapter 2), etc., etc. Elijah and Elisha were no greater heroes than David, but David's biography was written by a man who lived in his times and saw the events—possibly Abiathar. Neither Elijah nor Elisha was a greater prophet than Isaiah or Jeremiah, but Isaiah and Jeremiah wrote (at least in part) their own books, while we have no word written by either of the other two. Probably the stories were all based upon fact, but the incidents were pasesd on by word of mouth, sometimes from generation to generation, by people who were quite convinced that, if the LORD was particularly interested in a man, he would unquestionably show his concern by his miraculous intervention. And so the stories grew, nurtured by the faith of those who not only believed in the supreme power of the LORD, but who also were convinced that this was his way of showing it.

The accounts of Elijah and Elisha present us with the greatest concentration of miracle stories to be found in the Old Testament. Some of them (e.g., the raising of the dead boy,

1 Kings 17:17-24 and 2 Kings 4:8-37) are quite plainly the same story related to each of the prophets. The picture of Elijah seems, however, to come to us much clearer than that of Elisha. Partly for this reason, but more because he was thought to be the earlier of the two, the Jewish religion has always thought of him as the first and greatest of the prophets. As Moses represented the Law, so Elijah represented the Prophets. (Matthew 17:1-13.) Elijah was the one who was to return to the earth to indicate the coming of the day of the LORD. (Malachi 4:5.) And to this day, the ritual of the Feast of the Passover includes an opening of the door, so that Elijah may enter and announce the day of the Lord.

RELIGION OF THE PERIOD

The main development in the religion of Israel during this period, the first hundred years after the division of the kingdom, was the beginning of the sharp separation of the worship of the LORD and the worship of Baal. In the earlier days, the one had been strictly a religion of shepherds, and the other a religion of those who grew crops. There was of course a clash. Then, as the Israelites settled in the land, there was a process of adaptation. Many of the agricultural elements of Baal worship became incorporated into the worship of the LORD. As the number of practices common to both religions increased, the danger that the Israelites would take over all of the worship of Baal—or that the worship of Baal would take over all the Israelites—became greater. The work of Asa and his son Jehoshaphat was important in the south in preventing such a catastrophe: in the north it was Elijah who made the stand. Whatever happened on Mount Carmel, it convinced the people that the LORD was God. It may be that the work of Elijah (with his protégé Elisha) was the one great factor which preserved the worship of the LORD in Israel.

The picture of Elijah traveling forty days and nights to Mount Horeb, the home of the LORD, shows that the people did not at that time think of God as being present everywhere. When Elijah wanted to find him, there was one place for him to look. But the idea of social justice was beginning to emerge. In the time of David, his sin with Bathsheba and his murder of her husband had been roundly condemned. Now, in the time of Ahab, we find a prophet of the LORD daring to stand before the king and tell him that the LORD would punish him in a manner corresponding to his crime in the murder of Naboth. It was only a century before the time of Amos.

LITERATURE OF THE PERIOD

In this hundred-year period of the beginning of the divided kingdom, many of the accounts of the past were written down. All of the stories of the judges which had not previously been put on parchment were now committed to writing, as were the stories of Samuel, Saul, and David. But the stories of Elijah and Elisha were not written until a later date.

Some time in the latter part of the united kingdom the official scribes probably began keeping the court records. It was necessary to have an account of what the king had done and said, of what ambassadors had come, and of what treaties had been consummated. These records—one set preserved in the north and one in the south—later became the framework for the political accounts in the Books of 1 and 2 Kings. In references to them, they are called "the Book of the Chronicles of the Kings of Israel" and "the Book of the Chronicles of the Kings of Judah", respectively. (1 Kings 14:29; 15:31; and many other places.) These names are *not* to be confused with the Books of 1 and 2 Chronicles of the Old Testament, which were written much later.

One other very important piece of literature from this period was the J history, a combination of many previous fragments into one connected whole. This was one of the four major strands which, when woven together, formed the first great historical series of books in the Old Testament.

CHAPTER XIII

THE DIVIDED KINGDOM

The First Writing Prophets

THE HOUSE OF JEHU, 2 KINGS, chapters 9, 10, 13, 14

The king of Israel with the assistance of the king of Judah was besieging the city of Ramoth-gilead, and was wounded, just as had been his grandfather, Ahab, before him. Elisha commissioned his servant to anoint the aggressive Israelite general Jehu to be the king. The servant went to Ramoth-gilead and, summoning the general from a staff meeting, carried out his order. As soon as Jehu's fellow commanders knew of it, they swore allegiance to him and started toward the city of Jezreel, where the king was convalescing from his wound. The king of Judah was with him. Both kings came out in their chariots to meet Jehu to find out whether or not he came in peace, and, discovering his mission, fled. Jehu personally shot the king of Israel, and since the king of Judah was the son of Athaliah and the grandson of Ahab, he also was killed.

Jehu dared the people of Jezreel to select one of the descendants of Ahab for the throne and to defend him, but seeing that Jehu had the army behind him, they refused to take the chance. They cut off the heads of all the royal family and, at Jehu's order, placed them in two piles before the gate of the city, thus committing themselves irrevocably to his side.

Jehu distinguished himself in two ways. First, he tricked a great number of Baal worshipers into assembling for a sacrifice, and then had them murdered, destroying their temple. In the second place, he chose the wrong king in the struggle between Assyria and Damascus. The biblical record does not show it, but we have a monument of Shalmanezer III, king of Assyria, showing Jehu paying tribute to him. At the first opportunity, Damascus began paying back Jehu for his alliance with her enemy (in the time of Ahab, Israel and Damascus had been leaders of a coalition *against* Assyria), so that Israel lost one

section after another of its territory, all during the reigns of
Jehu and his son. Not until the reign of Jehu's grandson did
Assyria successfully attack Damascus, and so make it possible
for Israel to regain some of its lost territory. Once started, this
procedure continued through his reign and the reign of Jehu's
great-grandson, Jeroboam II. Because of this pressure upon
Damascus from Assyria, on its eastern border, there were no
troops available for use against Israel, so Jeroboam was very
successful in his international affairs. The repeated conquests
brought increasing wealth to Israel and, because it was rapidly
acquired and not evenly distributed, it tended to separate
sharply the economic classes. This was the first appearance of
a comparatively wealthy middle class.

After the long successful reign of Jeroboam II the nation
deteriorated rapidly. First one king and then another would
swear allegiance to the now-dominant power of Assyria, and
always the allegiance was broken and the necessary tribute
refused. Assassinations brought the country to the verge of
anarchy and finally, two decades after Jeroboam II, the city
of Samaria was besieged. In 722 B.C. it finally fell to the king
of Assyria, the leaders were transported to other conquered
provinces, and people of other languages and cultures were
brought in to take their places. So were the "ten lost tribes of
Israel" scattered, never again to be gathered together.

THE RULERS OF JUDAH, 2 KINGS, chapters 11—12; 15:1-7

Athaliah, daughter of Ahab and Jezebel of the northern kingdom of Israel, married the son of Jehoshaphat, king of Judah.
Her husband became king, and after his death her son came
to the throne, thus elevating Athaliah to the highest position
available to a woman—queen mother. But, as we have just
seen, her son was in the north, and was killed, when the revolt
of Jehu broke upon the land. Rather than retire from her high
position, Athaliah killed all the claimants to the throne of
Judah (her own grandchildren had for the most part been destroyed by Jehu) and seized the throne for herself. She overlooked one grandson Joash, a baby of one year, who was
promptly hidden in the temple by Jehoiada, probably an uncle
of the infant by marriage. After six years Jehoiada succeeded

in arranging a temple coup in which, by manipulating the guards of the temple and palace, the evil queen was killed and the seven-year-old boy was crowned. Under the regency of Jehoiada, and thereafter as long as Jehoiada lived, Joash served as a fairly good king, noted more for repairing the temple of the LORD than for any other thing.

The next king of importance was Azariah, elsewhere known as Uzziah. His reign, paralleling that of the northern king Jeroboam II, was peaceful, prosperous, and very long. Since those qualities do not make good material for the writing of histories, we are told almost nothing about this very successful king. Two other kings of interest were Ahaz and Hezekiah. As they were contemporaries and acquaintances of Isaiah, they will be considered later in connection with him.

AMOS, AMOS, chapters 1—7

The common use of the word "prophet" as a predictor sometimes causes us to overlook the fact that the basic meaning of the word is "spokesman." When Moses told the LORD he was unable to speak to Pharaoh, the LORD told him that he would make him as God to Pharaoh, and Aaron would be his (Moses') *prophet*. (Exodus 7:1f.) The prophet was expected to hear what the LORD told him, and then to proclaim it to the people. Sometimes in the early history, when the prophets were gathered in bands, they seem to have made known the LORD's will by their actions. Men like Nathan, Ahijah, Elijah, Micaiah ben Imlah, etc., spoke the word of the LORD. Some of the later prophets seem to have depended upon the written word alone. But the main idea was that the prophet gave the people the word of the LORD. Sometimes he felt that the LORD was about to punish the people: sometimes that the LORD wanted them comforted. In such cases there was an element of prediction present, but it was not the idea of prediction that was important; it was the fact that the prophet transmitted the word of God.

Amos preached by word of mouth, telling the people what he felt the LORD was revealing to him, but, because they did not listen—in fact, drove him from the kingdom of Israel—he wrote down what he had said, thus becoming the first writing prophet. Possibly because we have here for the first time the words practically as the prophet gave them; or perhaps because different times produced different leaders, we think of Amos as a different kind of man. Amos himself, acquainted with the type of man described by the word in his time, vehemently refused to be called a prophet. (Amos 7:14.) But we have disregarded his protest to the extent that, instead of thinking of Amos being like the prophets, we now think of the prophets being like Amos. He was the first of a new breed.

During the reign of Jeroboam II in the northern kingdom of Israel, the steady influx of wealth had made certain families extremely well-to-do, while the poor people, receiving no increase in silver or property, became comparatively worse off than before. The religious teachings of the times claimed that the LORD punished those who did not serve him, but rewarded those who did. This doctrine was twisted until the obverse of it came to be believed—that if a man was poor, he was being punished by the LORD (for wealth was the symbol of reward), and if he was wealthy, he was being rewarded for his good deeds. Since religion was pretty much the offering of the proper sacrifices in the correct way to the right god, it is plain that there was a cumulative effect. The rich man was able to offer beautiful sacrifices—the poor man was not. Also, if a man of wealth oppressed a poor man—cheated him in the market; by sharp practices robbed him of his land; in a case at law bribed the judge—he had merely to make the proper sacrifices, and his increased wealth would prove that the LORD was pleased with him. Thus the full weight of the religious establishment and the public opinion of the laity (especially the wealthy and thus more important laity) were marshalled solidly behind economic exploitation and corruption.

Amos the herdsman lived in Judah, but his preaching was done in Israel. That may be one reason why his message was heartless, predicting nothing but destruction ("will any part of Israel be left?—It will be as when a shepherd seeks a sheep taken by a lion and finds . . . two shin bones and a piece of an ear"). Amos was not preaching about his friends. He came down over the hills to the sanctuary of Bethel, where the important people of Samaria were worshiping, and began a series of short condemnations of the nations about Israel:

Thus says the LORD:

"For three transgressions of Damascus,
  and for four, I will not revoke the punishment;
because they have threshed Gilead
  With threshing sledges of iron."

—Amos 1:3

This may be a reference to the horrible custom of staking out prisoners of war upon the ground, and dragging over them the heavy sledges with transverse bars of iron on the bottoms, which were used to crush the last kernels of wheat out of the heads in the threshing process. In any case, Damascus had been the last power to oppress Israel, and there was doubtless great enthusiasm in his audience when Amos continued with a description of how the LORD would send the disaster of fire upon the ruling house of Damascus, and would destroy the cities and send the people into exile.

After cursing Damascus, Amos pronounced a judgment of doom upon Philistia, Tyre, Edom, Ammon, Moab, and Judah. Then he struck at Israel itself, because they "sell the righteous for silver, and the needy for a pair of shoes," and for sexual irregularity, which he interpreted as an offense against the LORD himself. It is quite possible that all these "oracles" were not delivered in the same order, or at the same time. But this is the order chosen—possibly for its psychological effect—when Amos wrote his book. Many scholars think the oracle against Judah is a later addition, made when the book was being preserved in Judah after the fall of Samaria, by another prophet who felt that his own people should not be without criticism.

The second part of Amos, chapters 3—6, contains a number of sermons. One points out that, just as we know in natural life that a certain effect is produced by a certain cause, so we shall know in the moral realm that when evil befalls a city, it is because of the punishment of the LORD (Amos, chapter 3). In another he condemns the wealthy hard-drinking women of Samaria, calling them the cows of Bashan and predicting that they, like cows, will be led out of the city into captivity with rings through their noses—the last of them with fishhooks. (Amos 4:1-3.)

The third part includes the series of visions: the locusts, the fire, the plumb line held before a wall which was not vertical, and a basket of summer fruit, all of them indicating destruction for Israel. (Amos, chapters 7—8.) There is good reason for believing the latter part of chapter 9 was written sometime after the fall of Jerusalem, but the rest, with the possible exception of Amos 2: 4f, was written by Amos himself, very close to 760 B.C. The destruction he described came crashing down on Israel in 722 B.C. when Assyria captured Samaria.

The great contributions of Amos include:

a. His dramatic insistence upon social justice.
b. His opposition to ritual as a substitute for righteousness:
    "I hate, I despise your feasts, and I take no delight in your solemn assemblies."

—Amos 5:21

c. His conception of the LORD as ruler over other nations as well as Israel—the oracles of chapters 1 and 2, and "Did I not bring up Israel from the land of Egypt, and the Philistines from Caphtor and the Syrians from Kir?"

—Amos 9:7b

d. The creation of the first book of the Old Testament to be written.

The greatest passage in the book is Amos 5: 21-24, which describes the disgust of the LORD with the cultic ritual of sacrifice instead of ethical righteousness, and closes with the greatest plea for justice ever given:

"But let justice roll down like waters, and righteousness like an ever-flowing stream."

HOSEA, HOSEA, chapters 1—4, 6, 7, 11, 14

Like Amos, Hosea preached in the northern kingdom Israel, but, unlike Amos, he lived in that country. Though he proclaimed disaster because of the people's sins, he did it with an aching heart, for they were his people.

Hosea was quite unfortunate in his choice of a wife, though her character was not revealed until at least two of her children had been born. The first one, a son, was named "Jezreel." The word means "the LORD has sown," and it was originally assigned to the most fertile valley in Israel. Later it became the name of a river in that valley, and a city situated on the river. It was the city in which the royal line of Ahab had sought refuge from Jehu, and beside whose gates their heads had been piled after the massacre. The name was given as an object lesson to the people of Israel, indicating through a play upon the meaning of the word that the LORD, who had sown, would reap vengeance from the house of Jehu, whose current ruler was Jeroboam II. Though Amos had been driven out of Israel something over a decade before for criticizing this same king, there is no record of royal retribution against Hosea.

The second child born to Hosea's wife, a girl, was named "Not pitied." We believe Hosea was uncertain whether or not he was the father, but if so, his uncertainty vanished before her third child was born. He was named "Not my people." Some time after this, Hosea's wife left him, either at his direction or at hers, presumably becoming a prostitute. Later Hosea saw her in the market place, for sale as a slave. He bought her as one would buy a cow, and took her to his home, though probably not to resume her former position as his wife.[1]

When Hosea tried to reason with himself, to discover how this horrible thing could have happened to him—how he could still have protected this woman, after what she had done to him— he found the answer to another problem which had been vexing him: "Why did the LORD continue to bless Israel with good crops and other evidence of his kindness, when the people played the harlot and worshiped false gods?" Because the LORD loved Israel! Thus was born the idea that the LORD loved his people, an idea never before recorded in the history of human thought. It was the nation that was loved, not the individual man. That concept of individualism had to wait another century, till the time of Jeremiah, to be born. Nor did it indicate that Israel,

---

1. Some scholars give other interpretations—e.g., that Hosea deliberately married a prostitute as an object lesson. The explanation given here is the one usually accepted.

because of the love of the LORD, would escape punishment. The penalty had to be exacted, but the LORD would carry it out with an aching heart:

> When Israel was a child, I loved him,
>   and out of Egypt I called my son.
> The more I called them,
>   the more they went from me;
> they kept sacrificing to the Baals,
>   and burning incense to idols.
>
> How can I give you up, O Ephraim!
> How can I hand you over, O Israel!
>   —Hosea 11:1-2, 8a

One phase of Baal worship involved a degrading sexualism. There were sacred prostitutes associated with the religion, and it is highly probable that a large proportion of the worshipers of both sexes carried out this ritual. It may well be that the harlotry of Hosea's wife was of this nature. If her actions were urged by false religious convictions rather than by her personal character, it is easier to understand how Hosea could still have loved her. This would also make even more understandable his intense bitterness against Baal worship, which shows up throughout his book. Hosea was the first writer ever to depict Israel as anything other than masculine, for traditionally Israel (Jacob) was the son of Isaac. This, however, is not the last time the figure of speech of the harlot is applied to God's chosen people.

The demand for righteousness and justice introduced by Amos was repeated by Hosea, but to it he added, out of his own personal agony, the marvelous idea that God can love mankind —in this case, Israel.

ISAIAH, ISAIAH, chapters 1—2, 5—9, 11, 28

One of the great books of all time is the Book of Isaiah, and one of the great prophets of the Hebrew people was Isaiah, the son of Amos (not to be confused with Amos the prophet). But since the book is to a large extent poetry—with some measures reaching the absolute peak of sublimity—and since frequently there is no statement in this poetry to fasten the passage unquestionably to any historical incident, there are now and always will be differences of opinion as to the occasions on which various sections of the book were written.   As we are told that Isaiah began his work in the year King Uzziah died (about 740 B.C.—Isaiah 6:1), and as Cyrus is mentioned as the messiah or anointed one (Isaiah 45:1—shortly before 538 B.C.), it is quite evident that one man did not write all of the book as we have it today.   There are many other problems of dating connected with the book.[2]

Isaiah, son of Amoz (ben Amoz, as the Hebrews said), was a citizen and statesman of Judah, the southern kingdom, and apparently was of the nobility—an intimate of the king.   At the beginning of his ministry he had a vision which, for the grandeur of his conception of the LORD, has never been surpassed:

> In the year that King Uzziah died, I saw the Lord, sitting upon a throne, high and lifted up; and his train filled the temple.   Above him stood the seraphim; each had six wings; with two he covered his face, and with two he covered his feet, and with two he flew, And one called to another and said:
>
> "Holy, holy, holy is the LORD of hosts;
>   the whole earth is full of his glory."
> And the foundations of the thresholds shook at the voice of him who called, and the house was filled with smoke. And I said: "Woe is me!   For I am lost; for I am a man of unclean lips, and I dwell in the midst of a people of unclean lips; for my eyes have seen the King, the LORD of hosts!"   (Isaiah 6:1-5)

After this acknowledgment of unworthiness, one of the seraphim touched his lips with a burning coal from the altar, purging him of his sin and guilt, and he was commissioned to go and to preach to a people who, he was warned, would neither listen nor understand.   This call, the basis for our

2. See Appendix, Note E.

great hymn "Holy, Holy, Holy," marked the beginning of
Isaiah's ministry: the latter part evidently was written after his
disillusionment, when he found, as have so many preachers since
his day, that the people disregarded his words.

Isaiah's early message was similar to that of Amos and Hosea
—that the LORD would punish the people for their sins. But
after about five years he became involved in a great political
question: in the struggle between the mammoth Assyrian empire and the coalition of the Northern Kingdom Israel and
Damascus (Syria), which side should Judah take? The king of
Judah, Ahaz, favored alliance with (i.e., practically submission
to) Assyria, but there were enough of his people who opposed
this course to encourage Israel and Damascus to invade his kingdom for the purpose of deposing him and placing upon the
throne a king who would make an alliance with them. The
statesmanship of the prophet convinced him that either of the
two courses would be disastrous for Judah. If an alliance were
to be made with the two small kingdoms, Judah would go down
with them to defeat; on the other hand, an alliance with Assyria was probably unnecessary, and the tribute involved in
such a course would ruin Judah financially. But Isaiah was a
prophet of the LORD as well as a statesman. If Judah made
an alliance with Assyria, not only would tribute be required;
the Assyrian king would demand that the new tributaries should
worship his god. We know this, because the alliance *was* made,
the tribute *was* required, and the king of Judah sent back home
to Jerusalem the specifications of the Assyrian-type altar which
had been erected in Damascus. (2 Kings 16:5-18.) To Isaiah,
all this seemed unnecessary, for he had invincible faith in the
ability of the LORD to protect Judah.

Isaiah, like others of the prophets, frequently used object
lessons to drive home his messages. At the time of this crisis
with Israel and Damascus, and Assyria, he confronted the king
of Judah and demanded that he ask a sign of the LORD, as deep
as Sheol or as high as the heavens. When the king refused to
ask a sign, Isaiah indignantly gave him one: a young woman
would bear a son and, by the time he was born, conditions
would be so good in Judah that the name "God is with us"

would be an appropriate name for him.[3]   Also, before he was old enough to know what things were good to eat and what were not, Israel and Damascus, which were attempting to invade Judah to depose the king, would be deserted. (Isaiah 7:1-17.) This same message was repeated in the next chapter. Taking a tablet, he wrote upon it *Maher-shalal-hashbaz* (the spoil speeds, the prey hastens), to indicate that the two countries, Israel and Damascus, which were so eager to invade Judah, would themselves soon be invaded. Not satisfied with writing this, Isaiah bestowed it as a name upon his son, so that people would constantly be reminded of his message. Is it possible that Isaiah was influenced by the symbolism of the names Hosea had given the children of his wife, only a decade earlier, in the kingdom of Israel?

Isaiah's message fell on deaf ears, or perhaps he spoke after the king had already taken action. The alliance with Assyria was made; Judah paid tribute to the colossus of the east; Damascus was captured and annexed to the Assyrian empire, and Israel (i.e., the North), in abject surrender placed a pro-Assyrian puppet on the throne. It may be this disillusionment which made Isaiah include in his description of his inaugural vision:

And he said, "Go, and say to this people:

'Hear and hear, but do not understand;
see and see, but do not perceive.'
Make the heart of this people fat,
    and their ears heavy,
    and shut their eyes;
lest they see with their eyes,
    and hear with their ears,
and understand with their hearts,
    and turn and be healed."
—Isaiah 6:9-10

In his disappointment and frustration Isaiah gathered about him his disciples and retired from public life. "Bind up the testimony, seal the teaching among my disciples." (Isaiah 8:16.)

---

3. See Appendix, Note F.

After enthroning a king who was acceptable to the Assyrians, the people of the Northern Kingdom Israel enjoyed a purchase peace for about a decade. Finally, however, their king was detected in an intrigue with Egypt, seeking to revolt from Assyria. It took the Assyrian monarch three years, but he captured the city of Samaria in 722 B.C. and deported the leading citizens to various other conquered provinces in his empire. This was probably the time when Isaiah, living in Jerusalem, only forty miles south of Samaria, came out of retirement and pronounced the doom of the LORD upon the northern capital:

> Woe to the proud crown of the drunkards of Ephraim,
> and to the fading flower of its glorious beauty.
> —Isaiah 28:1

In spite of the vivid object lesson of Samaria, the people of Judah tempted the same fate, trusting in the help of Egypt, and refused the tribute due the Assyrian king. In an attempt to forestall this action Isaiah walked naked and barefoot through the streets of Jerusalem, seeking to demonstrate that the Assyrians would make slaves of the Egyptians, and of all who depended upon them. (Isaiah, chapter 20.) In 701 B.C. Sennacherib, the ruler of Assyria, led his armies on a punitive expedition into Palestine.[4] The people of Jerusalem sought any means of escape short of unconditional surrender, but were unsuccessful. Just when hope was exhausted, Isaiah proclaimed that the city would not fall. (Isaiah 14:24f.) Whether because of a plague or an invasion of another part of his empire, Sennacherib fulfilled Isaiah's prediction by promptly moving his troops out of Judah. For another century Jerusalem was saved, but the king was more careful about paying the tribute after this experience.

King Hezekiah at one time suffered from a serious infection which both he and Isaiah thought would prove fatal. Just after Isaiah had left the sick man, he became convinced that the king would recover, so he returned and told him so, ordering that a poultice of figs be placed upon the infected area. (2 Kings 20:1-11; Isaiah, chapter 38.) It may be because of this re-

---

4. Many scholars date this expedition in 689 B.C. It is impossible to determine whether there were one or two such expeditions.

covery which was accredited to the LORD, or it may be because of Sennacherib's unexpected withdrawal from the siege of Jerusalem that Hezekiah instituted a reformation against false (Baal) worship in Jerusalem which was so thoroughgoing he destroyed a cult object from the temple known as the "bronze serpent of Moses." (2 Kings 18:1-6, See above, pp. 60-61.) On the other hand, it is possible that the reformation came *before* the siege of Jerusalem by Sennacherib, and that the religious zeal of Hezekiah was one of the reasons why Sennacherib invaded Judah.

One difficult problem about Isaiah is the authorship of so-called "messianic passages." Some of the most wonderful words ever written about peace and the ideal king are found in the book:

> The people who walked in darkness
>> have seen a great light
> those who dwelt in a land of deep darkness,
>> on them has light shined.
> Thou hast multiplied the nation,
>> thou hast increased its joy.
>
>> —Isaiah 9:2-3

> For to us a child is born,
>> to us a son is given;
> and the government will be upon his shoulder,
>> and his name will be called
> "Wonderful Counselor, Mighty God,
>> Everlasting Father, Prince of Peace!"
> Of the increase of his government and of peace
>> there will be no end,
> upon the throne of David, and over his kingdom,
>> to establish it, and to uphold it
> with justice and with righteousness
>> from this time forth and forever more.
> The zeal of the LORD of hosts will do this.
>
>> —Isaiah 9:6-7

> The wolf shall dwell with the lamb,
>> and the leopard shall lie down with the kid,

and the calf and the lion and the fatling together,
    and a little child shall lead them.
—Isaiah 11:6

He shall judge between the nations,
    and shall decide for many peoples;
and they shall beat their swords into plowshares,
    and their spears into pruning hooks;
nation shall not lift up sword against nation,
    neither shall they learn war any more.
—Isaiah 2:4[5]

These passages are characteristic of the work of postexilic prophets, whose main purpose was to encourage the people in their distress by painting a brilliant picture of the future. Most scholars therefore date them after the fall of Jerusalem in 586 B.C., although some attribute them to Isaiah the son of Amoz.[6]

The statesmanship of Isaiah availed the people of Jerusalem but little, for they did not listen to his advice. He urged absolute neutrality for Judah in the struggle between Assyria and the two small western nations, Israel and Damascus, but Judah made an alliance with Assyria—later to be regretted. About a third of a century later he urged that in accordance with their covenant, the alliance (and tribute) be continued, but the king did not heed him—hence the siege of Jerusalem by Sennacherib. On that occasion he said the city would not fall. However, after the city had been saved, they developed the idea that it could never be destroyed, a doctrine which, more than a century later, almost cost the prophet Jeremiah his life.

The two great permanent contributions of Isaiah were the concept of reverence toward God, as shown in his inaugural vision in chapter 6 and in his constant attitude of veneration toward the "Holy One of Israel"; and his sublime faith.

MICAH, MICAH 1:1-9; chapter 3; 6:6-8

Micah, the fourth of these eighth-century prophets, came from an agricultural area of southwestern Palestine, near the

---

5. Found also in Micah 4:3 and, reversed in meaning to indicate preparation for war, in Joel 3:10.

6. See J. A. Bewer, *Literature of the Old Testament* (rev. ed.; New York: Columbia University Press, 1938), pp. 114ff.

city of Gath. He seems to have had the rural man's distrust of cities, for a large part of his message was directed against Samaria and Jerusalem. He therefore must have preached before the destruction of Samaria in 722 B.C.—possibly about 725 B.C. The clearest statement of this attitude against the cities is an oracle against Jerusalem:

> Therefore because of you
> Zion shall be plowed as a field;
> Jerusalem shall become a heap of ruins,
> and the mountain of a house a wooded height.
> —Micah 3:12

But the high point of the book is the so-called prophetic summary. Amos had preached of the LORD's demands for social justice; Hosea had introduced the idea of the love or mercy of the LORD; and Isaiah had given his thrilling picture of his majesty, which made mortal man so painfully aware of his inadequacy because of his sin. Micah asked what the LORD demanded: was it burnt offerings of year-old calves? or thousands of rams? or ten thousand *rivers* of oil? or did he demand the sacrifice of his own son—"the fruit of my body for the sin of my soul?" Such practices were not unknown in Judah. At least two kings of that period were guilty: Ahaz and Manasseh. Then he switched to the positive, and summarized the other three eighth-century prophets:

> He has showed you, O man, what is good;
> and what does the LORD require of you
> but to do justice, and to love kindness,
> and to walk humbly with your God?
> —Micah 6:8[7]

RELIGION OF THE PERIOD

The religion of the period of the first four writing prophets involved a continuing struggle of the worship of the LORD against the worship of Baal. Though we have no record of events as spectacular as the dramatic contest of Elijah with the

---

7. The tendency of recent scholarship is to ascribe this reference to Micah himself. See Wolfe, *Interpreter's Bible*, VI, 899. Chapters 1-3 are usually thought of as his work.

prophets of Baal on Mount Carmel, the religion of Baal continued, and the prophets of the LORD valiantly opposed it. This opposition was one of the most important parts of the work of Hosea, and we can sense it very clearly in the work of Isaiah. There were undoubtedly some changes in what was called the worship of Baal because of the rise of Assyrian influence on Judah. In the previous period, the culture of Phoenicia, as introduced by the alliances of Omri and Ahab with Tyre, and as exemplified by the dynamic Phoenician princess Jezebel, who became the queen of Ahab, had been the dominant factor. In the current period, the subjection of Israel to Assyria during the last decade before the fall of Samaria, and the subservience of Ahaz (2 Kings, chapter 16) introduced many Mesopotamian practices. We even find Ahaz employing the abominable custom of child sacrifice, though we are not justified in claiming this as Assyrian in origin. Hezekiah did make a determined effort to stamp out Baal worship, but his son Manasseh seems to have undone all that his father had been able to accomplish.

The great development in religion, though, is of course the contributions of the writing prophets. Since they considered themselves primarily as spokesmen for the LORD (their customary byline was "Thus says the LORD") the demands they made of the people clearly reflect their conception of the nature of the LORD. When Amos condemned the people for social injustice, it was because he thought of God as demanding justice; when he criticized the emphasis upon cultic ritual instead of ethical righteousness, he added to the religion of Israel the conception of the LORD as a God who was not to be satisfied by the sacrifice of sheep instead of honesty on the part of the worshiper. There are one or two scattered references to the matter of justice before the time of Amos. Nathan criticized David for taking Bathsheba and killing her husband; Elijah cursed Ahab for having Naboth stoned to death. There are, however, some who think that something of the flavor of the accounts of these two incidents may come from the work of Amos or other eighth-century prophets, since the writer who revised and edited the historical books of Samuel and Kings lived later than these prophets. But the words of Amos are from Amos, so he is usually thought of as the great prophet of social justice.

While Amos added to the religion of Israel the concept of a LORD who demanded righteousness instead of ritual, and who was able to control nations other than Israel and Judah, Hosea added the idea of a God who loved Israel, and Isaiah introduced his magnificent picture of the attitude of reverence of man to God, and the absolute need of faith in him. Micah added nothing which was original, though his prophetic summary bolstered the contributions of the other three. All told, it is doubtful if any hundred-year-period in the history of mankind, except the sixth century B.C and the first century A.D., ever improved religious thinking as much as did the eighth century B.C.; and the great contributors were the prophets.

LITERATURE

Sometime between the time of Amos and the time of Hosea— that is, about 750 B.C.—the second great strand of Hebrew history, the E document, was written in the northern kingdom. A quarter of a century later the kingdom went down in ruin, as the capital city of Samaria had fallen. Fortunately a copy of this historical work, along with the prophetic books of Amos and Hosea, was preserved in Judah, where it was later (about 700) combined with the earlier J document to form a consolidated, but not harmonized, record of the traditional beginnings of both these nations. This combined record is called JE. It represents an early step in the development of the history of the Israelite people.

Another step toward completed history was the continuation of the "Chronicles of the Kings of Israel" in the north, and the "Chronicles of the Kings of Judah" in the south, which later served as the important structural outline for 1 and 2 Kings. But the most important writings were the great prophetic messages which have just been discussed—Amos and Hosea in Israel, and Isaiah and Micah in Judah.

CHAPTER XIV

THE REMAINING
KINGDOM OF JUDAH

Deuteronomy and the Reformation

WORSHIP OF THE LORD AND BAAL

After the fall of Samaria in 722 B.C., there remained only one of the two Hebrew kingdoms—Judah in the south, which consisted largely of the city of Jerusalem with a little territory around it. The official religion of this small kingdom had been alternating between worship of Baal and of the LORD. Away back in the time when Elijah had been preaching in the Northern Kingdom, Jehoshaphat, king of Judah, had been an ardent worshiper of the LORD. When his daughter-in-law Athaliah usurped the throne, Baal worship became official. Then, under her grandson Joash, it returned to the LORD. Ahaz, ruler during the early ministry of Isaiah, sometimes sponsored Baal worship, but his son Hezekiah instituted a great reformation in favor of the LORD. After his death the pendulum swung back again when his son Manasseh came to the throne. He sacrificed his own son by fire, and slaughtered many prophets of the LORD in the city of Jerusalem.

There were two reasons for this rotation of religions. Originally Baal had been the religion of the Canaanite agriculturists, and the worship of the LORD (Yahweh) had been the religion of the nomadic Israelite shepherds. Then, as the Israelites became more firmly settled in the land, and more at home in the pursuit of agriculture, they began to think of the LORD as controlling the conditions which governed the crops. By the time of Amos and Hosea we find this clearly stated in words attributed to the LORD:

"And I also withheld the rain from you
when there were yet three months to the harvest."
—Amos 4:7a
"And she did not know that it was I who gave her
the grain, the wine, and the oil. . . ."
—Hosea 2:8a

Since the two parties, Baal and the LORD, were political as well as religious; and since there was always a majority party in power, a minority group awaiting its opportunity, and a great bulk of people ready to swing either way, it is easy to see that two or three years of bad crops would bring the charge that the wrong god was being worshiped. The reasoning was not greatly different from what we have seen in our two-party political system in the United States. Each party claims to be the source of "prosperity," and only a year or two of depression before an election year has seemed adequate reason for a change in administration. However, in ancient Israel and Judah, violence was normally the means employed as the party in power sought to remain in power, and also the technique usually used by the new party as soon as it had come into authority.

Sometimes, however, the power of a foreign nation was an important factor in this alternation. Ahaz, at least a part-time worshiper of Baal, was urged to that position by the desires of the ruler of Assyria. (2 Kings 16:10-17.) Ahaz also was guilty of the worship of the powers of heaven, especially the sun, for he made altars upon the roof, and had chariots of the sun, and probably also statues of the horses of the sun. (2 Kings 23:11f.) These were forms of Assyrian worship, but the writer in 2 Kings undoubtedly considered them of a piece with the Baal worship— a form of apostasy from the worship of the LORD. Hezekiah, who opposed Assyria as well as he was able, was a great worshiper of the LORD. And it is likely that Assyrian pressure had a great deal to do with making Manasseh so complete a devotee of Baal.

One custom which made the transition from one religion to the other a fairly simple matter was the custom of using the same sacred place—usually a "high place"—for the worship of both gods. As these sanctuaries had been dedicated to Baal long before the Israelites had entered Palestine, many of the minor details of the Baal ritual were preserved and used, even in the periods when the LORD was being worshiped. Thus they were a constant threat to the religious stability of the country, as the people were accustomed at all times to the sanctuaries and to much of the ritual of Baal worship.

THE WRITING OF DEUTERONOMY

Manasseh was so ferocious when he persecuted the prophets of the LORD in his reaction against the religious practices of his father Hezekiah that he drove them underground. While in hiding, either in or near Jerusalem, about the middle of the seventh century B.C., they wrote a book. The backbone of it was the "Covenant Code." (Exodus 20:22—23:33.) Since the name of Moses was associated with this group of laws, they presented them as a series of talks by the great lawgiver, and since they were prophets, they enlarged them with many prophetic ideals from the great ethical prophets of the eighth century. Hosea in particular seems to have influenced them. His idea of mercy was added to the basic prophetic concept of justice and applied even to animals:

"You shall not muzzle an ox when it treads out the grain." (Deuteronomy 25:4.) They felt that, if an ox was used to thresh the grain, he was entitled to any stray head of the grain he could snatch as he plodded about the central stake to which he was hitched.

Usually in the religion of Israel the law was considered to be the province of the priests, and the sermon the province of the prophets. The priests were concerned with the fixed religion of the past, especially as it was defined by the law which *had been given* by the LORD. The prophets felt that the word of the LORD was given to *them* and they had the responsibility of delivering it to the people. Thus the priests were looking to the past, while the prophets considered primarily the present and future. There is certainly a place for both in religion, as we recognize in two of our great hymns: for the priestly attitude, "Faith of Our Fathers, Living Still"; and for the prophetic attitude, Whittier's great hymn, which, referring to the prophet Elijah, ends:

> Speak through the earthquake, wind, and fire
> O still small voice of calm!

Because of this difference in functions, there frequently were grave differences of opinion between priests and prophets. It was a priest who drove the prophet Amos out of the Northern Kingdom of Israel. As we shall see, it was a temple official (undoubtedly a priest) who scourged the prophet Jeremiah and put him in the stocks in Jerusalem.[1] And Jesus, who was a successor to the prophets, was bitterly assailed by the priests and especially the Pharisees, who were the ultra-legalists of his day.

However, there are two places in the Old Testament where the work of the prophet and the priest merges: in the Book of Ezekiel, who was both a priest and a prophet, and in this book, written during the persecution of Manasseh, by prophets whose great purpose was to emphasize the law of the LORD.

In addition to the Covenant Code and the teachings of the prophets, the writers borrowed generously from the great historical narrative JE, made half a century earlier by combining the J history with the E history, which had been brought to Jerusalem from the Northern Kingdom. This historical work furnished the background for the life of Moses, and the situations wherein he delivered the discourses which form the main part of the book.

Since these consecrated writers were of the group persecuted by the Baal-worshiping king, and since they realized that the continued presence of the "high places" as centers of worship provided focal points from which Baal worship could spread and take over the whole of the small kingdom of Judah, they strongly opposed their use, even for the worship of the LORD. If it was evil to use them, the LORD must have known it, and must have told Moses so. They therefore indicated many times in their book (e.g., Deuteronomy 26:2) that the LORD told Moses he would pick out one place where they should worship and where his name would be known. The name of Jerusalem could not have been given, for the writers felt that the LORD had been talking to Moses in the wilderness two centuries before the Hebrews had captured the city, but it is easy to see that that is the place to which they referred. This is called the doctrine of "Centralization of Worship." It could not possibly have been effective in the days of the United Kingdom, as too much territory was involved. But by the time of Manasseh the Northern Kingdom was gone, and Judah had shrunk so much in area that it was quite feasible for all its citizens to travel to Jerusalem for worship, which was what the

---

1. See below, p. 172. See also Jeremiah 20:1-6.

prophet-writers desired. Eventually, this is the reason why Jesus was taken to Jerusalem as an infant after his circumcision, and went there later on the occasions of the annual passover feasts. (Luke 2:21-24, 41f.)

It is doubtful that the writers expected their book to become the law of Judah. The laws are stated, but usually there are no definite punishments assigned for specific violations. It seems rather to have been a book of idealism—a picture of the requirements the prophets would have liked to have seen in effect in Judah. The penalty for worshiping false gods was quite definite and very severe (Deuteronomy 13:6-17), and this of course would have included worship of Baal. It is evident that, under a Baal-worshiping regime, it would have been fatal to have been caught with the book in one's possession. It was therefore hidden in the temple at Jerusalem until a safe time for its revelation. It may have been genuinely lost. At any rate, it was not made public until the eighteenth year of Josiah's reign.

THE REFORMATION, 2 KINGS, chapter 22; 23:1-30

Josiah was the last great king of Judah. He came to the throne at the age of eight, but was probably under the shadow of the last great monarch of Assyria, Asshurbanipal, until the time of the latter's death. It was not by chance that the book of the law was "found" in the temple in 621 B.C., a short time after the death of the Assyrian king. As soon as Josiah was certain that this book, written in hiding by the prophets during Manasseh's evil reign, was indeed the word of the LORD, he felt free to start reforming the religion of the people. He was more afraid of the wrath of the LORD than he was of the displeasure of Asshurbanipal's successor. As soon as the prophetess Huldah had affirmed that the book of the law (probably the central part of the book of Deuteronomy as we have it) was indeed the word of the LORD, there was consternation in Jerusalem. In Deuteronomy 28:15-68 we have two solid pages of violent curses upon the people if they did not keep the law. If any part of this section, or Deuteronomy 13:6-17, or Deuteronomy 17:2-7, was included in that book read to the king and then to the people, their terror is easy to understand. They had not kept the law—they had never even heard it!

Immediately after this the reformation was started, with all the authority of the 26-year-old active king behind it. Priests of the evil religions who had sacrificed children in flames were burnt upon their own altars. One sacred place near Jerusalem, the valley of Hinnom (Ge Hinnom) was strewn with the bones of the dead and made a dumping ground for garbage and refuse—hence forever unsuited as a place of worship. The evil odors, and the perpetual fires for the burning of rubbish caused the place eventually to be known as a synonym for the later conception of Hell, "Gehenna." The high places all over the kingdom were destroyed, and, in accordance with the book of the law, all worship was concentrated in the temple at Jerusalem.

RESULTS OF THE DEUTERONOMIC REFORMATION

Few books in the history of literature have had the importance of the Book of Deuteronomy. Some of the results of the reformation it inspired are as follows:

a. At least for the balance of the life of Josiah, the worship of the LORD was the only worship in Judah.

b. All worship was centered upon Jerusalem and the temple. Though this was a real safeguard for the religion at first, it was only a third of a century before the city and temple were destroyed, thus raising a grave problem for later religious leaders.

c. Since the book was hailed as the word of the LORD, and was available in tangible form, this was the beginning of the religion of a book. After the destruction of Jerusalem and the removal of the people into exile in Babylon, the possession of such a book, and the acquaintance with a book religion were of inestimable importance.

d. The adoption of this book of the law as sacred (the word Deuteronomy is Greek for "Second Law") was the beginning of the idea of religion as law—or legalism. Eventually legalism became the most prominent characteristic of Israelite religion.

e. As a result of the Book of Deuteronomy and the reformation, there was developed a new philosophy of history, the
idea that the LORD controlled all history, and rewarded Israel
for its righteousness by victory, or punished it for its sin by
abandoning it to defeat.   Two groups of writers having this
philosophy edited the great historical writings to conform to
their ideas: one group writing about 600 B.C., and another
group re-editing the material about fifty years later.   The
results of this moralizing treatment of history are seen principally in the Books Joshua, Judges, 1 and 2 Samuel and 1
and 2 Kings, and the Book of Deuteronomy itself.

CHAPTER XV

THE REMAINING
KINGDOM OF JUDAH

The Fall of Jerusalem, and Jeremiah

THE CONFLICT OF WORLD POWERS

The relationships of the great powers, one to another, became very complicated about the time of Jeremiah. Yet they must be understood if we are to appreciate the words of the prophets, and the actions of Judah, which once again was caught between the hammer and the anvil. For centuries Assyria had been the dominant world power, increasing steadily in strength. She reached her peak in the reign of Asshurbanapal about the middle of the seventh century B.C. The second great power was Egypt. Always fearful of Assyria, she sought eagerly to protect herself by alliances with the small countries in and near Palestine which separated her from the rapidly approaching southern boundaries of Assyria. If a country was free, Egypt offered an alliance and urged it not to submit to Assyria; if it already was under subjugation, Egypt urged revolt and promised to send aid—aid which seldom arrived. Sometimes a clear-thinking statesman like Isaiah could see the comparative strengths of the two great competitors; sometimes the ruler on the throne of Assyria seemed weak, and a revolt was attempted—almost always with disastrous results. Thus Damascus, Israel, and many other small nations ceased to exist, while Judah continued only because heavy tribute was paid.

In 661 Asshurbanipal, the last great king of Assyria, conquered and destroyed Thebes, the capital of Egypt, and ruled the country of the Nile for a short time. However, Egypt soon regained freedom, and resumed her plotting. Meanwhile Babylon, on the lower Euphrates River, which had for centuries been a vassal of Assyria, was struggling to revolt, gaining temporary independence and then losing it. Ambassadors from this country also sought alliances with the small Palestinian states, so that the over-all picture is one of constant change, with an interlacing network of intrigue involving Assyria, Babylon, Egypt, Moab, Judah, various Philistine cities, and, before 732, Damascus and Israel. Sometimes a city would achieve independence for a short time, only to be recaptured, punished and thrust back into a condition of vassalage. But after the middle of the seventh century, Assyria was definitely on the way down, and Egypt and Babylon were rising to take her place.

In 625 B.C. Babylon finally threw off the yoke of Assyria, and kept growing much stronger as her former master grew weaker. Then, in 612 B.C., the combined forces of two or three peoples conquered Nineveh, the Assyrian capital. Babylon was joined by the Medes from the northeast, and possibly by the Scythians. These were a mobile mass of barbarians from the steppes of southern Russia who had recently overrun much of western Asia, threatening, with lightninglike drives, even as far as Palestine and Egypt. This coalition destroyed the central authority of the Assyrians, although they retained for several years a few fortress cities in western Asia.

Probably from fear of the new Babylonian power, Pharaoh Necho, ruler of Egypt, became allied with Egypt's former master, Assyria. In 608 B.C., on one of his expeditions through Palestine to aid his partner, he met and killed Josiah of Judah. Three years later he came north again for the same purpose. This time he was thoroughly defeated at Carchemish on the upper Euphrates River by the Babylonian forces under the crown prince Nebuchadnezzar, in one of the decisive battles of world history.[1] Nebuchadnezzar was unable to exploit his victory, as his father died at that time in Babylon, and it was necessary for him to return to take over his own kingdom. Later the Babylonian king came back to western Asia and annexed all of it, but Egypt regained sufficient strength to resume her intrigues with the smaller conquered nations, so that it was necessary for Babylon to send one expedition after another to keep the new provinces in line. Two of these resulted in the downfall of Jerusalem in 597 B.C. and in 586 B.C.

1. For an analysis of this period, see W. F. Albright, "The Seal of Eliakim and the Latest Preexilic History of Judah, with some observations on Ezekiel," *Journal of Biblical Literature*, LI, Part II (June, 1932), especially pp. 85-93.

JOSIAH AND HIS SONS, 2 KINGS, chapters 22—25

In the last chapter we saw that Josiah, after the death of powerful Asshurbanipal, was sufficiently master of his own country to institute the most thoroughgoing religious reformation of its history—the Deuteronomic reform of 621 B.C. Since he carried this reformation into the territory which had formerly been the northern kingdom of Israel, it is evident that he had either been able to conquer this area in his own name, or, as is more likely, he ruled this territory and Judah also as a subject of Asshurbanipal's successor.[2] Then, after the fall of Nineveh in 612 B.C., Josiah switched his allegiance to the rising nation of Babylon. That is why, when the Egyptian Necho went north through Palestine to fight alongside what was left of the Assyrian army against Babylon, Josiah felt it necessary to oppose him at Megiddo—thus meeting his death.

Three months after the death of Josiah, Pharaoh Necho, who had killed him, was returning southward to Egypt. Summoning the son of Josiah who had been placed upon the throne at Jerusalem to appear before him, he accused him of being pro-Babylonian like his father. He therefore loaded him with chains and took him to Egypt, placing his half brother Jehoiakim, who was pro-Egyptian, upon the throne. Sometime after Carchemish, when the Babylonians were overrunning Palestine, Jehoiakim switched his allegiance to Nebuchadnezzar, but after three years he switched back. As soon as Nebuchadnezzar could get his other affairs in order, he started for Jerusalem to punish Jehoiakim, but before he reached the city, Jehoiakim died—possibly assassinated by his own countrymen because his anti-Babylonian policies were bad for the nation. Upon his death his son Jehoiachin was placed on the throne, but he promptly surrendered to the advancing Babylonians. He was given reasonable treatment, probably because he had saved Nebuchadnezzar the annoyance of a long siege. Transported to Babylon, he was freed from prison by a later king (2 Kings 25:27-30), and treated with respect until his death. It was through him that the line of David was traced by later writers. Most of the important people and craftsmen were deported

---

2. Cf. Albright, *The Jews, Their History, Culture and Religion*, p. 44f.

with the king in 597 B.C. in what came to be known as the first
captivity. Among them was a young man who had been trained
for the priesthood—Ezekiel.

An uncle of the deported king, who was the third son of
Josiah to reign and the full brother of the man who had been
taken in chains to Egypt by Pharaoh Necho for being pro-Babylonian, was the next ruler of Jerusalem. He was given the
name Zedekiah, and installed by Nebuchadnezzar after solemn
oaths of fealty. For a while he remained faithful. Then he
revolted, and history repeated itself. Nebuchadnezzar again
besieged the city of Jerusalem. Egypt made a futile effort to
interfere, but the situation was hopeless. The royal family
sought flight at night, and traveled as far as the plains of
Jericho, where they were captured and brought back before
Nebuchadnezzar. There Zedekiah was forced to watch his
sons killed; then he was blinded, loaded with chains, and taken
to Babylon where, according to Jeremiah's book, he remained
in prison till his death. (2 Kings 25:1-7; Jeremiah 52:4-11.)

Thus we have three sons and one grandson of Josiah on the
throne at Jerusalem in this period:

a. The first son, Jehoahaz, who ruled only three months
after his father's death, and, because he was pro-Babylonian,
was deported to Egypt by Pharaoh Necho.

b. The second son, Jehoiakim, who, being pro-Egyptian,
was put upon the throne by Necho. He ruled eleven years,
and died as Nebuchadnezzar was marching on Jerusalem.
He was possibly assassinated because his pro-Egyptian policies had made trouble for Jerusalem with the now-dominant
Babylonian king.

c. The grandson, Jehoiachin, son of Jehoiakim, who ruled
only three months before surrendering to Nebuchadnezzar.
He was put on the throne possibly as a result of a palace
revolt against his father, because he did not share his father's
anti-Babylonian policies. His surrender instituted the first
captivity in 597 B.C.

d. The third son of Josiah to rule, given the name Zedekiah, was the full brother of Jehoahaz and presumably like-

wise pro-Babylonian, hence acceptable to Nebuchadnezzar. Later, military successes of the Egyptians against the Babylonians induced him to revolt against his Mesopotamian master, which action resulted in the fall and destruction of Jerusalem. Although the first captivity caused the removal of far more citizens of Jerusalem to Babylon, it was the captivity of 586 B.C. which came to be known as the beginning of the "exile."

THREE MINOR PROPHETS, NAHUM, chapters 1; 3; HABAKKUK, chapters 1—3; ZEPHANIAH, chapters 1; 3.

After three-quarters of a century of silence, the voice of prophecy was again heard in Judah in this, the last period before the exile. As there were four prophets in the eighth century: Amos, Hosea, Isaiah and Micah; so there were four in the seventh century: Nahum, Habakkuk, Zephaniah, and Jeremiah, though much of the work of Jeremiah was accomplished after 600 B.C.

Nahum wrote when the destruction of Nineveh was imminent—and it brought no desolation to his soul. Yet it is difficult to criticize the prophet for his grim satisfaction because retribution was coming to the cruel oppressor of all Asia. The book could not have been written before 661 B.C., because it describes the destruction of Thebes, which Assyria conquered at that time. Probably some time in the decade before the destruction of Nineveh in 612 B.C. would suit best. The poetry is bold and powerful, with extremely vivid descriptions. There is no very great religious value present. Judah will no longer suffer, but the main theme of the book seems to be "Nineveh will be destroyed—Hallelujah."

There is much disagreement among scholars about the Book Habakkuk. It seems to deal with the Chaldeans or Babylonians, which would place it somewhere around 600 B.C. However, some think it discusses the Greeks at the time of Alexander the Great, 332 B.C. The majority favor the earlier date, but most students agree that the psalm in chapter 3 was written later. It is a beautiful picture of the power of God, by someone who must have been acquainted with the Song of Deborah. (Judges 5.) The first two chapters were not written at one time. First

we have a question asked of the LORD: "Why does injustice
prevail?" Then the answer, that the LORD is raising up the
Chaldeans to punish the oppressors. Then, presumably, a considerable time elapses, during which it is seen that, instead of
being a satisfactory answer to the question, the cruel Chaldeans
have made the problem much greater. Therefore the LORD
will punish them. But, in the meantime, the righteous man
will live because of his faithfulness.

Two ideas of extreme importance are brought up in this little
book. The first one is called the "problem of evil" or the
"problem of suffering" and is concerned with Habakkuk's question: "Why does injustice prevail?" It will be discussed in
connection with Jeremiah, a contemporary of Habakkuk, and
with other later writers.[3] The other one is his statement: "The
righteous shall live by his faith (or faithfulness)."[4] Six and a
half centuries after Habakkuk climbed onto his watch tower
and talked with God (Habakkuk 2:1-4), Paul the apostle was
engaged in a terrific argument with conservative Jewish members of the Christian Church. They held that, in order to be a
Christian, it was necessary to conform to all the intricate requirements of the Jewish law—fasting, food laws, circumcision,
Sabbath observance, etc. Paul insisted that a man was saved
not by what he did—"works," or observance of the law—but
by what he believed—that Jesus was the Christ or Messiah. In
his letters to the churches of Galatia and Rome he used this
proof-text from Habakkuk: "The righteous shall live by his
faith." Thus these words from a somewhat obscure prophet
became perhaps the most convincing argument in the persua-
sion, first of Paul, and then of the Christian Church as a whole,
that Christianity was *not* subject to the Jewish law. Had it not
been for this stand of Paul, it is probable that Christianity
would have remained only a sect of Judaism. Martin Luther
also used this passage, as quoted in Paul's letter to Galatians,
as a powerful argument against "indulgences" at the time of
the Protestant Reformation.

---

3. See below, pp. 195-197.

4. The correct translation here is certainly "faithfulness" (as shown in the footnote of
RSV) or "fidelity." Many years later when the Greek translation was made, the word
used was one which could be translated either "faithfulness" (fidelity) or "faith"
(belief). Paul used this Greek translation, and went by the latter meaning.

A century and a third before the time of Zephaniah, the wealthy people of the Northern Kingdom of Israel had been most complacent. Sometimes by honest, sometimes by dishonorable methods, they had collected their wealth. Since they were financially able to offer fine sacrifices, they considered themselves righteous and thought their success was the blessing of the LORD upon them because of their careful observance of religious ritual. They looked forward to the day of the LORD, when they expected God to take over complete charge of the world and to reward them even more than he had done. To them, religion was ritual sacrifice, not righteousness toward their fellow men. Amos had bitterly opposed this philosophy, and had insisted that the day of the LORD was to be not a time of rejoicing, but a day of judgment; not light, but darkness. (Amos 5:18ff.) Now, in the Southern Kingdom, many years after Amos, we find the prophet Zephaniah preaching the same thing as Amos had preached but doing it more vehemently. The people were terrified by the approach of the wild hordes of Scythians who threatened to engulf all of Judah. Zephaniah interpreted the threat as the punishment of God, the coming day of the LORD, which was to be a horrible experience for the Judahites. His magnificently powerful poem on this theme (chapter one, especially vss. 14-18) is the greatest thing in the book. It eventually became one of the great hymns of the mediaeval church—"Dies Irae," or "The Day of Wrath." One verse in the earlier part of the chapter,

> "At that time I will search Jerusalem with lamps,
>   and I will punish the men
> who are thickening upon their lees,
>   those who say in their hearts,
> 'The LORD will not do good
>   nor will he do ill.' "

—Zephaniah 1:12

is reminiscent of the cynic philosopher, Diogenes, going about with a lighted lantern in the daytime, seeking an honest man. It demonstrates that, in those days, there were skeptics who denied that the LORD took any part in the destiny of mankind, in exact opposition to the Deuteronomistic philosophy of history, which pictured everything as being controlled by the LORD.

There is no reason for thinking Zephaniah preached over any great length of time. He seems to have utilized the common fear of the Scythians to drive home upon the people of Judah the idea that the LORD would, by utter destruction, punish them for their sins. Possibly the passing of the Scythian threat and the glories of the middle part of Josiah's reign made the prophet of doom unpopular, so that, if he did write more, it was not preserved. Even if that is the case the three chapters we have were preserved, and after the oppression by the Babylonians had begun, the truth of Zephaniah's message was appreciated.

JEREMIAH, JEREMIAH, chapter 1; 13:1-11; 18:1-11; 19:1-9; chapters 20; 28—32; 36; 38; 40; 41:1-3

There are many people who think no prophet greater than Jeremiah ever lived—unless Jesus of Nazareth be considered a prophet. For a third of a century he underwent the pressure of unpopularity, and sometimes bitter persecution. He watched his beloved Jerusalem sink from the high point of Josiah's reign to the two times it was surrendered to the Babylonian army of Nebuchadnezzar, and all but the most worthless of its citizens were marched into captivity. He saw the morale of the people disintegrate from the great dedication of the early days of the Deuteronomic Reformation to the point where the only apt description of them was a basket of bad (probably rotten) figs, so bad they could not be eaten. He was beaten, put in the stocks, imprisoned, placed in danger of death—yet he continued to preach the word of God. He cursed the day upon which he was born, but when he tried to remain silent instead of preaching, he felt a fire within his bones which forced him on in his unappreciated ministry. (Jeremiah, chapter 20.)

It is generally assumed that Jeremiah began to preach in 626 at the time of the Scythian threat—at the same time and for the same reason that Zephaniah preached. One description of his call to the ministry is a vision he had of a boiling caldron, facing from the north, which brought destruction to all in its path. (Jeremiah 1:13f.) This is usually interpreted as referring to the Scythians, though some now hold that, from the very first of his ministry, Jeremiah realized that the threat against Judah from the north was the Babylonian empire.[5]

Whether or not he began his work as early as this, Jeremiah was probably preaching by the time of the Deuteronomic Reformation, five years later. Here the prophet seems to have changed his mind. He must have supported the reform at first, for some of his early pronouncements were against the "high places," which were prime targets of the reformation. Also we should expect that if he was in favor of the reformation, he would have been unpopular with the people of his home town of Anathoth. This town had been a religious sanctuary, probably since the time Abiathar had been sent there by Solomon, and the reformation prohibited worship any place except at the temple in Jerusalem. We are told that the young men there tried to kill Jeremiah. (Jeremiah 11:21ff.)

But though Jeremiah seems at first to have supported the great reformation, he apparently became dissatisfied with its accomplishments and turned against it. He proclaimed in no uncertain terms that the LORD would destroy the temple in Jerusalem, treating it as he had treated Shiloh, the ancient sanctuary of the Hebrew federation of tribes in the days before the institution of the monarchy. (Joshua, chapter 18, 1 Samuel, chapters 3—4), which had been destroyed by the Philistines. This powerful sermon of Jeremiah appears both in chapter 7 and in chapter 26. It would have cost the prophet his life had not someone remembered the words of Micah predicting the same thing: "Zion shall be plowed as a field; Jerusalem shall become a heap of ruins." Likewise, in his greatest chapter (31), Jeremiah spoke of the inadequacy of the great covenant the LORD had made with the people when he brought them out of Egypt (the high point of the Book of Deuteronomy), saying that a new covenant would be made, and the law would be put within the people, written upon their hearts. However, this passage may have been written a long time after the institution of the reform.

5. See *The Interpreter's Bible*, Vol. V, p. 779. Hyatt doubts the existence of the Scythian threat against Judah, and suggests 626 B.C. as a possible date for the birth of Jeremiah.

But if Jeremiah changed his position in relation to the Deuteronomic Reformation, he certainly did not change it in regard to the political situation. He seems to have been one of the first to appreciate the rising power of Babylon, and like Isaiah before him he consistently opposed any tendency of the kings of Judah to rely upon Egypt, in spite of the occasional success of Egyptian arms in southern Palestine. Once again, the kingdom might have been spared untold agony if the words of the prophet had been heeded. And if Jeremiah was consistent in his political activity, he certainly steered a true course also in his moral efforts. There was no compromise with wrong, even though the priests, the nobles, and the king himself were involved.

On one occasion in the reign of Jehoiakim the prophet felt himself ordered by the LORD to record all his prophesies against Israel, Judah, and the other nations, so he dictated them to his scribe Baruch and ordered him to read them to the assembled people in the temple on a fast day. For some unknown reason, Jeremiah was not able to be in the temple himself. Word of the messages was given the king, who ordered them read to him in the presence of his princes. As rapidly as a section was read, the king cut it from the scroll and put it in a fire, until all had been destroyed. He ordered Baruch and Jeremiah seized, but they escaped. Jeremiah then cursed the king, saying that he would have no son who would succeed him upon the throne, and his own body would receive no burial (Jeremiah, chapter 36 and 22:18f), and dictated the prophecy over again to Baruch. This second edition is probably the nucleus of the Book of Jeremiah as we have it today, though many things were added to it later, both by Jeremiah and by others.

It may be that the beginning of the disagreement between Jeremiah and the king Jehoiakim was a difference of opinion about Babylon. Jehoiakim had been placed upon the throne by the pharaoh of Egypt, whereas early and consistently Jeremiah recognized the power of the new Mesopotamian empire. Possibly as early as the battle of Carchemish, Jeremiah began to think of Babylon as the agent of the LORD, and to place his trust in her. Certainly after the first surrender, when vows of

fidelity had been made in the name of the LORD, he considered
disloyalty to Nebuchadnezzar of Babylon equivalent to revolt
against God.   This first surrender came almost immediately
after Jehoiachin had inherited the throne, subsequent to the
death of his father Jehoiakim.   The Babylonian army was en-
route to Jerusalem, and the young king was persuaded to cast
himself upon the mercy of Nebuchadnezzar.   Three months
after his coronation, Jehoiachin and most of the important
people of Jerusalem were led into Babylon in the first captivity.

The uncle of the exiled king, Zedekiah, who next came to
the throne, was pro-Babylonian, and remained faithful to Nebuchadnezzar for a number of year.   Finally, however, the
Egyptians became more powerful in their military activities,
and the anti-Babylonian pressure upon the king in Jerusalem
increased.   Because of this propaganda, and a similar and contemporary unrest in Babylon, Jeremiah again became active
along political lines.   When another prophet, Hananiah,
preached that the LORD would destroy the power of Babylon
and return the exiles from that land, Jeremiah put a wooden
yoke upon his own neck, to illustrate the manner in which the
LORD had placed the yoke of Babylon upon the neck of Jerusalem.   After Hananiah had removed and destroyed the yoke,
Jeremiah announced that the LORD had removed the yoke of
wood so that he could replace it with one of iron. When Hananiah died that same year, it was quite natural that his death
should have been attributed to the fact that he opposed Jeremiah.   Jeremiah then wrote a letter to the people in captivity in
Babylon, telling them to settle down in the country, for it would
be seventy years (i.e., a long, long time) before the LORD would
return them to Jerusalem.   (Jeremiah, chapters 28—29.)[6]   This
passage was later of great importance to the writer of the Book
of Daniel.

When Zedekiah finally did revolt against Nebuchadnezzar,
Jeremiah violently opposed the action, and when the army of
Babylon appeared before Jerusalem, he urged all the military
forces to cease resistance.   He was imprisoned in a cistern,
from which the water—but not the mud—had been exhausted.

---

6. Some scholars think the story of a letter to the captives in Babylon was written by
a later writer.

His life was saved only by the intervention of an Ethiopian eunuch who received permission to pull him out of the mud into which he had sunk. He was then imprisoned in the court of the guard and given a daily ration of bread, as long as there was any left in Jerusalem. (Jeremiah, chapters 37—38.)

Before the final capitulation of the city, a relative of Jeremiah offered him a piece of land. The prophet purchased it and carefully completed the deed of sale, directing his secretary Baruch to enclose it in a jar. This was probably very similar to those in which, six centuries later, the members of a monastic order hid their most precious manuscripts in the caves about the Wâdī Qumran (the "Dead Sea Scrolls"). This was to insure preservation of the document for future years, a clear proof that Jeremiah expected the eventual restoration of Judah, so that land would once again be bought and sold there. (Jeremiah 32:6-16.) It supplements the attitude expressed in his letter to the Babylonian captives, telling them that eventually the LORD would re-establish them (or rather, their descendants) in Judah.

When Jerusalem finally fell in 586 B.C., the Babylonians rewarded Jeremiah for his consistent support by giving him his choice of remaining in the city or going with the captives to Babylon. He chose the former, and apparently worked diligently with Gedaliah (whom the Babylonian king had appointed governor over the captured province) in an effort to restore some of the lost dignity of Jerusalem and Judah. But a wild-eyed patriot assassinated Gedaliah, and a number of other people. Some of the citizens asked Jeremiah to inquire of the LORD if they should flee to Egypt or remain in Jerusalem to face possible punishment by the Babylonians for the disorder. It took Jeremiah ten days to determine what was the will of the LORD. When he told the people they were ordered to stay in Judah, they fled to Egypt, taking Jeremiah as a sort of hostage. Perhaps they were wise, for we are told there was a small number of people taken to Babylon by Nebuchadnezzar in a *third* deportation, in the twenty-third year of his reign, which would be just the right time for a punishment of Judah for the death of the governor, Gedaliah. (Jeremiah 52:28ff.) When in Egypt, these refugees from Judah further trampled on Jeremiah's heart by forsaking the worship of the LORD, sacrificing to other gods, and the women burning incense to the "Queen of Heaven." When the prophet remonstrated with them, they replied that when they had done so in Judah and the streets of Jerusalem, there had been plenty of food, and no evil times. He then predicted that the pharaoh of Egypt would be captured by the Babylonians, and Nebuchadnezzar would set up his throne on the stones upon which they were standing. (Jeremiah, chapters 43—44.) Tradition tells us that Jeremiah was slain in Egypt by his own countrymen.

The figures of speech of Jeremiah are wonderfully vivid. One of the pictures of his call to be a prophet is the vision of a huge caldron boiling in the north, its contents threatening to engulf the land. He was told to wear a loin cloth for a time, and then to bury it. Later, on digging it up, he found it had rotted—a symbol of Judah and Jerusalem: safe so long as they cling to the LORD, but destroyed when they leave him. (Jeremiah 13:1-11.) The comparison of the people remaining in Jerusalem to a basket of bad figs (Jeremiah, chapter 24) and the breaking of a jar to simulate the LORD's destruction of Jerusalem (Jeremiah, chapter 19) are particularly brilliant, but the finest of his figures is the parable of the potter's wheel, which pictures the remaking of the house of Israel, after the nation had failed in the LORD's first attempt to make it into a useful vessel. (Jeremiah 18:1-11.)

Two of the greatest problems of mankind are treated by Jeremiah. First, he seems to have been a firm believer in predestination—the idea that the LORD has predetermined everything about a man's life so that what he is going to be has been settled before his birth. It is difficult to imagine a clearer statement of this than is given by the prophet about his ministry, in words attributed to the LORD:

"Before I formed you in the womb I knew you,
and before you were born I consecrated you;
I appointed you a prophet to the nations."
—Jeremiah 1:4f

Jeremiah was not happy about his work. He even accused the LORD of deceiving him when he led him into his ministry (Jeremiah 20:7f), and finally cursed the day on which he was born. (Jeremiah 20:14f.) But he did feel that it was possible, for a time, to reject this control of the LORD. In his parable of the potter's wheel, the potter was thwarted in his first plan, yet used the same clay to make another vessel. (Jeremiah 18:1-11.) Even so, although Judah refused the role to which it had been predestined, the Potter would remake the country to serve his own designs.

The other great problem was the problem of evil, or the question "Why do the righteous suffer?" This has been mentioned above, and will be discussed more thoroughly below, in the treatment of Second Isaiah and the Suffering Servant.[7] The people of Judah had been taught for many years that, if a man did wrong in the eyes of the LORD, he would be punished. From this idea there developed two corollary beliefs:

a. If a man did right, he would be rewarded, and

b. If a man suffered misfortune, it was because the LORD was punishing him for his misdeeds.

Since reward and punishment were judged on a material basis, and righteousness was associated with sacrifice and ceremony, the reasoning in the early days was that the successful man was righteous, and the unsuccessful man guilty of some sin in the sight of the LORD. Amos and a few others sought to discredit this view, but the general tendency was to assume that, if a person had misfortune, there was some sin, perhaps unknown, which had caused it. Any protestation could be disregarded, as the words of a sinner. On the other hand, no successful man was willing to deny that it was his own good character which had insured his success.

But as conditions grew worse, questions began to arise, reaching a climax in the death of Josiah. How could the anointed of the LORD, who had ruled thirty-one years in "that fierce light which beats upon a throne," and had instituted and carried on the Deuteronomic Reformation, rooting out all Baal worship and destroying the high places, have been an evil man? And yet he was slain when forty years of age, by a heathen pharaoh

7. See below, pp. 195-197.

who knew not the LORD. Was God unjust? Or was he not powerful? Was it simply that he did not care? The problem has been with mankind from that day to this, and probably always will lack a satisfactory answer. Today, one says that suffering is an instructive and purifying influence; another that there really is no absolute suffering—it is the mental inability to adjust; another that, as in the case of Lazarus and the rich man in the New Testament (Luke 16:19-31), all these things will be compensated after death. But these explanations would have been of no value to the man of ancient Judah. He was a practical man, and did not want to suffer if he did not deserve it; he certainly did no rationalizing about whether or not there *was* evil—he had experienced it; and it was not until long after this that the Jews clearly believed in a life beyond death.

The first hint we have of this problem in the Old Testament comes from two prophets who were preaching at, or shortly after, the time of Josiah's death. Neither attempted an explanation, although Habakkuk, when he asked:

> O LORD, how long shall I cry for help,
>   and thou wilt not hear?"

was told that the LORD was rousing the Chaldeans to take care of things. (Habakkuk 1:2-17.) He did have faith that, eventually, all would come out all right. Jeremiah merely asks the obverse of the question—not why do the righteous suffer, but why do the wicked prosper?

> Righteous art thou, O LORD, when I complain to thee;
>   yet would I complain to thee;
> Why does the way of the wicked prosper?
>   Why do all who are treacherous thrive?"
>   —Jeremiah 12:1

This eternal question was the inspiration for some of the finest thinking done by the chosen people. It reached its flower in the writings of the Second Isaiah and the Book of Job.

Jeremiah in a marvelous way repeated in his life and in his message the teachings of the earlier prophets—particularly Hosea. This similarity to Hosea may come out of the fact that each endured a great emotional ordeal: Hosea the disruption of his home and Jeremiah the degeneration of the people of Judah and the fall of Jerusalem. But there are three other great contributions which come from Jeremiah himself.

Jeremiah emphasized the pure, direct, unmediated worship of the LORD by man. The people had just been reminded by the discovery of the Book of Deuteronomy that Moses had given them a covenant engraved on tables of stone, which their fathers had broken. Jeremiah told them that there would come a time when the LORD would make a new covenant with the house of Israel and the house of Judah, and that this covenant would be written upon their hearts, and they would all know him. (Jeremiah 31:31-34.) This would not require a priest to intervene between man and God. Jeremiah was not on very friendly terms with the priests. Probably Jeremiah, when he spoke of the LORD writing his law on the hearts of men, thought of writing on tablets or tables, as he had when he spoke of the LORD writing about the sin of Judah, engraving it upon the tablet of their heart with a pen of iron, and the point of a diamond. (Jeremiah 17:1.) The word "table" here is the same as used in Deuteronomy, e.g., when Moses destroyed them because of the sin of the people (Deuteronomy 9:17); but the tables of their hearts they could *not* destroy.

The second great contribution is an idea closely related to the first—that the LORD is concerned, not only with the nation but with the individual within the nation. When Hosea had taught about God's love for Israel, he was not talking about the individual man, but about the nation. But Jeremiah felt himself to have been rejected by men. He was hated by the common people, by the priests outside Jerusalem, by the temple authorities within Jerusalem, by the rank and file of the army, the military commanders, the nobles, and the king. During part of his reign Zedekiah was not harsh with him, and his scribe Baruch, the Ethiopian eunuch who saved him from the cistern and the governor, Gedaliah, may have been on friendly terms. Aside from these, and a king who ruled only three months, we know of no person in Judah who does not appear to have been against him. He did not even have a wife. He seems to have been driven to find companionship with the

LORD. He talked to him, argued with him, and even criticized
him:

> Wilt thou be to me like a deceitful brook,
> like waters that fail?
>   —Jeremiah 15:18b

There was a saying, popular in Jerusalem in Jeremiah's time,
that the punishment of the people was because of the sins of
their fathers, but Jeremiah said that would no longer be true—
the penalty assessed to each would be because of his own sins:
"In those days they shall no longer say:

> 'The fathers have eaten sour grapes,
> and the children's teeth are set on edge,'

But everyone shall die for his own sin; each man who eats
sour grapes, his teeth shall be set on edge." (Jeremiah 31:
29-30.)

As a result of Jeremiah's emphasis upon the individual, and
especially because of the teachings of his greater successor,
Jesus of Nazareth, that not a sparrow falls to the ground without the Father's will, and that the hairs of our heads are num-
bered (Matthew 10:29-30), we find it difficult to imagine a
time when this was not a commonly accepted idea—yet Jeremiah was the originator.

In addition to these two great contributions to religious
thinking—the idea of simple direct worship of the LORD, and
of the LORD's relationship to an individual—Jeremiah made one
more great contribution of which he was not even aware. All
through his life, Jeremiah was a man of sorrows. He endured
opposition and persecution, but his greatest cross was to see what
happened to his people:

> O that my head were waters,
>   and my eyes a fountain of tears,
> that I might weep day and night
>   for the slain of the daughter of my people!
>   —Jeremiah 9:1

It is no wonder he was called the "weeping prophet." But all through his life he was faithful to his highest ideals. Receiving no reward, he gave himself completely for the people of Judah.

> But I was like a gentle lamb
>   led to the slaughter.
> I did not know it was against me
>   they devised schemes, saying,
> "Let us destroy the tree with its fruit."
> —Jeremiah 11:19

True, he fell somewhat short of perfection by asking vengeance upon his enemies in the next verse, but the complete sacrifice he made still stood. Two generations later the greatest of the prophets pictured his people as the "Suffering Servant of the LORD" in what may be the most important passage ever written. (Isaiah, chapter 53.) He seems to have drawn his picture of the Servant from the life of Jeremiah, and even to have used some of Jeremiah's words to describe him.[8]

LITERATURE OF THE PERIOD

The four books of prophecy just described—Nahum, Habakkuk, Zephaniah, and Jeremiah—form the prophetic works of the period. In addition to these authors, there was another group of writers called the "Deuteronomic School," interested in historical literature. Their ideas, shaped rigidly by the original Book of Deuteronomy, discovered in the eighteenth year of Josiah's reign (621 B.C.), and by the great Deuteronomic Reformation which he instituted, centered about two fixed beliefs:

a. The LORD was the only God, at least for Israel, and the one great sin was to worship other gods. A corollary to this was the rule that the only lawful place to worship was at Jerusalem, at the temple of the LORD.

b. All the history of Israel (and Judah) was determined by the LORD for moralistic purposes. If the nation, or any part of it, was defeated in battle, it was because of its sin (worshiping false gods). If the people recovered from bondage, it was because they repented of their sin, and the LORD had mercy upon them.

---

8. See below, p. 196.

Most of the writings of these men were of an editorial nature; i.e., they took older writings, and enlarged them, putting upon them their philosophy of history. Because of this moralistic interpretation, it is often rather easy to separate the original writings from the editorial additions of the Deuteronomistic writers.

A number of the books of the Old Testament bear the stamp of these editors. We have seen above how the J history, which started with the story of creation and continued at least until the time of the judges (and possibly to Solomon), and the E history, which started with the story of Abraham, were finally united, about 700 B.C. That part of the JE history which is included in the first twelve chapters of the Book of Joshua was carefully revised by the Deuteronomistic or D editor. The stories of the judges, found in the first sixteen chapters of the book of that name, were even more carefully worked over by this same editor, who was responsible for the book very much as we have it today.

It is difficult to determine the underlying strands in the books of 1 and 2 Samuel. Possibly they are a continuation of J and E. At any rate, there are at least two major accounts in the first part of 1 Samuel, one much earlier than the other. There are certainly other materials also to be found. But it was the Deuteronomistic editor who organized the whole into combined form.

We know of a number of sources for the books of 1 and 2 Kings. One was, "The Book of the Acts of Solomon." (1 Kings 11:41.) There were, of course, official court records for both kingdoms, after the division of Solomon's kingdom. It was either to these records, or to books compiled from them, that the editor had reference when he said "Now the rest of the acts of . . . behold, they are written in the Book of the Chronicles of the Kings of Israel" and ". . . in the Book of the Chronicles of the Kings of Judah." (1 Kings 14:19, 29, and many other references.) Other probable sources are some kind of record kept in the temple, and the groups or "cycles" of stories about Elijah, and about Elisha, and about Ahab. Of these, and possibly other materials, the editor built his great history.

The date usually ascribed to this Deuteronomistic editor is about 600 B.C., though some think it should be about ten years earlier than that—after the Deuteronomic Reformation, but before the death of King Josiah.[9]

Thus we have a great deal of literary activity shortly after (or possibly shortly before) the death of Josiah. It sought to interpret history from a religious point of view. As a result of these intensely earnest editors, a large part of the Book of Joshua, and the Books of Judges, 1 and 2 Samuel and 1 and 2 Kings began to assume shape. These editors also greatly enlarged and possibly completed the Book of Deuteronomy, which had been their original inspiration.

A half-century later another group of men with the same ideals and purposes did some further work editing these same books. Among other things they mention that thirty-seven years after King Jehoiachin had been imprisoned in Babylon, at the time of the first captivity, he was released from prison and given a place at the king's table. Since this account is included in 2 Kings 25:27-30, the final revision could not have taken place before 560 B.C. This revision left the books concerned—part of Joshua, and all of Deuteronomy, Judges, 1 and 2 Samuel, and 1 and 2 Kings in their final shape, except for any inadvertent errors in copying the manuscripts through the centuries.

---

9. See, e.g., for the earlier date, Snaith, *The Interpreter's Bible*, Vol. III, p. 11; for the later date, Robert H. Pfeiffer, *Introduction to the Old Testament* (New York: Harper & Brothers, 1941), p. 379.

PART FOUR

THE EXILE

CHAPTER XVI

EZEKIEL AND

SECOND ISAIAH

EZEKIEL, EZEKIEL, chapters 1—5; 8; 18; 24; 33; 37; 40; 46

The fall of Jerusalem in 586 B.C. marks the end of an epoch. Except for the Maccabean Period, about four centuries later, in which the struggling little nation enjoyed a hundred years of semi-independence under the friendship of Rome, it was the last of Judah as a nation. It also marks the virtual end of a type of prophecy. Beginning with Amos, the prophets before the exile without exception chose as their main theme the condemnation of the people because of their sin. This was because the prophet considered himself the spokesman of the LORD. If the people had been following his will, there would have been no need for a spokesman. However, after the fall of Jerusalem, what the people most needed was hope, so the prophetic message, almost without exception, was largely a message of comfort.[1] Of the two great prophets of the Exile, Second Isaiah accomplished all of his ministry after the fall of Jerusalem, so the element of comforting predominates. Part of Ezekiel's work (the first 24 chapters) is dated before that event, and the balance after.[2] We therefore find strong condemnation of the people in the pre-exilic part, but a message in which hope is very prominent in the latter part.

It should be remembered that only one half of Ezekiel is truly exilic. The first captivity began in 597 B.C., and Ezekiel began to preach five years later, but six years before the second captivity, which is the date accepted for the exile. It seems simpler to consider all of Ezekiel in the one period of the exile,

---

1. The Book of Malachi, though late, does seem to follow the pattern of pre-exilic prophets in that it deals largely with criticism of Judah because of sins.
2. There are many difficult problems about Ezekiel. A number of scholars think the book is much later than the exile. There is good reason for thinking there was at least a revision of the book by a later writer. We shall follow the traditional dating, i.e., the fifth year of King Jehoiachin's captivity, or 592 B.C. for the beginning of the book.

181

rather than to separate the two parts of his work. This is especially true since, for Ezekiel and those to whom he was preaching in Babylon, some of the problems of the exile had already begun before 592.

It is often difficult to distinguish between what actually happened to Ezekiel, and what he saw in a "vision." The opening verses of his book definitely place him in Babylon, by the river Chebar—probably a canal. (Ezekiel 1:1ff.) But most of the first part of the book deals with the sins of the people of Jerusalem, before the fall of that city. He tells of being lifted by the Spirit by a lock of his hair, and transported to Jerusalem. (Ezekiel 8:3f.) Likewise, he was lifted up and brought to the house of the LORD, which, of course, was in Jerusalem. (Ezekiel 11:1.) He was told to preach to Jerusalem about her abominations (Ezekiel 16:1ff), and against her sanctuaries. (Ezekiel 21:1f.) Are we to assume that he left Babylon, preached in Jerusalem, and then returned to Babylon? During the reign of Zedekiah in Jerusalem (i.e., between the beginning of the first captivity and the fall of Jerusalem) the king on at least one occasion sent messengers to Babylon. (Jeremiah 29:3.) It is possible that Ezekiel was able to make a similar trip in the opposite direction. It is equally possible that he remained in Babylon all the time, and that his descriptions of activity in Jerusalem were "visions."

There were three great problems of religion which faced the people of Judah when they came to Babylon after the fall of Jerusalem. The first of the three pertained equally to those of the first captivity. The Book of Deuteronomy had taught that the LORD was to be worshiped in only one place—the temple at Jerusalem—and that restriction had been one of the basic principles of the Deuteronomic Reformation. How then could the displaced people from Jerusalem worship their God in Babylon? The answer of Ezekiel to this first great problem was his vision, given in the year 592, five years after the first deportation from Jerusalem, and recorded in chapter one of his book, with many references to it later on in the book.

The first thing described in the vision was the stormy wind, with a cloud and great brilliance about it, and fire flashing out.

From the very beginning, the LORD had been associated with the stormy wind and with fire. The vision of Moses was of a bush on fire. (Exodus, chapter 3.) It was by a pillar of cloud through the day, and a pillar of fire at night that the LORD led Israel out of Egypt. (Exodus 13:21f.) The LORD drove back the waters of the sea with a strong east wind, so Israel could escape from the Egyptian army. (Exodus 14:21f.) Both the cloud and the fire were present on Mount Sinai when Moses received the Commandments. (Exodus 19:9, 16-19.) It was by a storm that the LORD defeated the hosts of Sisera. (Judges 5:4f.) These and many other passages indicate that the early conception of the God of Israel was that of a storm god, with clouds, wind, and lightening indicating his presence and power. But this vision of Ezekiel also indicated controlled movement. There were grotesque animals, each with multiple wings and four faces: one the face of a man, one of a lion, one of an ox, and one of an eagle. Each animal also had hands. (Ezekiel 1:5-28.) Although these creatures were somewhat more elaborate than the five-legged winged bulls of Mesopotamia, they undoubtedly show Babylonian influence. They were called "cherubim." (Ezekiel, chapter 10.) Beneath each animal was a "wheel within a wheel" (probably one wheel directed straight ahead, and another at ninety degrees from it, to permit movement north, south, east or west, according to the will of the LORD).

Above the creatures was a "firmament"—a base or platform —on which was the sapphire throne of the LORD. This vision appeared in the north, the direction from which any person coming to Babylon from Jerusalem would appear. It was certainly interpreted as proof that the LORD was not limited to his temple in Jerusalem—that, in spite of the restrictions of Deuteronomy, the Israelites in Babylon could still worship their God. This vision was for the benefit of those of the first captivity, but its influence was still available to help those who came to Babylon after the fall of Jerusalem.

The second problem was the question: "Why worship a God who was unable to save Jerusalem, the only great city where he had been worshiped?" Half of the Book of Ezekiel is devoted to criticism of the people because of their sins (largely the worship of false gods) and the prediction of the fall of Jerusalem. In this he was aided by the work of Jeremiah in Jerusalem, who preached the same thing. When the last days of Jerusalem approached, Ezekiel was ordered to make no public display of his grief, and at that time his wife died. It is not quite clear, but it is probable that this was an object lesson for the people about him: that he was so stunned by his grief over the city that he could not make the outcry customarily expected over the death of a wife. (Ezekiel 24:15-27.) A later account of this same unusual dumbness states that the word of the destruction of Jerusalem was brought to Ezekiel some months after its fall by an escaping survivor, which would tend to bear out the idea that it was in Babylon that Ezekiel received the message. (Ezekiel 33:21f.) If that is correct, those who had been in Babylon had heard Ezekiel, just as those who had been in Jerusalem had heard Jeremiah, and all had the prophetic assurance that, when the city of David fell, it fell not because the LORD was unable to save it, but because he insisted upon its destruction as a punishment for its sins.

The third great problem was the question whether or not it was worth while to hold on to the culture (including the religion) of Israel, when the people were living in so distant a land. Aside from its religion, the culture of Israel had always been rather barren. The land for the most part was not fertile; the craftsmen were not skillful; and when Solomon had built the temple, he had had to import workmen to get men capable of erecting it. But at least some of the exiles must have been acquainted with the city of Babylon. This was the time of the building of the Hanging Gardens of Babylon, one of the Seven Classic Wonders of the World. Why not forget about the provincial culture of Jerusalem, and adopt the thrilling new civilization—and religion—of Babylon? Ezekiel combated this tendency in two ways: First, he made it difficult to follow the faith of Israel. By making the ritual more intricate, and the ceremonial laws more rigid and complicated, he tended to separate his people from the surrounding Babylonians. Probably a great many of the Sabbath laws come from this time, and perhaps some of the simpler dietary laws. Thus a wall of religious observance was built, and law began to be emphasized. This new tendency in religion came to be known as the religion of Judah, or Judaism. Ezekiel is commonly called the "father of Judaism." A man who is a devotee of this religion is properly called a Jew. It is a religious, not a racial term, when used correctly.

The other technique used by Ezekiel was to try to keep alive an interest in an ultimate return to Jerusalem. How interesting it would be if we could believe that the letter sent by Jeremiah, stating that "After seventy years" the exiles would return, had had an influence upon Ezekiel in this respect. One step intervening before any return would be the removal of other nations which had appropriated much of the land of Palestine. There are many oracles against such nations found in the latter part of the book of Ezekiel—some of which may have been written by him. But more to the point are the descriptions given by Ezekiel of the temple of the LORD which would be built,[3] and the list of laws by which the new nation was to be ruled. This utopia was to be a true theocracy. It would have the LORD as the ruler.

The most vivid teaching about the restoration is Ezekiel's vision of the Valley of Dry Bones. (Ezekiel, chapter 37.) The bones represented Israel, which was to be restored by the LORD. Bone was to be joined to bone; sinews, flesh, and skin were to be added; and the nation was to be brought to life in one body, both Judah and the Northern Kingdom. This is not a teaching of life after death for the individual, but for the nation. However, Ezekiel does carry on the teaching of Jeremiah about the individual's relation to the LORD. The same saying about sour grapes quoted by Jeremiah is also given by Ezekiel:

" 'The fathers have eaten sour grapes, and the children's teeth are set on edge' " (Ezekiel 18:2) and he says it will never be used again. The doctrine of individual responsibility is carried even further by this later prophet, who says that even if Noah, Daniel, and Job were in a land which the LORD was punishing,

---

3. No temple of those specifications was ever built, but the plans must have helped keep up religious interest, and, eventually, a temple *was* built.

they would be unable to save their own children. Only the great men themselves would avoid destruction. (Ezekiel 14: 12-20.) Yet the wicked by repentance can achieve salvation. (Ezekiel 33:10-16.) Ezekiel's own responsibility is shown in the discussion of the watchman. If in time of danger he sounds the alarm and the people of the city do not heed, theirs is the responsibility. But if he does *not* sound the alarm (i.e., if Ezekiel does not preach about the sins of the people), their blood will be required at his hand. (Ezekiel 33:1-6.)

The figures of speech—or object lessons—of Ezekiel are extremely vivid. A number of them, all with the same general message, are found in chapters 4 and 5. The prophet drew upon a brick a picture of the siege of Jerusalem, placing an iron plate between himself and the city, to indicate that the siege would come, and the LORD would not help. He lay 390 days upon his left side, to indicate the number of years for the punishment of Israel, and 40 days on his right side for the years of punishment of Judah. He made bread under foul conditions, and ate it, rationed by weight, to indicate shortage of food and unclean circumstances in captivity. He used a sword as a razor, dividing the hair cut off, to indicate the inhabitants of the city. One part he burned, one part he cut with a sword, and one part he scattered to the wind. He wrapped a few hairs in his robe and then destroyed most of those. Only a very small number would be saved.

The great work of Ezekiel was to shepherd the people of Judah at the time of their exile in Babylon, but he also marked a clear beginning of a new tendency in literature. In the late years of the pre-Christian era and on through New Testament times a type of writing called "apocalyptic" was very popular. The best examples of it in the Bible are the Books Daniel and Revelation. One important characteristic of these writings is the use of visions of grotesque figures, which are supposed to reveal a message not clear to any except to the group for which it is written. Ezekiel is not an apocalypse, but, if our dating of the book is correct, it is the first writing of the style which was eventually responsible for apocalyptic writing. The vision of the mobile throne of the LORD, in chapter one and elsewhere, is a style of writing not previously encountered.

SECOND ISAIAH, ISAIAH, chapters 40—43; 47; 52; 53; 55

As previously stated, Isaiah is a complicated book which very few scholars today consider to be the work of a single man.[4] It is generally taken for granted that chapters 40—50 were written by one author, shortly before the fall of Babylon in 538 B.C. The final part of the book, chapters 56—66, was written either by the same, or, more likely, by a different man, some years later. This final section (Third Isaiah) has somewhat the same style as Second Isaiah (chapters 40—55), but the background is Jerusalem after the return from Babylon in 538, and the aims of the book are different.

Since it is an exilic book, we should expect to find comfort the main purpose of Second Isaiah, and it is unnecessary to go beyond the first word of the first verse to find it:

> Comfort, comfort my people, says your God.
> Speak tenderly to Jerusalem, and cry to her
> that her warfare is ended,
>   that her iniquity is pardoned,
> that she has received from the LORD's hand
>   double for all her sins.
>
> —Isaiah 40:1-2

If the first two verses set the theme of comfort, the rest of the chapter and the two succeeding ones give in summary form the message of the writer. Israel had sinned against the LORD, and had been punished by the exile into Babylon. Now the LORD will restore his people. Let the way be prepared—a highway in the desert for God. Lift up the valleys, depress the hills, and make the rough places a level plain, that Israel may return to Jerusalem. The glory of the LORD has spoken, and, though mankind may wither as the grass, the word of the LORD endures forever.

The power of the Creator, God, is portrayed in majestic lines, equalled only in the greatest part of the Book of Job (chapters 38—41), and excelled not even there. The folly of those who

---

4. See Appendix, Note E.

worship idols is portrayed by a crushing mixture of humor and logic. The product of the skilled craftsman, an idol which cannot move, is contrasted with the Holy One of Israel who calls out by name the starry host of heaven. He is the one who gives power to the faint. He is the one who has stirred up a leader from the north and from the east, who will trample kings under his foot, as a potter treads upon his clay. But Israel is the servant of the LORD. He must not be dismayed, for the LORD is his God, and he will uphold him with his victorious right hand.

The rest of Second Isaiah—chapters 43 through 55—is largely an elaboration of this theme of the first three chapters: the illimitable power of the LORD will, by the conquering agent he has stirred up, restore Israel his servant, who has by now doubly paid for his transgressions. In Isaiah 44:28 and the next verse, 45:1, the one who will accomplish the LORD's will is identified as Cyrus, called in the former verse the LORD's shepherd, and in the latter one his anointed. He is the one who is to destroy the power of the Chaldeans or Babylonians (43: 14; 47:1-9), as indeed he did in 538 B.C.

The servant of Second Isaiah was quite plainly the people Israel (41:8, 44:1). There are four poems which are usually called the "Servant Songs"—42:1-4; 49:1-6; 50:4-9; and 52:13-53:12—which describe this servant of the LORD, and tell of what he is supposed to accomplish. The first and the last of these are the best known and the greatest; the last one is by some considered one of the most important passages ever written.

Second Isaiah realized that Israel had sinned against the LORD, yet he felt that the punishment of the fall of Jerusalem and the exile had been out of proportion to the guilt involved. In the very beginning of his book, he had stated that Jerusalem had already received of the LORD's hand double for all her sins. (40:2b.) This undoubtedly was the generally accepted idea of the captives. Few people suffer great tragedies without feeling that they are not entirely deserved. But why should they so suffer, if the LORD is good? Once again, we have the problem of evil.

The fourth Servant Poem presents its answer to this question: "Why do the Righteous Suffer?" in a short drama which pictures representatives of the various nations inquiring the reason for the suffering of the humble but righteous servant of the Lord—Israel:

> Who has believed what we have heard?
>   And to whom has the arm of the Lord been revealed?
> For he grew up before him like a young plant,
>   and like a root out of dry ground;
> he had no form or comeliness that we should look at him,
>   and no beauty that we should desire him.
> He was despised and rejected by men;
>   a man of sorrows, and acquainted with grief;
> and as one from whom men hide their faces
>   he was despised, and we esteemed him not.
>
> —Isaiah 53:1-3

Then, after the question had been asked, the answer came from the very ones who had asked it. It was for their sakes that Israel had suffered, so that their transgressions could be paid for:

> Surely he has borne our griefs and carried our sorrows,
>   yet we esteemed him stricken, smitten by God, and afflicted,
> But he was wounded for our transgressions,
>   he was bruised for our iniquities;
> upon him was the chastisement that made us whole,
>   and with his stripes we are healed.
> All we like sheep have gone astray;
>   we have turned every one to his own way;
> and the Lord has laid on him the iniquity of us all.
>
> —Isaiah 53:4-6

This was of course a message of comfort. The suffering was over, and more than repaid the sin committed by Israel. The balance of the account was for the redemption of other nations. Israel would receive a reward—"a portion with the great." (53:12a.) It may well be that this ideal of suffering for the sake of others—vicarious suffering—was inspired by a knowledge of the life of Jeremiah, who through all his existence had suffered for the sake of other people. There is even some similarity in language between this poem and Jeremiah's writings:

> But I was like a gentle lamb
> led to the slaughter.

> . . . .
>   "let us cut him off from the land of the living."
>   —Jeremiah 11:19

and:

> "like a lamb that is led to the slaughter
> . . . .
> that he was cut off out of the land of the living."
>   —Isaiah 53:7f

But, whether or not the original idea or prototype of the servant who suffered for others came from the life of Jeremiah, the ideal presented was too noble to be adopted for the future by the people of Israel, just as it is too noble for any nation today. Israel was concerned almost solely with the welfare of Israel. Five and a half centuries later, though, there was a young Jew who planned his lifework, and was satisfied only with the noblest ideal his people could furnish. He knew the scriptures of Israel, and he loved the Book of Isaiah. When he was invited to read in the synagogue, that was the scroll he chose. (Luke 4:16f.) Ever since his time, it has been recognized that the 53rd chapter of Isaiah was a prophecy of Jesus of Nazareth. Certainly it was. It was the ideal after which he patterned his life. He made it come true.

In addition to this lofty ideal of suffering for others—of infinite importance, because of the use Jesus later made of it —and the majestic picture of the LORD, especially as contrasted to the silly idea of the idols worshiped by those about them, there are two more great contributions of the Second Isaiah to religious thought. One of them is the idea of the message of the LORD going to people other than Israel. There are only three writings in the Old Testament which are liberal enough to think of any particular good in any nation other than Israel. These three are Ruth, Jonah, and Second Isaiah. Israel was of course the chosen people (Isaiah 43:20f), and would be restored by the LORD:

> How beautiful upon the mountains
> are the feet of him who brings good tidings,

who publishes peace, who brings good tidings of good,
    who publishes salvation,
    who says to Zion "Your God reigns"

. . . .

for the LORD has comforted his people,
    he has redeemed Jerusalem.

—Isaiah 52:7-9

Babylon was the country which had oppressed Israel, so the LORD would punish her bitterly (Isaiah, chapter 47), but the task of Israel was to be a beacon light to the nations, that they might find salvation in the LORD.

he says:

"It is too light a thing that you should be my servant
    to raise up the tribes of Jacob
    and to restore the preserved of Israel;
I will give you as a light to the nations,
    that my salvation may reach to the end of the earth."

—Isaiah 49:6

The other great contribution of Second Isaiah to religious thought is the statement of monotheism. Probably Amos had thought of the LORD as the only God, since he spoke of him as controlling the destinies of other nations, but he did not unequivocally say so. The first flat definite statement of this idea we have comes from Second Isaiah:[5]

Thus says the LORD, the King of Israel
    and his Redeemer, the LORD of hosts:
"I am the first and I am the last;
    besides me there is no god."

—Isaiah 44:6

Not once, but several times is this statement made. (43:10; 45:12-14; 46:9.)

Thus we have this wonderful work of art, made malleable in the forge of captivity, and shaped on the anvil of experience by the hammer of a man's invincible faith in his God. A poet of the highest order, he presents a magnificent picture of the

---

5. There are passages in Deuteronomy (4:35; 6:4) which may be earlier than Second Isaiah, or may be later, and influenced by the prophet. It is difficult to determine when we do have a clearcut statement of monotheism. Sometimes the passage means merely that *for Israel* there is only one God.

majesty and power of the one and only God, and portrays him as being universal to the extent that all men—of whatever nation—can find salvation in him. And he offers as a solution to the problem of evil the explanation that Israel suffered in expiation of the sins of other nations so that they also might know the one true God, the Holy One of Israel. It is no wonder that the Great Unknown of the Exile was the favorite prophet of Jesus of Nazareth.

OTHER LITERATURE

There is a collection of five short poems about the fall of Jerusalem, four of which may very well have been written during the period of the Exile. An ancient tradition assigns these five poems—the Book of Lamentations—to Jeremiah. There are many reasons for not accepting this tradition, although at least two of the poems were probably written while Jeremiah was still alive. The first four chapters of Lamentations (each chapter being one poem) are written in the acrostic form. Each stanza in each poem begins with a different Hebrew letter, and, as there are twenty-two letters, there are twenty-two stanzas. With two exceptions, these initial letters in the poems are kept in the common order of the Hebrew alphabet, i.e., the first stanza begins with the letter *aleph*, the second with *beth*, and so forth. This form is not uncommon in Hebrew poetry, and it interferes with the spontaneity of the writer less than would be expected. In the third chapter the acrostic arrangement is even more intricate, each stanza consisting of three lines, all of which have the same initial letter. In this it resembles the most elaborate acrostic in the Psalms, number 119, which has 22 stanzas of 8 lines each, all lines of stanza one beginning with the first letter of the alphabet, *aleph*; all lines of the second stanza beginning with *beth*, and so forth. This structural resemblance to a late psalm bolsters the general opinion that the third chapter of Lamentations was written much later than the other four.

Chapters one, two, four, and five of Lamentations were probably written during the exile, and two and four are very likely by the hand of a man who saw the fall of the city.[6] These two poems are among the most poignant in all the Bible:

> Arise, cry out in the night,
>   at the beginning of the watches!
> Pour out your heart like water
>   before the presence of the Lord!
> Lift your hands to him
>   for the lives of your children
> who faint for hunger
>   at the head of every street.
> Look, O LORD, and see!
>   With whom hast thou dealt thus?
> Should women eat their offspring,
>   the children of their tender care?
> Or should priest and prophet
>   be slain in the sanctuary of the Lord?
>   —Lamentations 2:19-20

and

> Happier were the victims of the sword
>   than the victims of hunger,
> who pined away, stricken
>   by want of the fruits of the field.
> The hands of compassionate women
>   have boiled their own children;
> they became their food
>   in the destruction of the daughter of my people.
>   —Lamentations 4:9-10

Even in translation it is possible to get something of the rhythm of the Qinah meter, the slight break a little past the middle of the line, so that the two parts are not evenly balanced. This meter, which adds so much to the pathos, was customarily used by the Hebrews for elegies and other similar verses.

It is usually impossible to assign one of the psalms to a definite historical incident, but there can be no doubt but that Psalm 137 came from the Israelites in Babylon at the time of

---

6. Bewer (*op. cit.*, p. 189) holds that the author of these two poems was one of the band who, with the king, Zedekiah, sought to escape at night when the defense of Jerusalem no longer seemed possible. Lamentations 4:18-20, seems to support this view.

the exile.   The deep despair when their captors made sport of
them was followed by a heart-warming statement of the place
of the lost Jerusalem in their memories:

> By the waters of Babylon,
>   there sat we down and wept,
>   when we remembered Zion.
> On the willows there
>   we hung up our lyres.
> For there our captors
>   required of us songs,
> and our tormentors, mirth, saying,
>   "Sing us one of the songs of Zion!"
>
> How shall we sing the LORD's song in a foreign land?
> If I forget you, O Jerusalem,
>   let my right hand wither!
> Let my tongue cleave to the roof of my mouth,
>   if I do not remember you,
> if I do not set Jerusalem
>   above my highest joy!"
>
>   —Psalm 137:1-6

The desire for vengeance is quite understandable, but it is un-
fortunate that the beauty of the first part of this psalm drops
to it in the final verses—

> Happy shall he be who takes your little ones
>   and dashes them against the rock!
>   —Psalm 137:9

There is a distinctive little code of laws in Leviticus, chapters 17—26, which seems to fit into the earlier part of the period
of the Exile.   It includes laws of many types: ritualistic, ethical, sexual, agricultural, etc., but the principal idea seems to
be that the laws should be obeyed in order that the people of
Israel would be different or separate from the people about
them.   That is one of the basic meanings of the word which is
translated "holy":

> "you shall be holy to me; for I the LORD am holy,
> and have separated you from the peoples, that you
> should be mine."   (Leviticus 20:26.)

Because of this emphasis, the group is called the "Holiness Code," frequently given by the initials HC. Like so many of the laws of Israel, the code was ascribed to Moses, although it is quite evident that the collection comes from the time of the Exile. Nevertheless there may be included within it some regulations which came from antiquity. The similarity of these laws and the purpose behind them to the laws and purpose of Ezekiel is so great that there is no question but what one influenced the other. However, scholars are divided as to whether the Holiness Code was earlier than the legal part of Ezekiel and therefore influenced it, or whether it was later and influenced by it. It was a part of the growing legalism which formed so important a tendency in the late Judaism.

In addition to the above writings of the period, there was, about the middle of the Exile, the final editorial work of the Deuteronomic School, which put the books Deuteronomy, Judges, 1 and 2 Samuel and 1 and 2 Kings into the shape they now possess. The Book of Deuteronomy may have received its final editorial work at the hands of this group, or it may have been completed a half-century earlier.

PART FIVE

THE
PERSIAN PERIOD

CHAPTER XVII

THE TEMPLE

THE POLITICAL SITUATION

Some of the brilliant political predictions of the Second Isaiah came true, and some did not. Cyrus the Great did capture Babylon and did overthrow the domination previously enjoyed by the Chaldean kings. He did permit conquered peoples to return to their own countries, as described in the book of Ezra (Ezra 1:1-3, a repetition of 2 Chronicles 36:22f) and confirmed by Cyrus' own records, although in them he ascribed his victory to Marduk, a god of Babylon, who was described as being offended at the last Babylonian king.[1] But the return of the Israelites to Jerusalem lacked all the glamor Second Isaiah had anticipated. Only a small portion of the Jews returned, for it was a long, dangerous, expensive journey, and there was little assurance of a restoration at the end of it. Indeed, for many years—even centuries—those of the chosen people who had adopted Babylon as their homeland and had remained there continued to think of themselves as the center of Judaism. Even in New Testament times and later, Mesopotamia was an important source of Jewish thought.

In 538 B.C., as soon as it was permitted, a small band of hardy pioneers, probably under the leadership of one of the sons of Jehoiachin,[2] made the long hard journey, ostensibly with the main purpose of rebuilding the temple of the LORD. Many difficulties hindered the accomplishment of this task. Homes had to be reconstructed and crops had to be planted in a country which was none too fertile. Likewise, it is very unlikely that the people who were occupying the land were willing to turn it over to former owners without considerable argument.

---

1. See Finegan, *Light from the Ancient Past* (Princeton, Princeton University Press, 1946), p. 191.
2. See Albright, *The Jews, Their History, Culture and Religion*, Harper, p. 49f.

Even though the newcomers had full legal rights, and were accompanied by an official of the Persian government, the empire had been but recently acquired, and there certainly were few means of establishing justice at that time in a city so far from the seat of power. The rights of the returning Jews had to be protected by force or by bargaining. As a result of these difficulties, after eighteen years little or nothing had been done toward the rebuilding of the temple. Cyrus the Persian, after the conquest of Babylon, ruled very successfully until he was killed in 529 B.C., fighting in the eastern part of his empire. He was succeeded by his son Cambyses, whom he had chosen to inherit his throne. According to the record carved on the great rock at Behistun by Darius the Great, Cambyses did not ascend to the throne until after he had killed his own brother Bardes (or Smerdis, to give him another of his names). However, there are other records which do not tally with this.[3]

In 525 B.C. Cambyses conquered Egypt, and three years later, while on his way back to Mesopotamia, was informed that an usurper who claimed to be his brother Bardes had seized his Persian throne. At this point Cambyses died—probably by his own hand. The usurper achieved a great deal of popularity by temporarily remitting tribute. However, within eight months he was killed by a coalition of nobles led by Darius, a young man of the royal blood who, though not of the same line of the family as the rulers, had been nevertheless a protégé of both Cyrus and Cambyses. Darius then seized the throne, and he had a difficult task. Many widely scattered parts of the empire revolted against the new ruler, but his military and administrative genius succeeded in restoring order within a few years.

HAGGAI, HAGGAI, chapters 1—2

There were four Jewish men associated with the rebuilding of the temple: Zerubbabel, the grandson of the former king of Jerusalem, Jehoiachin; Joshua the high priest; and two prophets, Haggai and Zechariah. Political analysts of the time saw

---

3. For a more detailed account, see A. T. Olmstead, *History of the Persian Empire* (Chicago: University of Chicago Press, 1948), pp. 107ff; or see *Cambridge Ancient History* (New York: Macmillan Co., 1926), IV, pp. 19, 173ff.

many events which must have seemed to them to herald the approaching dissolution of the Persian empire. There had been four different kings upon the throne in the preceding decade, two, at least, of them having met violent deaths. The two years of the reign of Darius had been marked by rebellions in all parts of the empire. It looked like a most auspicious time for the Jews to seek to regain their independence. How unfortunate for the chosen people that they could not know history would call the currently reigning Persian monarch "Darius the Great."

One essential for a group about to attempt so dangerous a course as rebellion is a national institution about which the people can rally, and nothing else could have served the Jews so well in such an emergency as the temple of the LORD. Haggai seems to have seen this, and to have done everything possible to promote its restoration. For eighteen years the body of exiles had been back in and near Jerusalem, but the temple was yet in ruins. They had had poor crops. How could they expect anything else, if they dwelt in comfortable (?) houses, while the LORD had no home? The ruins contaminated the whole country. Let them reconstruct the temple,[4] and he would shower them with good crops and other blessings. The last three verses of the book hinted that, among the blessings, might be included the "overthrow of the throne of kingdoms (Persia?)," and named Zerubbabel as the "signet ring" chosen by the LORD, i.e., the "servant" who would achieve their independence.

ZECHARIAH, ZECHARIAH, chapters 1—6

All the work of Haggai was done within a single year, the second of the reign of Darius (520 B.C.). Just before his last pronouncement, Zechariah began to speak the word the LORD had revealed to *him,* continuing in his ministry two years, to 518 B.C. Only the first eight chapters of the book are to be attributed to him, and those chapters consist largely of visions, some of which are not easily understood. As in the case of Haggai, the purpose was to urge the rebuilding of the temple—

---

4. The author of Ezra 4 held that an earlier attempt had been made to rebuild the temple, but a complaint to the Persian ruler from adversaries of the Jews had forced abandonment of the project.

a task not accomplished until 516 B.C., two years after Zechariah's last message.

One of the visions (chapter 4) pictures a golden lamp stand with seven lamps and a bowl upon it, and two olive trees, one on either side of the bowl. The branches of these trees were said to represent the two anointed ones who stood beside the LORD of the earth, i.e., Joshua the priest and Zerubbabel the governor. The two offices for which the ancient Hebrews anointed candidates were the priesthood and the kingship, and especially the latter. We have many stories of how a prophet or priest anointed a selected man by pouring oil on his head, signifying his appointment by the LORD to be king—Samuel anointing Saul (1 Samuel 10:1) and David (1 Samuel 16:13), and Zadok anointing Solomon. (1 Kings 1:39.) Joshua the priest could have been anointed without any complaint from the Persian rulers. What cared they if the Jews dedicated one of their number to the priesthood? But anointing Zerubbabel was another matter entirely. He had been made governor because he was a prince of the royal blood, and thus could have been better able to keep order among his people. He was of the line of David, a descendant of the kings of Jerusalem, a member of the tribe of Judah. If he were to be anointed, it would be that he might serve, not as a priest, but as a king, and Darius most certainly would not have stood for that. After all the wonderful things said by Zechariah about Zerubbabel, there was an ominous silence. We hear nothing more about him, and it is probable that his friends, who sought to honor him by making him a king so that he could free Jerusalem, succeeded only in accomplishing his death on the charge of treason to the Persian monarch.

THE MESSIANIC HOPE

The words of the prophet were preserved. Whatever happened to Zerubbabel, the literature of Israel from that time forward contained the picture of a hoped-for ruler of the house

5. Another name applied to Zerubbabel is the "Branch." (Zechariah 3:8 and 6:12.) This is most likely a play on words, for the name Zerubbabel means "that which was sown in Babylon." In other words, Zerubbabel, born in Babylon of the line of David, was the "Branch" in whom the royal line of David would be restored. (The word appears in a similar connection in Jeremiah 23:5 and 33:15.)

of David, anointed by the Lord.[5]   The Second Isaiah had spoken of Cyrus as the anointed one, but Cyrus was a Persian. From the time of Zechariah on, the anointed one was thought of, not as a foreign king, but as a king of Israel, of the line of David.   No king who was not of that line had sat on the throne at Jerusalem.   This expected king was to be the anointed of the LORD, and the more the political position of the Jews deteriorated, the larger was the amount of help they expected from the LORD to bring it to pass.   Eventually they thought the anointed one would be a heavenly king, sent to Israel by God.

The word for "anointed one" in Aramaic, the language spoken by the Jews in the late years before the Christian era, is "Messiah."   This continuing hope for a God-given king to rule in Jerusalem is therefore termed the "Messianic Hope."   It became the greatest solace of the people in the years of their greatest political distress. When the New Testament was finally written in the Greek language, the Greek word for the "Messiah" was used—the "Christ."   When they wrote of Jesus as the Christ (at first the article "the" was used in this connection), they meant Jesus the Messiah, or Jesus the Anointed One—that is, Jesus the King.

CHAPTER XVIII

THE WALLS AND THE LAW

Biblical Sources

The best biblical source we have for the history of the chosen people in the Persian period, after the building of the temple, is the memoirs of Nehemiah, found chiefly in the first seven and the thirteenth chapters of the book of that name. The account is accurate and vivid, and is accepted by scholars as the work of Nehemiah, with the possible exception of the list of names which is found in the seventh chapter, and also in Ezra, chapter 2. The memoirs of Ezra (the last two verses of Ezra, chapter 7, plus the next two chapters) are not so straightforward. Some scholars do not accept them as the work of Ezra.

Nearly two centuries after Nehemiah, a very interesting author (or group of authors) wrote a history of Israel from the time of Adam through the time of Ezra. He used many different sources for this work, including the two memoirs just mentioned.[1] It was originally one connected book, but we know it today as the four books, 1 and 2 Chronicles, Ezra, and Nehemiah. The author of this history is commonly called the "Chronicler." Because he was so far removed from the events he described, and because there were so few sources available to him for the period after the rebuilding of the temple, this part of the Chronicler's history is quite confusing. The following reconstruction is one of those generally accepted.

Nehemiah, Nehemiah, chapters 1-2, 4-6, 13

In the twentieth year of the Persian king Artaxerxes I (that would be 444 b.c.), the king's cupbearer, an Israelite eunuch[2] named Nehemiah, was greatly worried about the vulnerability of the Jewish city Jerusalem. The walls of the city were in

---

1. See below, p. 231.
2. Albright, *The Jews, Their History, Culture and Religion*, p. 51.

ruins, and her enemies were crowding in about her. Because of his great anxiety, Nehemiah appeared before the king with a sad countenance—a most dangerous proceeding. However, instead of showing wrath, the king inquired the reason for the melancholy attitude, and graciously appointed the cup-bearer to be a temporary governor of Jerusalem, with orders to rebuild the walls. He promptly started on his journey to accomplish this.

When Nehemiah arrived in Jerusalem, after having reported to the governors of the "Province beyond the River," he re-mained quiet a few days until after he had made an almost solitary night inspection of the ruined walls. In spite of strong opposition from Sanballat, the governor of Samaria, and some other leaders nearby, Nehemiah succeeded in restoring the walls within an unbelievably short time. The entire task was subdivided and assigned to various families, and, in spite of the fact that some were forced to stand under arms for the protection of the workmen, the project was soon satisfactorily completed.

During this period Nehemiah also put considerable pressure on some of the wealthy Jews who had been levying heavy interest charges upon their brethren, and foreclosing mortgages against the poor. He claimed that he and his co-workers had not even touched the allowances they were allowed to collect as the ruling group. Strict orders were given to keep the gates securely closed until well on in the morning, and ap-parently the country was run in a most efficient manner.

Upon completion of his term of office Nehemiah returned to Persia. Twelve years after his first appointment he was again dispatched to Jerusalem to serve as governor. (Nehemiah 5:14; 13:6f.) The account seems to indicate only a short interval of time between these two terms, but the conditions found upon his arrival again at Jerusalem suggest that he had been away for some time, as his formerly strict rule had been seriously relaxed. A noble of the Ammonite people had been granted quarters in the temple itself, where none but Jews were allowed to appear; the fees due the Levites had been with-held, and as a result these workers and others had forsaken their tasks and returned to their own fields; Sabbath laws had been disregarded; Jews had married foreign women, and their children not only were uninstructed in the religion of their fathers—in many cases they could not even speak their native tongue. But the crowning irritation was when he found the son of the high priest married to the daughter of his arch-enemy, Sanballat, who had led the opposition to most of Nehemiah's reforms. He immediately drove the young couple out—if the Jewish historian Josephus can be believed, San-ballat made the man high priest of Samaria—and promptly corrected all the other evils. Our record of Nehemiah's diary ends here so abruptly that it is quite evident the later editor did not give its original conclusion.

EZRA, EZRA 4:1—10:17

The historical accounts found in the Book of Ezra simply cannot be reconciled with other biblical records. Although the whole structure of the book seems to demand that Ezra be dated as arriving in Jerusalem some time after Nehemiah, it is stated that he came in the seventh year of Artaxerxes, whereas Nehemiah was placed in the twentieth year of Arta-xerxes. One way of solving this discrepancy is to assume that Nehemiah came in the twentieth year of Artaxerxes I (i.e., 444 B.C.), while Ezra arrived in the seventh year of Artaxerxes II (398-397). The Chronicler or historian who picked up his information from the diaries of Nehemiah and Ezra and other sources was not only unable to distinguish between Artaxerxes I and II—he was confused about the order of the entire line of Persian kings. In Ezra 4:23f he points out that because of a letter of Artaxerxes the work on the house of the LORD ceased until the second year of King Darius. It is true that the second year of Darius was the date of the work on the temple (Haggai 1:1 and Zechariah 1:1), but the first Artaxerxes did not come to the throne until half a century after this date. And in the latter part of the fourth chapter of Ezra the Chronicler confused the rebuilding of the temple (520-516 B.C.) with the rebuilding of the wall (accomplished by Nehe-miah in 444 B.C.). It is quite evident that the pious man (or men) responsible for the present form of this narrative material lived so long after the compiling of the sources that he was unable to fit the various incidents into their proper backgrounds, or, indeed, even into their chronological order.

The best reconstruction we can give is that, nearly half a century after Nehemiah had rebuilt the walls and made Jerusalem safe, and had given some impromptu rules against intermarriage with Gentiles, Ezra, a trained scribe who had probably been educated as a priest, arrived in Jerusalem armed with two weapons: a commission from the reigning Persian monarch Artaxerxes II, and either a body of legal writings from the Priestly document, or, possibly, the entire first five books of our Old Testament.

Ezra was dismayed by the number of marriages between Jewish men and gentile women, and by the general ignorance all the inhabitants had of the law (largely ritual)—which was probably then for the first time expounded in Jerusalem. He called all the inhabitants together under penalty of forfeiture of their property, forced renunciation and divorce of their foreign wives, and read to them the law. (Ezra 10:1-17; Nehemiah, chapter 8.) The impression is given that all these mixed marriages were promptly dissolved. The law became from that time forward a more and more important part of the religion of the Jews, thus carrying on and intensifying the influence of Deuteronomy, the Holiness Code, and Ezekiel. The "Great Assembly" of Ezra, at which he read the law to the people, was in some ways the prototype of the later synagogue, whose main function was the reading and explaining of the law. Although later and greater leaders took a more liberal attitude toward religion, and tended to regard legalism as interfering with its higher development, it is quite possible that without the steady conservative influence of men like Ezekiel, Nehemiah, and Ezra, the religion of the God of Israel might have perished from the earth.

CHAPTER XIX

THE LITERATURE OF

THE PERSIAN PERIOD

Although a great deal of the literature of the Jews was written in the Persian period (538-332 B.C.), the historical references are not so clear as in the literature of some other periods, so it is difficult to be exact in the dating. But, for the most part, it is not too important what the specific time was. This is fortunate, for there is a great difference of opinion in the matter. Many scholars disagree regarding some books as to whether they were written in this period, or in the Greek period after 332 B.C., or even before the Exile in 586 B.C.

The three great poetical works of the Old Testament, Job, Psalms and Proverbs, were written over a considerable length of time. Quite possibly the early part of Job, and certainly many of the Psalms and Proverbs were written in the Persian period. However, none of the three books was completed before the Greek period, so they will be considered under that heading.

THE HISTORICAL WRITINGS

The most important historical work was the completion of the first historical series described above. The combined Judah-Ephraimitish history had been partly revised by the Deuteronomistic editor, with the addition of the Book of Deuteronomy, shortly before the first captivity of Jerusalem in 597 B.C. Then a half-century later, about the middle of the Exile, another group of Deuteronomistic editors in Babylon made a further revision, leaving the books Deuteronomy, Judges, 1 and 2 Samuel and 1 and 2 Kings in the shape they now possess.

Although the Book of Deuteronomy is largely a collection of laws, there was a strong prophetic influence upon the revisers. All history was interpreted by them as a manifestation of the judgment of the LORD: if Israel lost in war, it was because of sin; if Israel won, it was because of righteousness. There was also a prophetic sense of justice, involving particularly the rights of the poor. These things show up in the books revised by these editors.

But there was another type of thinking done by some of the Israelites in Babylon at the same time. The authors of the Holiness Code and Ezekiel had stressed observance of ritual law as the high point of obedience to the LORD. Emphasized by the priests and scribes during the next 600 years, this became one of the most important elements of Judaism. A century and a quarter after Ezekiel, a group of Jewish priests in Babylon wrote another strand of the great historical work. Their history, like the Judah history, began with the story of creation. (Genesis, chapter 1.) This story, which was completely separate from the one in the Judah history (Genesis 2:4-4), was based upon an already ancient Babylonian legend about a struggle among the gods.[1] This Priestly story, although it did take some ideas from the crude Babylonian record, is one of the most magnificent things ever written. All the rest of the Priestly writings are dull and repetitive in style, but here the majesty of the theme—the creation of the world by the command of God—is so great it inspires the account. Usually, however, this writer is prosaic and legalistic, and much concerned with genealogical tables.

A half-century after this history was written (i.e., about 400 B.C.), a group of priests, influenced by the same motives, wove this new material into the earlier strands (JED). They then revised all that had not been revised by the Deuteronomistic editor, thus completing those books in the series which had not already been completed by D—Genesis, Exodus, Leviticus, Numbers, Joshua. All the books in our Old Testament from Genesis through 2 Kings, with the exception of Ruth, were then finished.

It was either the Priestly document with its abundance of ritualistic laws, or the first five books of the Old Testament

---

1. This legend, which we have today as a series of clay tablets, is called the *"Enuma elish"* from the first two words on the first tablet. It is quoted in a number of books—e.g., Finegan, *Light from the Ancient Past*, pp. 50-53; George A. Barton, *Archaeology and the Bible* (Philadelphia: Amer. S. S. Union, 1937), pp. 279-294.

which contain the Priestly document that Ezra brought from Babylon to Jerusalem with him and read to the returned exiles there.

The accurate memoirs of Nehemiah and the considerably less accurate memoirs of Ezra were written in the Persian period, but the books of Ezra and Nehemiah which resulted from those memoirs were not written until the Greek period. However, there was a sharp literary reaction against the work of Ezra which resulted in one—possibly two—of the smaller books of the Old Testament.

Although the Book of Ezra gives the impression that all the marriages of Jewish men with gentile women which were in effect at the time Ezra arrived in Jerusalem from Babylon were promptly dissolved by divorce, there were undoubtedly many who opposed such action. One of the most effective bits of propaganda ever written is the beautiful short story which came out of this opposition. It may be that the Book of Ruth was based upon an ancient incident in Hebrew history, but most scholars hold that the story as we now have it was written in or after the time of Ezra to combat his teachings about marriage.[2] It also gives us many interesting glimpses of the social customs of the time when it was written—all the more attractive because they portray a period of peace.

The basic custom about which the Book of Ruth rotates is the levirate law. This provided that if a man died leaving a wife but no son, his nearest of kin bore the responsibility of marrying his widow. The first son born of that marriage took the name of the former husband, and presumably his property rights. Thus the widow was cared for, and the line of succession was assured.

In the story of Ruth a family of four—father, mother, and two sons—were forced by famine to leave their home in Bethlehem in Judah to go to the country of Moab.[3] There the two sons married, but soon after they and their father died. In the course of time Naomi, the mother, feeling her welcome grow-

---

2. See, e.g., Harry M. Orlinski, *Ancient Israel* (Ithaca, N. Y.: Cornell University Press, 1954), pp. 136ff; contra, Pfeiffer, *op. cit.*, pp. 718f.

3. There is a Hebrew pun involved here. The word "Bethlehem" means "House of Bread" or "House of Food." The family left because, even in the house of food, there was no food. It is not the only pun in Ruth.

ing thin, decided to return to her own home. One daughter-in-law remained in Moab, but the other, Ruth, determined on going to Bethlehem with Naomi. The older woman pointed out that she did not have another son to give Ruth for a husband, but Ruth insisted on accompanying her in the following lyrically beautiful words:

> "Entreat me not to leave you or to return from following you; for where you go I will go, and where you lodge I will lodge; your people shall be my people, and your God my God; where you die I will die, and there will I be buried. May the LORD do so to me and more also if even death parts me from you." (Ruth 1:16-17.)

The custom of gleaning was a predecessor of our community chest. After the owner of a field had cut his crop the first time over, the grain that had been missed belonged to any poor person who wanted to reap it. Ruth went out to glean, to provide food for her mother-in-law and herself, and selected the field of Boaz. Intrigued by the fair gleaner, Boaz ordered his servants to leave plenty of grain for her. When she returned home, Naomi told Ruth that Boaz was a kinsman of her late husband and therefore bore a responsibility under the levirate law.

Another custom was for the people to leave their homes in the small walled cities, where they normally stayed for mutual protection, and to spend the nights sleeping on the threshing floor in the harvest season, where they could guard their grain. Naomi told Ruth to spend the night there, and to pull a corner of the blanket of Boaz over her, to show all that she claimed to be of the same family. As there was one other kinsman more closely related, and there was probably property of the former husband involved, it was necessary to secure a release. Boaz therefore summoned the other kinsman to the presence of the elders in the gate of the city—the only place where there was room for an assembly—and in words of those days told him "to speak now or forever hold his peace." When for any one of a half-dozen reasons he refused to marry Ruth and thus to fulfill requirements of the law, a sandal was passed from him to Boaz, a custom indicating the sealing of the contract—possibly because, property rights being involved, the sandal conveyed the right to walk upon the land.

Boaz married Ruth, and to them was born a son, Obed, who eventually became the father of Jesse, and then the grandfather of David, the king of Israel. Surely no one would hesitate about a marriage with a non-Jewish woman when this beautiful story portrayed a Moabite girl who, by her fidelity and industry, proved herself worthy of marrying a landowner of Judah and becoming the great-grandmother of Israel's greatest king.

Another book of this time, which is sometimes considered history but is really a short historical novel, is Esther. It presents as its heroine a beautiful Jewish girl who married the Persian monarch and, with the aid of her uncle Mordecai, saved the Jews from near-extermination by Haman, the evil premier. Because he hated him, Haman prepared a high gallows for Mordecai, but, through the clever maneuvering of Esther, and the discovery of the record of how Mordecai had once saved the life of the king, Haman himself was hanged, and Mordecai was made second in rank to the king. According to the story, the Jews killed over 75,000 of their enemies, and observed the occasion as the Feast of Purim (Purim means "lots"), which is recognized to this day. This beautifully constructed story seems to come from the time of Ezra, and is the exact antithesis of the liberal and tolerant Book of Ruth. There are no great spiritual values in Esther—only the exaltation of nationalism and the supremacy of the Jews over their enemies.

THE PROPHETIC WRITINGS

The prophetic works from the early part of the Persian period are of course Haggai and the first eight chapters of Zechariah, all dated between 520 and 516 B.C., in the second decade of the period. Later on there were three additions to Zechariah: chapters 9-11; 12-14; and the Book of Malachi. These three sections start in a similar manner, with the expression: "An Oracle—the word of the LORD, etc." In the third of these additions, the expression "My messenger" (Hebrew "Malachi"), which is the first unusual word in the passage, was assigned as the name of the book, after it was again separated from Zechariah.[4] The Book of Malachi is unusual among postexilic books of prophecy because it is chiefly a condemnation of the people for various misdeeds—marital infidelity, offering defective sacrifices, withholding of tithes, and so forth. However, in the last two verses it refers to the coming terrible day of the LORD, and promises that Elijah will be sent to turn the hearts of the people before that day. Late Jewish thinkers believed that, having been taken up to heaven (2 Kings 2:1-12) in a fiery chariot, Elijah had never died, and was therefore available to return to earth. This concept, supported by the passage under discussion in Malachi, is still recognized today in the observance of the Passover Feast, where a cup of wine is set out for Elijah, and an inquiry is made as to whether or not he is at hand for that observance of the feast. This same reference was behind the question sent by John the Baptist as to whether Jesus was the Expected One or Messiah (Luke 7:19), and the entire idea that John, who in many ways was like Elijah, was the forerunner of Jesus. (Mark, chapter 1.)

The Book of Malachi is usually dated about the middle of the fifth century B.C., shortly before the time of Nehemiah. The other two additions to Zechariah (Zechariah, chapters 9-11 and 12-14) are most often dated two and a half centuries later, in the Greek period.

The Book of Obadiah is a portrayal of the hatred of the Jews against the people of Edom, who had turned against them at the time of the fall of Jerusalem, and had become like the strangers who had carried off the wealth of Jacob and "cast lots for Jerusalem." The latter part pictures the destruction, in turn, of Edom. The author used as a source the same writing as was used by the author of the middle part of Jeremiah, chapter 49. The Book of Obadiah cannot be later than Joel, for Joel 2:32 is a quotation from Obadiah 17.

The latter part of the Book of Obadiah, portraying the day of the LORD as marking the vengeance of the Jews upon their

4. Bewer apparently holds to this view, that Malachi was at one time added to Zechariah, chapter 14. See Bewer, *op. cit.*, p. 407. Dentan, *The Interpreter's Bible*, VI, 1089, believes otherwise.

enemies, shows a tendency toward the apocalyptic style of the later writers. This tendency is much more pronounced in the Book of Joel. The most impressive thing in this writing is the picture of a locust plague and the devastation it created upon the countryside. Probably inspired by the armorlike plates on the locusts, and the seriate ranks in which they moved, the author imagined them as the mounted army of the LORD, wreaking vengeance upon the foes of Israel. In a figure of speech exactly the opposite of one appearing twice elsewhere (Isaiah 2:4; Micah 4:3) he called for militarization:

> Beat your plowshares into swords,
>   and your pruning hooks into spears.
> —Joel 3:10

One of his greatest passages, quoted in the description of the day of Pentecost in Acts 2:17, pictures the effect of the spirit:

> "And it shall come to pass afterward,
>   that I will pour out my spirit on all flesh;
> Your sons and your daughters shall prophesy,
>   your old men shall dream dreams,
>   and your young men shall see visions.
> Even upon the menservants and maidservants
>   in those days, I will pour out my spirit."
> —Joel 2:28-29

This salvation was only for Israel. The entire picture was a vivid portrayal of the LORD taking care of his own chosen people—and of no one else.

But there was one small book, always listed among the prophetic writings, which *was* concerned with the welfare of other people. It is one of the tragedies of literary interpretation that the little gem of a book, Jonah, which contrasts so sharply the generous attitude of God with the narrowness of some of the Jews of the author's time, should be known through the centuries primarily as the story of a great fish. (There is no mention of a whale in the book.) Jonah, representing the Jewish people, was ordered to go to Nineveh, which for centuries had been the hated oppressor of Israel and practically everything else in western Asia, and to preach of its destruction for its

sins. Jonah deliberately took a ship in another direction—
possibly toward Spain. Unwilling to be so thwarted, the LORD
sent a storm, and after the sailors had found by casting lots that
Jonah was the cause of their misfortunes, they threw him over-
board. After the fish had escorted him to the shore, the LORD
repeated Jonah's orders. This time they were carried out.

Jonah preached so effectively that the entire city of Nineveh
repented in sackcloth and ashes. The LORD pardoned Nineveh,
but Jonah, since his predictions of disaster were not carried out,
sulked in a hut near the city. The LORD sent a plant to grow
over his hut to shade it, and then, after the prophet had de-
lighted in the comfort it produced, destroyed it by a worm.
When Jonah complained of this, the LORD showed him how
indefensible his position was, objecting to the saving of a city
great enough to include 120,000 young children, yet complain-
ing about the destruction of one vine which he had not even
planted.

The Third Isaiah (chapters 56—66) belongs also in this period. With the exception of the Servant poems and their bearing upon the problem of evil, almost everything said about the
Second Isaiah can be said to a lesser degree of this later book
also. Even the style is similar so that many think the writer
to have been a student of the Great Unknown of the Exile.
Indeed one great scholar insists that he was the same man.[5]

RELIGIOUS TENDENCIES

There were five tendencies in religion which began to develop or continued to develop in the Persian period. The most
advanced of these was the tendency toward legalism, which
had already become well established during the exile. The
work of Ezekiel and the Holiness Code had influenced the
priests, and they had written the Priestly Code, which had
influenced others. These priests had edited earlier writings,
leaving the legalistic stamp on the historical material. Thus
there were many to whom the highest responsibility was strict
obedience to the law, which by now was attributed chiefly to
Moses. This tendency continued through the Greek period,

5. C. C. Torrey, *The Second Isaiah* (New York: Charles Scribner's Sons, 1928), p.
53 and most of the rest of the book.

becoming eventually the chief driving force of the scribes and the Pharisees.

Opposed to this legalism was a sweet-tempered liberalism which very likely found its origin in the enlarging concept of God. It is difficult to think of a God over all the universe who is concerned with only one nation, and it was this separatist idea which was the basis for the legalism. No writer in the Old Testament had a more significant conception of God than did Second Isaiah, nor was any more concerned with the welfare of non-Jewish people than he. That same reasonableness continued over into the Persian period in the writings of the Book of Jonah, and the Book of Ruth. Also, although it is not opposed to legalism, Third Isaiah tends more to the liberal attitude.

The development of apocalyptic thought was accelerated during the Persian period in such books as Zechariah, chapters 1—8, Joel and Isaiah, chapters 24—27, though the impassioned longing for the day when the LORD would destroy everything except his chosen people did not fully seize Israel until after the middle of the Greek period, and then only in a time of bitter persecution. The other two tendencies, the plaintive appeal of the humble, unpretentious ones found in the Book of Psalms, and the tendency to exalt wisdom, found especially in Proverbs and Job, both began in the Persian period, but did not blossom into full flower until the time of Greek domination.

PART SIX

THE GREEK PERIOD

C H A P T E R   X X

T H E   M A C C A B E E S   A N D

T H E   B O O K   O F   D A N I E L

ALEXANDER THE GREAT AND HIS SUCCESSORS

Alexander not only made the world over, he painted it another color.   Other conquerors had made their conquests, ruled their empires, and then left them for later strong men to repeat the process.   But the world could never again be the same after Alexander.   In an unbelievably short time he conquered what of the world seemed to him worth conquering, and then, with the key of the Greek language, opened the doors of the barbarian lands to the culture of Greece.   The Hellenization of the Mediterranean was begun by the phalanxes of Alexander; it was completed when the legions of Rome brought the best of that culture in chains to the Tiber, to serve as slave-educators of their less-worthy rulers.

The Macedonian did not leave a competent successor.   After his death in 323 B.C. there was a struggle among his generals to see who would receive the legacy of his empire.   Eventually that part with which we are concerned was divided between two of them: Ptolemy (after whom his successors were named) who claimed Egypt, and Seleucus, ancestor of the Seleucids of Syria, most of whom were named either Seleucus or Antiochus. And as had always been the case, Palestine was the bone of contention between Egypt to the south and west, and Syria to the north and east.

Though there were struggles over Palestine by these two protagonists, Egypt ruled the country most of the time before 198 B.C., and Syria ruled it after that time.   During most of the Egyptian domination much of the control of Israel was in the hands of the Jews themselves, and on the whole they were not subjected to many hardships.   Indeed, when later the Syrian rulers were less lenient, the Jews, like their ancestors in the

219

wilderness under Moses, began to long to be once again under the rulership of Egypt.

The process of Hellenization of the Jews proceeded at a pace slower than that of the rest of the Mediterranean because of the rigid control of their daily lives by their religion. The work of Ezekiel, Ezra, and the Priestly writers was still bearing fruit. Yet there was a tendency among the young to follow the popular Greek customs. One activity abhorrent to the conservative older Jews was the holding of athletic games, where the contestants appeared clad only in sandals and a peculiar flat hat. Occasionally these hats were seen as symbols on young Jews even in Jerusalem.

One of the Greek rulers of Syria, Antiochus IV (Epiphanes) who came to the throne in 175 B.C., had the great ambition to create a strong Greek empire in the east which would rival Rome in the west. He tried to hasten the Hellenization of the Jews in Palestine, and succeeded only in making them resist. Since they had had complete freedom of religion while under Egyptian control, and now were opposing the Greek religion, he interpreted their objections as a loyalty to Egypt, and hence a disloyalty to himself. He stirred up considerable trouble by appointing an ineligible man to be high priest, an office which had always been filled by the Jews with a man of their own selection. When he tried to conquer Egypt and had defeated the Egyptian army, he was ordered back to Palestine by a Roman legate and found it necessary to obey him. He took his spite out on the people of Jerusalem when he returned. On one occasion he found the populace celebrating a somewhat premature announcement of his death, and turned his soldiers loose on them, killing thousands. Jews were deported from Jerusalem and heathen families brought in, in an attempt to break the Jewish resistance. Regular inspections were made, and possession of a copy of the Jewish law or the circumcision of infants was punished by death. On at least one later occasion, when an army was sent against the leader Judas, foreign merchants accompanied it to get first chance at the purchase of slaves. The outer walls of Jerusalem were destroyed so that the city could not be defended, but those of the old city of David, in the center of the more modern city, were refortified as a citadel for the Greek garrison. Although Judas was able to take the outer city rather early in the Maccabean period, the citadel remained in the hands of the Greek rulers until the time of Simon in 142 B.C.[1]

Finally Antiochus committed the unforgivable sin against Jewish religion. On the 25th of Kislev (a month corresponding roughly to December) he caused a sow to be sacrificed to Zeus on the altar of the LORD in the temple at Jerusalem. Nothing could have been more abhorrent to a religious Jew than this act, which was called the "abomination of desolation."

THE REVOLT

A short time after this incident, an elderly priest named Mattathias Hasmonaeus refused to make a sacrifice to Zeus, and killed both another Jew who did not refuse, and the official who was in charge. He fled to the hills with his five sons, and was soon joined by others with like sympathies. He died within the year, but was succeeded by his son Judas, who was so successful in guerrilla warfare against the Greek soldiers that he was nicknamed Maccabaeus (the Hammer). This term was used for the successors to Judas—first his brothers, then the the descendants of his brother Simon—until Roman times, though the descendants of Simon are frequently called Hasmonaeans.

Before the death of Mattathias there had been one sad lesson to learn. Some of his troops were attacked by the heathen enemy on the Sabbath day, and, in accordance with their religion, they refused to defend themselves—being slaughtered almost to a man. This resulted in a more realistic attitude, and henceforth it was recognized that military necessity took precedence. About this time these patriots, who were interested in freedom, were joined by another group called the "Pious" (Chasidim) whose concern was primarily the right to worship God in accordance with their law. It was a very successful combination.

By masterful disposition of his troops and by sheer bravery of his men, Judas was able to win some important battles

---

1. See Emil Schürer, *A History of the Jewish People in the Time of Jesus Christ* (New York: Charles Scribner's Sons), I, pp. 206-214.

against terrific odds. In a short time he secured control of a large part of Jerusalem (but not of the citadel). He then tore down the desecrated altar in the temple and rebuilt it, ceremonially cleansing the rest of the temple area, and reinstituted the morning and evening sacrifices on 25 Kislev, 165 B.C.—three years to the day from the abomination of desolation. That ceremony is celebrated to the present time under the names "Feast of Lights," "Feast of Dedication," or "Chanukah."

DANIEL, DANIEL, chapters 1; 2; 5—9; 11; 12

Shortly after the cleansing of the temple a book was written to keep alive the faith of those who were struggling against Antiochus Epiphanes. It claimed to have been written 400 years earlier during the Babylonian exile by a young man called Daniel who, with three other Jewish youths, was miraculously saved by the LORD in a series of adventures because of his fidelity. Though the traditions of these four men may have come from the time of Nebuchadnezzar, it is quite evident that the book, as we know it today, was written within the first six months after 25 Kislev, 165 B.C. Among other indications as to time, we find a knowledge of the temple cleansing on that date, but ignorance of the manner of death of Antiochus Epiphanes in 164. These hero stories cover the first six chapters of the book.

The second half of Daniel is straight apocalyptic writing in which the main character (Daniel, of course) was told by visions, interpreted by a heavenly being, that the end of the present age was at hand. In Jeremiah 29: 1-14 we find a letter ostensibly written to the exiles in Babylon, telling them that the captivity would last seventy years. In Daniel this was explained by the heavenly being as referring to seventy *weeks* of years—i.e., 490 years—and that period was supposed to cover all the history of Israel from the exile to the end of the domination of the Seleucid kings, and to have nearly elapsed. If only the Jews could hold on a little longer, and remain faithful to the LORD, he would bring the present age to an end and they, like Daniel and his friends, would have their reward. These things were supposed to have been told Daniel shortly after 586

B.C., as predictions of what would happen to Israel nearly 490 years later.

The writer of the book, who actually lived and wrote in 165 B.C., was quite confused about the earlier history, picturing Daniel as a contemporary of both Nebuchadnezzar in 586 B.C. and Darius after 522, making Belshazzar the son of Nebuchadnezzar, and changing the order of the empires. But his record of the later history, close to the time when he lived, is accurate and detailed. It is not uncommon to find a book written thus with the name of some great earlier hero ascribed to it. The purpose was not to mislead, but to present in vivid form what the writer felt was the truth of God—and the Book of Daniel accomplished wonderful things in preserving the faith of these people in troublous times. This book is not only an apocalypse, portraying in vivid pictures what the author thought would be the end of the age: it also is a pseudepigraph or book whose authorship was ascribed to a hero who lived centuries before it actually was written. There are many such among the ancient writings of the Jews.

CHAPTER XXI

OTHER LITERATURE

OF THE GREEK PERIOD

SECOND HISTORICAL SERIES

Except for the Book of Daniel which we have just discussed as belonging explicitly in 165 B.C., there are not too many of the writings of the Old Testament which need, in order to be understood, to be dated definitely in the Greek period. Indeed, some are difficult to date in any period. We considered Esther under the Persian period, largely because of the intimate knowledge its author had of the Persian court, but some very good scholars think it comes much later.[1] However, the editing of the Books Ezra, Nehemiah, and 1 and 2 Chronicles quite definitely belongs in the Greek period, though before Antiochus Epiphanes. The diary of Nehemiah, and probably also of Ezra, was early, but the work of the editor shows clearly that a long time had elapsed between the time of Nehemiah and the time when the diary had been rewritten into the form of a book:

> These were in the days of Joiakim the son of Jeshua, son of Jozadak, and in the days of Nehemiah the governor and of Ezra the priest the scribe. (Nehemiah 12:26—see also 12:47.)

THE SONG OF SOLOMON

The general interpretation of "The Song of Songs, which is Solomon's" is that it is a collection of poems picturing in rather frank language the delights of married love. It was probably sung at the wedding feast, and, in its desire to exalt the most important person there—the groom, not the bride—it refers to him as the most glamorous person in Hebrew history, King Solomon. It is because of this tribute to the bridegroom that the idea of Solomonic authorship has become affixed to the

---

1. See, e.g., Pfeiffer, *op. cit.*, p. 742.

poem. This tradition that Solomon was the writer helped the book to get into the Hebrew canon, but it would not have been adequate to secure its acceptance had it not been for the allegorical interpretation which also was affixed—that the entire book was merely a poetic portrayal of God's love for Israel. Later, the Christian Church accepted the allegory, merely changing it to refer to Christ's love for the Church. It is of interest to us to see a different side of Israelitish nature, but there is little of spiritual value to be derived from it.

THE PSALMS, PSALMS 8, 19, 23, 24, 51, 130, 139

There are almost none of the psalms which can be dated, yet the value of most of them is so great that the dating is quite unnecessary. They are an accumulation of the religious poetry of Israel, gathered together over centuries, and covering many of mankind's deepest emotions. There is no dependence of one upon another: each must be considered by itself—coming spontaneously out of the heart of the psalmist, and revealing his childlike confidence in God.

Sometimes the awe and reverence felt toward the LORD, the Creator, is the theme:

> When I look at thy heavens, the work of thy fingers,
>   the moon and the stars which thou hast established;
> what is man that thou art mindful of him,
>   and the son of man that thou dost care for him?
> —Psalm 8:3-4

Sometimes it is the pitiful cry of the oppressed, asking help from the only One who can bring it:

> I say to God, my rock;
>   "Why hast thou forgotten me?
> Why go I mourning
>   because of the oppression of the enemy?"
> As with a deadly wound in my body,
>   my adversaries taunt me,
> While they say to me continually,
>   "Where is your God?"
> —Psalm 42:9-10

Sometimes it is a plea for forgiveness, with an expression of deep contrition:

> Have mercy on me, O God,
>   according to thy steadfast love;
> according to thy abundant mercy
>   blot out my transgressions.
> Wash me thoroughly from my iniquity,
>   and cleanse me from my sin!
> For I know my transgressions,
>   and my sin is ever before me.
> Against thee, thee only, have I sinned,
>   and done that which is evil in thy sight.
>   —Psalm 51:1-4

And sometimes it is the calm, placid assurance that the LORD will take abundant care of him:

> The LORD is my shepherd, I shall not want;
>   he makes me lie down in green pastures.
> He leads me beside still waters;
>   he restores my soul.
> He leads me in paths of righteousness
>   for his name's sake.
> Even though I walk through the
>   valley of the shadow of death,
>   I fear no evil;
> for thou art with me;
>   thy rod and thy staff,
>   they comfort me.
>   —Psalm 23:1-4

The power of the Psalms comes from the fact that a man of faith from the distant past speaks directly to a man of need today. We know not who the psalmist was, and only as much of his circumstances as may be gleaned from his song, but his message can be received.

These hymns, collected through the years, were eventually gathered into five groups, probably because by that time there were five books of the Law. They were used for a number of purposes: many for private devotions; some for the praise of the LORD (a number are called "Hallels," or songs of praise—

Hallelujah means literally "Praise ye the LORD"); some to mark the progress of the pilgrims in their ascent to Jerusalem and the temple; many as responsive chants in the temple itself. Among the names ascribed to the Book of Psalms are "The Hymnbook of the Humble" and "The Hymnbook of the Second Temple."

PROVERBS, PROVERBS, chapters 10, 13, 20, 22, 31

Like the psalms, the contents of the Book of Proverbs were collected through the years. As we have them now, they are in a number of collections variously ascribed to Solomon; "the Wise"; Agur the son of Jakeh of Massa; and King Lemuel of Massa. It is doubtful that Solomon wrote any of them, though it is possible that a few came from his pen. More likely is it that we have here one or two groups of proverbs with which he was familiar—possibly collected by his orders—so that they are called "Proverbs of Solomon."

Some of these proverbs have a touch of Jewish piety about them:

The fear of the LORD is the beginning of wisdom (Proverb 9: 10a), but many are of the international type, which treat of wisdom but not religion, and might come originally from any one of a number of oriental countries. Of the three great so-called "Wisdom" books of the Old Testament, Job, Proverbs, and Ecclesiastes, only Proverbs and Ecclesiastes use the typical maxim form, and probably no book ever written used it as effectively as Proverbs. The short concise rules for daily living, the somewhat more labored advice of a father to his son to avoid women, the pungent comments of the writer about people of whom he disapproves:

> Like a gold ring in a swine's snout
> is a beautiful woman without discretion.
> —Proverb 11: 22

give it a distinctive flavor, in spite of the many dissimilar elements of which it is composed. The book is no longer read so frequently as in former years, but it deserves a better fate. However, one chapter does retain its popularity. It is becoming difficult to read aloud any selection in the Bible about women without settling on the latter part of chapter 31 of Proverbs. Perhaps this is only a proverbial bit of longing for the days before women's rights were so firmly enunciated.

ECCLESIASTES, ECCLESIASTES, chapters 1—4, 7, 11, 12

One of the most interesting writers in the Old Testament is the author of Ecclesiastes—Koheleth. The word refers to one who calls out, and is usually translated "the Preacher." He was, when he wrote, a man who had lived long without finding any great satisfaction in life, except perhaps the satisfaction of writing about his disillusionment. He must have found pleasure in writing, for he did it so cleverly.

The theme of the book is "Nothing matters—much:" the byword is "Vanity of vanities, all is vanity." This refers not to the common idea of vanity as pride, but to the basic concept of emptiness. Nothing in life is worth while. Some scholars hold that beneath the cleverness of Koheleth there was a desire to drive his readers back to a firmer faith in God,[2] but more fail to recognize this motive.

Since the one person in Israelitish history who had had the greatest opportunity to enjoy all kinds of pleasure was King Solomon, that was the name selected as a nom de plume. Wealth, power, wives, glory, even wisdom had been at the disposal of this monarch, according to the established tradition. If, therefore, *Solomon* had been unable to find happiness, the search was fruitless, so Koheleth wrote as though he had been Solomon.

This writing was late. If there were no other indications of that, then the infiltration of Greek thought would prove it. Only from the Greeks could we get such a combination of Cynic and Epicurean philosophy. But there is nothing crude about it. There are means through which a man can achieve some pleasure, and he should use them, but not to excess. And the pleasure itself will be a passing experience. There is no denial of God. Indeed, only through God can

---

2. See Fleming James, *Personalities of the Old Testament* (New York: Charles Scribner's Sons, 1939).

man have any pleasure—yet, after all, it is scarcely worth while:

> There is nothing better for a man than that he should eat and drink, and find enjoyment in his toil. This also, I saw, is from the hand of God; for apart from him who can eat or who can have enjoyment? For to the man who pleases him God gives wisdom and knowledge and joy; but to the sinner he gives the work of gathering and heaping, only to give to one who pleases God. This also is vanity and a striving after the wind. (Ecclesiastes 2:24-26.)

The most popular passage in the book is the poem on old age in chapter 12 beginning:

> Remember also your Creator in the days of your youth, before the evil days come, and the years draw nigh, when you will say, "I have no pleasure in them." (Ecclesiastes 12:1.)

Then follow one upon another a series of beautiful figures of speech depicting old age, ending in the eighth verse with the same refrain:

> Vanity of vanities, says the Preacher; all is vanity.

The name of Solomon in the book gave it prestige and an ostensibly early date, but in itself was not sufficient to secure its inclusion among the sacred books of Israel. Sensing this, some unknown writer inserted what have been called "pious additions" which, bolstering the religious teachings of the book, accomplished this aim. The most prominent of them, placed strategically at the end of the book, is:

> The end of the matter; all has been heard. Fear God, and keep his commandments; for this is the whole duty of man. For God will bring every deed into judgment, with every secret thing, whether good or evil. (Ecclesiastes 12:13-14.)

Job, JOB, chapters 1—7, 28, 38, 39, 42

Job did not know the answers to all the questions about God, and we do not know the answers to all the questions about Job. To begin with, the book was not written all at one time, nor all by one man. Some parts seem to be much earlier than others, and some parts—possibly all of it—appear to come from Edom, rather than from Israel. In most places the book seems not to believe in any life beyond the grave:

> "For there is hope for a tree,
>   if it be cut down, that it will sprout again,
>   and that its shoots will not cease.
> Though its root grow old in the earth,
>   and its stump die in the ground,
>   yet at the scent of water it will bud
>   and put forth branches like a young plant.
> But man dies, and is laid low;
>   man breathes his last, and where is he?
> As waters fail from a lake,
>   and a river wastes away and dries up,
> So man lies down and rises not again;
>   till the heavens are no more he will not awake
>   or be roused out of his sleep."
>
> —Job 14:7-12

Yet there is one passage which is very similar to an ancient inscription at Ras Shamrah which very likely does refer to the death and resurrection of the god Baal:

> "For I know that my Redeemer [or Vindicator] lives,
>   and at last he will stand upon the earth;
> and after my skin has been thus destroyed,
>   then without my flesh I shall see God."
>
> Job 19:25-26

The traditional interpretation of this passage for many years has been that it was a prediction of Jesus, the Redeemer, though the word "vindicator" is a much more accurate translation. If, as seems likely, there is a connection between the verse and the Canaanitish inscription about Baal, we must admit at least the probability of some idea of life beyond the grave. The only other passages in the Old Testament with a similar idea are Isaiah 26:19 and Daniel 12:2-3, both of which are very late.

The theme of Job is the problem of evil: the question "Why do the righteous suffer?" If God is good, and God is powerful, why does he permit it? In the first of the book, Job appears as a wealthy, respected, righteous sheik, who was so careful about making sacrifices that, when the day came for one of his many sons to sacrifice, Job made an extra offering, just to be certain that it was not overlooked.

In an assembly of semidivine beings, the LORD was boasting about how righteous a man his servant Job was. The Satan[3] asked why he should not be righteous, because he had everything a man could ask for. The LORD said that was not the reason for the goodness of Job, and gave the Satan permission to strip everything from him—except that he could not touch the person of Job—to prove his point. Then follows the picture of various messengers coming in to tell Job of his misfortunes which the Satan has arranged—the loss of his flocks and herds, his sons and daughters (everything except his wife). This was the incident which probably gave Shakespeare the idea for his scene in *The Merchant of Venice* in which the messengers came one after the other to tell Antonio of the loss of his various ships until he was a ruined man. Yet Job did not turn against God:

> Then Job arose, and rent his robe, and shaved his head, and fell upon the ground, and worshiped. And he said, "Naked I came from my mother's womb, and naked shall I return; the LORD gave, and the LORD has taken away; blessed be the name of the LORD."

In all this Job did not sin or charge God with wrong. (Job 1:20-22.)

When the LORD asked again about Job, the Satan insisted that it had not been a fair test, because he had been unable to touch the person of Job:

> Then Satan answered the LORD, "Skin for skin! All that a man has will he give for his life. But put forth thy hand now, and touch his bone and his flesh, and he will curse thee to thy face." (Job 2:4-5.)

---

3. The Hebrew text uses the article, "The Satan," indicating that, as late as the writing of the Book of Job, the term described not an evil spirit, but a being who held a recognized function in the assembly which met with God. The footnote *"the adversary"* in the Revised Standard Version for Job 1:6 is really a better translation than "Satan."

The Lord gave the Satan that permission, but forbade him to kill Job, so the next test was that he was afflicted with loathsome sores. His only relief was the momentary pleasure of scratching the afflicted parts with a piece of broken pottery. Even his wife urged him to curse God and die.

When Job was in this extremity, he was visited by three of his friends who came to console with him. They remained in tactful silence for seven days, but then adequately made up for their former lack of speech. Each of the three spoke in turn, with a reply by Job after each speech. After these six, there was a second round of speeches and then parts of a third cycle. The theme of the comforters was that Job must have sinned or God would not have punished him—the common philosophy of the day. Therefore Job should confess his sin, and the Lord would no longer punish him. But Job, knowing that he was guiltless, refused to lie by admitting sin.

After these speeches there is an unattached poem (chapter 28) about wisdom. The author visited a mine, and was tremendously impressed by the cleverness of the men who operated it. He pointed out that they could do the ingenious tricks necessary to gain the products of the mine—but where was wisdom to be found? After a glowing tribute to wisdom, he claimed that it is to be found only through God:

" 'Behold, the fear of the Lord, that is wisdom;
and to depart from evil is understanding.' "
—Job 28:28

Job then spoke at length about how he had fallen from his former high estate. After this another man appeared and gave over again the same arguments as Job's three friends had given (but did not give them so well). Then the Lord spoke to Job out of the whirlwind. These passages, contrasting the majesty of God with the insignificance of Job, are the high point of the book:

"Where were you when I laid the foundations of the earth?
Tell me, if you have understanding.
Who determined its measurements—surely you know!
Or who stretched the line upon it?

On what were its bases sunk,
   or who laid its cornerstone,
when the morning stars sang together,
and all the sons of God shouted for joy?"

—Job 38:4-7

When the author switched from the heavenly bodies to unusual animals like the ostrich, the hippopotamus, and the crocodile, he was probably even more impressive to his ancient readers, but not nearly so moving to those of the present age.

Job, after this tremendous speech of the LORD, admitted that he was beyond his depth, and asked forgiveness:

"I had heard of thee by the hearing of the ear,
   but now my eye sees thee;
therefore I despise myself,
   and repent in dust and ashes."

—Job 42:5-6

The LORD then condemned the friends, praised Job, and rewarded him by giving him double of all he had had before in flocks and herds, three more daughters, and seven more sons, plus gifts from his own brothers and sisters.

The Book of Job does not solve the problem of evil—probably because it is insoluble. But it does wrestle with it honestly, bringing it out clearly into the open so that it may be understood. And it gives a wonderful picture of a suffering man standing stubborn in his integrity, until he is forced to admit that the problem is beyond him. The ways of God are beyond the ways of man. The character in literature always picked for comparison with Job is Prometheus.

RELIGIOUS TENDENCIES

There were no new religious tendencies which developed during the Greek period—only a continuation of those mentioned as growing during the Persian period. The legalism which had so clearly marked the Priestly writings was continued and even intensified by the Chronicler, in his editing of the Second Historical Series—1 and 2 Chronicles, Ezra, and Nehemiah. This series helped swing the common religion into the orbit of the priest, though the greatest force in that direction was always the Law attributed to Moses—partly Deuteronomic from the sixth century B.C., but even more of the Priestly flavor from the fifth century.

There was nothing of scripture written in this Greek period to promote liberal thinking, aside from an occasional passage in the Psalms—which are almost impossible to date anyway. Yet some effects of the earlier liberal writers seem to have carried on, for there were liberal thinkers toward the end of the period whose words have come to us.

The apocalyptic thought, of course, was greatly intensified, because of the persecution which produced the Book of Daniel, and because, after it had been written, the Book of Daniel itself was a strong influence. The tendency to emphasize the humble ones continued in many of the psalms written in the Greek period, and probably the numbers of these unpretentious ones greatly increased, though we have few means of proving it. There was a rigidity about those influenced by the other tendencies which makes it easier to recognize them. The meek may inherit the earth, but they do very little advertising.

The interest in wisdom was greatly intensified. The completion of the Books of Proverbs and Job occurred during this time, and they spread their influence far. Even non-Palestinian Judaism was concerned with the rapidly growing exaltation of wisdom—perhaps even more so than the Jerusalem variety.

Of the five movements, the one which seems to have lost ground in the Greek period is the liberal one; the two which gained most were the adoration of wisdom and apocalypticism; very likely the same oppressions which increased this apocalyptic thinking among some people tended almost to the same extent to develop an attitude of peaceful, humble nonresistance on the part of the meeker souls; legalism remained as strong as it had been before.

PART SEVEN
UNDER ROME

C H A P T E R   X X I I

T O   T H E   T I M E   O F   C H R I S T

The Political Situation

After the cleansing of the temple in 165 B.C., Judas Maccabaeus continued the struggle against the mercenary soldiers of the Seleucid kings with considerable success until he was killed, four year later. He was succeeded as leader by his brother, Jonathan. As there were two claimants to the Syrian throne, Jonathan manipulated the situation, using the Jews as a balance of power and gaining, in return for his support, concessions first from one side and then from the other. After his death, the third of the brothers to become leader, Simon, continued his policy and obtained complete freedom for Judah. He then retained that freedom by becoming and remaining a firm friend of Rome, which was not averse to having another small nation in western Asia.

After Simon the leadership became hereditary, with some of his descendants developing into strong and efficient rulers and some becoming weak ones. Violent cruelty was by no means unknown. Two primarily religious, but partially political, parties, the Pharisees and the Sadducees, entered the picture, and each was in turn supported by various rulers. After the death of a vigorous queen who had been supported by the Pharisees, her two sons, each the leader of one of these parties, engaged in a struggle for the throne. At this point one of the most skillful adventurers in history appeared— Antipater from Idumea, the later name of the country of Edom. He successfully supported one of the brothers, Hyrcanus II, who is best known as having held the office of high priest for over a third of a century.

In 63 B.C. Pompey made Judea a part of the Roman Empire, but Antipater, by ingratiating himself into the favor of whatever man was in power in Rome during those exciting days,

238   THE CHOSEN PEOPLE

remained a force to be reckoned with in the land of Judea.
Eventually he was poisoned, but his son Herod, likewise a man
of no mean ability, finally succeeded in becoming the King of
Judea. Commonly known as Herod the Great, he ruled his
country with a strong hand, erecting beautiful buildings (including the reconstruction of the Jewish temple), levying and
collecting heavy taxes, making himself cordially hated by
the Jews, and, according to Matthew, striving desperately to
kill the King of kings who he feared would supplant him. A
short time after the birth of Jesus, Herod died.

THE PEOPLE

The two most prominent parties in Judea in the late days
before the Christian era were the Pharisees and the Sadducees.
At times they were bloody enemies; at no time was there any
sympathy one for the other. The word Pharisee means the
separated ones. That is, by their righteousness and observance
of the law they were separate from other ordinary people.
This is, of course, the end result of the tendency begun when
Ezekiel, by giving the law in Babylon, strove to keep the Jews
separate from the Babylonians. The Pharisees considered it
necessary to keep both the written law and the oral interpretations made of it by the various great rabbis. They believed
in a resurrection of the body after death. For the most part
they were not wealthy. They were the teachers in the synagogue schools, where the boys were taught to read the Torah.
The synagogue was largely in their hands.

The Sadducees probably received their name from Zadok,
the priest who succeeded Abiathar when the latter made the
mistake of supporting Adonijah instead of Solomon as a successor to David. They were the group from which the temple
priests—especially the high priests—came, and were somewhat
more worldly than the Pharisees. They did not believe in a
resurrection of the body. In general they were wealthier than
the Pharisees.

The Essenes were a rigid monastic group who out-Phariseed
the Pharisees in their devotion to legalism. They were very
strict about their ablutions. Possibly John the Baptist belonged
to this sect. There are many scholars who claim flatly that the

men who operated the Qumran monastery were Essenes, and that the "Manual of Discipline" was the code by which these people were governed.[1] In any case, they had many characteristics in common with the Essenes, who are much better understood today because of the studies carried on in connection with the Dead Sea Scrolls.

The Herodians were those who supported the rule of Rome as exercised by Herod and his family. They probably were the successors to the earlier Hellenists, who could see good in gentile culture, and very likely represented the wealthy group whose wealth had come largely through the Roman administration.

The Zealots were the exact antithesis of the Herodians. Bitterly opposed to all that was Roman as an affront to the rulership of their God, they were in some cases willing to kill to get rid of Roman institutions. They were largely influenced by the messianic hope.

The Am-haarez, or people of the land, were not necessarily the poor, though in some cases they undoubtedly were. There were too many other things for them to do for them to spend the time necessary to be Pharisees. They were not antireligious, but did not practice religion except to a small degree. To this group belonged the great rank and file of the people.

The Humble were the unpretentious ones, who were meek in their appeal to God. Frequently they were downtrodden and oppressed. They were the ones who did not assert themselves, and were in no sense an organized group. They were the ones who were to "inherit the earth."

Of these seven classes of people, the first five mentioned were fairly cohesive groups, in some cases—e.g. the Essenes—being thoroughly organized. The last two, the Am-haarez and the Humble, were chiefly to be distinguished by their lack of distinguishing characteristics. One of them included those content to live without too much concern for religion, the other was composed of those nonaggressive souls who got along as best they could under the circumstances, leaving matters in the hands of their God.

---

1. See Appendix, Note G. See also F. W. Cross, Jr., article "The Dead Sea Scrolls," *Interpreter's Bible*, XII, pp. 657f, especially footnote 69.

THE GREAT EXPECTATION

These, then, were the chosen people at the close of the pre-Christian era. Probably the largest part of them were the Am-haarez, those who made no great commitment along any religious lines. But there was one tremendous anticipation which was experienced by nearly all of them. Certainly the Herodians were not so eager as, for example, the Humble, yet they were all Jews. They all thrilled to the stories of the ancient King David, and the glories of King Solomon. The pictures painted by the postexilic prophets had not yet come to pass. The Romans *had* brought peace, but it was a peace without freedom. It seemed that their famed justice was not for the Jews. Surely it could not be much longer before the day of the Lord would come—first Elijah, the forerunner, and then the Messiah, the Anointed One, the King, then his rule, which, according to some, would last a thousand years—the millennium. Then, after the centuries of injustice had been recompensed, would come the new heaven and the new earth. Surely, the LORD would not much longer delay the sending of his Anointed. The popular literature of the day was of the apocalyptic type. The people could be triggered into action by the claim of messiahship on the part of any leader—as indeed they were, more than once. Small wonder that, when Peter finally blurted out the belief that Jesus was the Christ (Greek for Messiah), Jesus charged his followers to tell no man about it. (Mark 8:29-30.)

The tragedy of the Jews was that they did not understand. From Ur of the Chaldeans to Bethlehem they had been led, for they were the chosen people. Chosen for what? For service through suffering. Yet the service was performed. They were great, not because of their armies but because of their faith. And century after century those individuals of the greatest faith gave to mankind new beauties and new hope. Out of the wreckage of their national ambitions rose, century after century, a constantly more wonderful conception of God, culminating at last in the person of the Greatest of all. He was not what they had expected; he was not what they wanted; but finally the Messiah of the chosen people did come.

CHAPTER XXIII

THE CANON

THE TORAH OR LAW

In Chapter II we found that the first great historical series, consisting of the combination of the J, E, D, and P histories, was finally completed about 400 B.C. The books of the Old Testament composing this series are Genesis, Exodus, Leviticus, Numbers, Deuteronomy, Joshua, Judges, 1 and 2 Samuel, 1 and 2 Kings. Shortly after their completion, the first five of these came to be considered the work of Moses, written by him practically by dictation from the LORD. If they were given by the LORD, they could not be changed, not even in a single letter, and were in every respect holy. They were called the Torah, a word which means instruction or law, and were the first part of Scripture to the Hebrew people. To them they have always been the most sacred part.

THE PROPHETS

The second group of books to be considered sacred was the Book of the Prophets. The first reference we find to this collection in ancient literature is dated about 200 B.C., so we assume that to have been the time it became considered sacred. There are two groups within this collection: the Former Prophets and the Latter Prophets. The Former Prophets, which were always called by that name, are not what we would call prophets at all, but are the historical books of the first historical series which were not included in the Torah; i.e., Joshua, Judges, 1 and 2 Samuel and 1 and 2 Kings. Since 1 and 2 Samuel were considered one book by the Hebrews, as were 1 and 2 Kings, they thought of the Former Prophets as being four in number.

The people who organized this literature loved order and balance. Therefore, when the Latter Prophets were selected, they had to have four. Three were chosen: Isaiah, Jeremiah, and Ezekiel; and then, for the fourth, they grouped the rest of the prophets and called them the "Book of the Twelve"—the ones we speak of as Minor Prophets. There were at that time only eleven, so the last one, Zechariah, was split. It was recognized that there were three additions which had been made to the original book (chapters 1—8), so the third one was broken off, and given as a name the first distinctive word appearing in it: "My Messenger," or, in the Hebrew, "Malachi." Since there were traditionally twelve tribes of Israel, and twelve months of the year, there had to be twelve prophets in this final section of the Latter Prophets.

For nearly 300 years these were the only parts of the Old Testament which were officially considered to be sacred. Some other writings—the Psalms, for instance—were held to be of great value, but were not technically a part of the Word of God. When Jesus spoke of the "Law and the Prophets," he was speaking of the Jewish Scriptures. When in the story of the transfiguration Jesus appeared in the vision flanked on one side by Moses and on the other by Elijah, Moses represented the Law and Elijah the Prophets. It was only six days after Peter had stated that Jesus was the Christ (Messiah), the Son of the Living God. To the people of that time, the story meant that the Scriptures testified that Jesus was the Messiah.[1]

The Writings

A generation later the temple was destroyed, and the greatest unifying factor in Judaism was lost. It was partly because of this, and partly because the Christians were beginning to select certain of their books as having unusual spiritual value, that the Jewish leaders organized a council at Jamnia, near what was left of Jerusalem, to determine once and for all which books were sacred—that is, which were the Word of God and therefore could be read in the synagogue. Only books which they believed had been written before the death of Ezra were eligible, for they thought him to have been the last man to whom the LORD had given his message to be written down.

1. Matthew 16:13—17:13.

This brings out the importance of names like that of Solomon being attached to late books like the Song of Solomon and Ecclesiastes.

There were four groups of the books finally selected at the Council of Jamnia in A.D. 91. Three poetic books, Job, Psalms, and Proverbs formed one; the second historical series, 1 and 2 Chronicles, Ezra and Nehemiah composed a second; five books which were read aloud, each at its own designated feast (Ruth, Esther, Ecclesiastes, Song of Solomon, and Lamentations) and were called the Festival Rolls, or Megilloth, were a third; and the Book of Daniel, which had not been written until after the selection of the Prophets, though the name Daniel affixed to it made it seem to be much earlier than Ezra, was the fourth. This third division of the Hebrew Scriptures was called the Writings—sometimes the Greek word for Sacred Writings, Hagiographa.

There was a reed which was very common, straight and rigid, so that it was frequently used by ancient carpenters as a rule or measure. Its name in Greek was *kanon*. Hence these books, which were sacred, were called the measuring stick or rule—the Canon.

THE HEBREW CANON
THE LAW (about 400 B.C.)

Genesis, Exodus, Leviticus, Numbers, Deuteronomy
THE PROPHETS (about 200 B.C.)

Former Prophets	Latter Prophets
Joshua	Isaiah
Judges	Jeremiah
Samuel (1 and 2)	Ezekiel
Kings (1 and 2)	Book of the Twelve

Hosea	Nahum
Joel	Habakkuk
Amos	Zephaniah
Obadiah	Haggai
Jonah	Zechariah
Micah	Malachi

The Writings (A.D. 91)

Books of Poetry

Job   Psalms   Proverbs

Second Historical Series

1 and 2 Chronicles   Ezra   Nehemiah

Festival Rolls (Megilloth)

Ruth   Esther   Ecclesiastes   Song of Solomon   Lamentations

Apocalypse

Daniel

THE APOCRYPHA

Over a period of a couple of centuries, beginning about 300 B.C., the Jews who had left Palestine to settle in Egypt translated their sacred writings into the Greek which was, after their dispersion, their common language. There was a tradition, based upon a letter said to have been written by a man named Aristaeus, that this translation had been made by 72 scholars, six from each tribe of Israel, miraculously guided by the LORD, so that, though there were 36 different sets of translated manuscripts, the sets tallied one with another, word for word. Because of this tradition, the translation is frequently called the Septuagint.[2] Frequently the Latin numeral LXX is used. In reality, this letter was written long after the time of Ptolemy II, which is the date ascribed. Its purpose was to bolster the authenticity of the Greek version. Instead of being divinely inspired and infallible, the different parts are of varying degrees of excellence, some books being very well translated, while others are not. Since these translations were made in Egypt several centuries before the Council of Jamnia (Palestine), which in A.D. 91 determined which books would be included in the third part of the Hebrew Scriptures, there are a number of books in the Septuagint which are not in the Hebrew Canon.

Around A.D. 400 one of the greatest scholars of the Christian Church, Jerome, made a translation of the Bible into the com-

---

2. The Latin word for 70. The other two seem to have been overlooked. The accent is upon the first syllable.

mon language of the people, which at that time was Latin.   It was, and still is, called the Vulgate, from *vulgus*, meaning "crowd."   As he depended heavily upon Greek manuscripts of the Septuagint, it included some books, such as 1 and 2 Maccabees, 1 and 2 Esdras, Judith, Tobit, The Wisdom of Jesus ben Sira (also called Ecclesiasticus) and a number of others, which are not in the Hebrew Canon.   These books are in the Roman Catholic Bible, which is derived from Jerome's Vulgate Translation, but are not in the Protestant Bible, which agrees exactly with the Hebrew Canon, though the books are not given in the same order.   They are called the Apocryphal Books of the Old Testament.

THE CONCLUSION

Thus ends our task, a recounting of the narrative history of Israel, the chosen people. Out of the ancient Near East they came, a group of Semitic tribes. They struggled as nomads into Palestine and called it their home, though more than once large groups were forced out by hunger, sometimes finding refuge in Egypt.

At the close of their most important Egyptian sojourn, they met their great leader, who had just found the God who had chosen them, and whom they were to follow. Out of bondage, into the covenant, and on through the wilderness they followed, till at last they came to the Promised Land.

Uniting with other tribes and becoming more consolidated within their own group, they abandoned their nomadic life, settled into agricultural pursuits with the attendant temptation of an agricultural religion, and selected a king who, under their God, was to rule them. From the greatness of David and the splendor of Solomon they sank to the futility of the sons of Josiah. First after Solomon came the division of the kingdom; then the destruction of the North; then the exile of Judah. The glory of the chosen people was departed, but it was to be:
"Not by might, nor by power, but by my Spirit, says
the LORD of hosts."

As the kings became feebler, the prophets became greater. One after another, in their troubled lives, they found new characteristics of the God they served, and proclaimed them to the people: justice; universalism; mercy; a concern for the individual—qualities we would think his followers always would have known.

After the return from Babylon the longing for a king, an anointed one, was again kindled. But the power of the surrounding nations made it evident that the anointed one would have to come chiefly by the power of God.

They worshiped their God, these chosen people, and gathered their books, and hoped for the One to come. And because they had been chosen, and because they worshiped, and because they gathered their books, and because they hoped, the world has been blessed. And, although it did not happen as they had expected it to happen, the Anointed One did come.

THE APPENDIX

Note A. The Name of God

The personal name for the God of the ancient Hebrews was probably Yahweh. The four letters with which it was written, YHWH, are all consonants. Originally there were no written vowels in the Hebrew language, each scribe memorizing the pronunciation of the words as he had been taught them, using the written consonants as a guide. Eventually, at least two centuries after the time of Christ, tiny symbols, now called "vowel points," were placed above or below the consonants to indicate what vowel was to be spoken, but these points were not considered a part of the sacred revealed text. Long before these vowel points had been invented, the word YHWH, the name of God, was considered too sacred to pronounce, so the word *Adonai* meaning "Lord" was substituted in reading aloud.

The sacred consonants of the Hebrew scriptures, being considered a revelation from God, could not be changed, but the scribes who copied them had no scruples against putting the *vowel points* for the word *Adonai* below the *consonants* YHWH, as an aid in pronunciation. That is the way the word appears today in the Hebrew Bible. Many books about the Old Testament indicate the spelling "Yahweh." People of the Jewish faith today prefer the term *Adonai* or *Adonoi*. The English King James or Authorized Version (KJV) translates it "Lord," in all capitals, as does the new Revised Standard Version (RSV). The American Revised Version (ARV) uses "Jehovah," made by combining the consonants YHWH and the vowels of the word Adonai.

The word YHWH is so ancient, we are uncertain as to its derivation, but it probably is related to the verb "to be," which may be the reason back of the expression "I AM WHO I AM," or "I AM WHAT I WILL BE." (Exodus 3:14.) In Moffat's translation of the Old Testament he recognizes this, and uses the expression "the Eternal." Albright[1] believes that it may be associated with the "causative" form of the verb—that is, that it refers to the One who causes things to be, or the "Creator."

---

1. W. F. Albright, *From the Stone Age to Christianity* (2nd ed.; New York: Doubleday and Co., 1957), p. 15f.

Note B. The Idea of "Spirit"

The Hebrew word for *wind,* like the Latin word *spiritus* and the Greek word *pneuma* (see, e.g., our word *pneumatic*), combines the meanings of wind, breath, and spirit. God was thought of as an invisible power: the wind was an invisible power. How natural that the wind should be the demonstration of God's power. Also, breath was wind, and breath was life. When a man could breathe, he was alive. Therefore the ancient Hebrew thought of this spirit of the LORD as

    a. The power which gave a man life, and
    b. The force which enabled him to do great and otherwise unexplicable things.

These two ideas of the function of wind are present in our own thinking. Compare the two English words, *inspiration* and *respiration,* both from the Latin root *spirare,* to breathe. The second term means to breathe in and out—inextricably associated with living; the former may mean either to breathe in, or to have the spirit of God breathed into one. This term, spirit of God, is used frequently throughout the Old Testament to describe the expression of his power working through men. In the New Testament the concept becomes known as the Holy Spirit.

Note C. Further Discussion of the Covenant

Not until modern times did anyone question that the Ethical Decalogue of Exodus, chapter 20, so familiar to all churchgoers, was the code representing the Israelite part of the Covenant of Sinai. Then there began a tendency to consider this marvelous little code to be the work of the prophetic movement, which started nearly five centuries after Moses.

A trend in the opposite direction started in 1934 with Albrecht Alt, who was the first great scholar to apply to the Old Testament a new technique of literary examination, seeking to reconstruct the political and sociological background from its literary form.[2] Alt claimed that the form of the commandments of the

---

2. This reconstruction of the background from the structure of the passage is called "Form Criticism" (Form-Geschichte). It has been very useful in the New Testament where, to mention one application, much of the purpose and technique of the early church can be inferred from an analysis of the sermons in the Book of Acts. In the Old Testament the laws of the Israelites—both civil and ritualistic—lend themselves readily to this method of study. Alt's book is *Die Ursprünge Des Israelitischen Rechts,* Leipzig, 1934.

Ethical Decalogue ("You shall not") is very ancient, in contrast to the "case" type of law ("If a man borrows anything from his neighbor, and it is hurt or dies—etc.").

A recent writer about this Decalogue is George E. Mendenhall, in a small book, *Law and Covenant in Israel and the Ancient Near East,* published originally in *The Biblical Archaeologist,* May and September, 1954, now reprinted 1955 by "The Biblical Colloquium" of Pittsburgh, Pa. He claims (p. 36ff) that the consolidation of a group of tribes into a political and religious organization by such means as a covenant with a god was entirely in keeping with the customs of Palestine in the time of Moses. Likewise, the engraving on stone, and the depositing of the agreement at a sacred shrine (here, the ark) was a natural procedure.

There are two separate stories of the Decalogue. The account in Exodus, chapter 20, describes the tables given by the LORD to Moses, and broken by him when he found the Israelites worshiping the golden calf. The other account in Exodus, chapter 34, containing quite different commandments which are concerned with Israelitish religious ritual ("You shall not boil a kid in its mother's milk," vs. 26), is presented as written down by Moses himself, at the time of his second ascent of Mount Sinai to receive the law. Earlier scholars, before the reversal of opinion just described, had assumed that the ritual laws were earlier than the ethical laws of Exodus, chapter 20, an assumption which is now being seriously questioned.

There is an ancient and somewhat more comprehensive list of laws called the "Covenant Code" found in Exodus, chapters 21—23 (sometimes the last four verses of Exodus, chapter 20 are included). This may represent a similar covenant made to protect the rights of the people as well as to unify the tribes at the time of the establishment of the monarchy under Saul, although Exodus, chapter 24, seems to assign it to the time of Moses.

Other references to covenants between Israel and the Lord are the story of Abraham's covenant of the circumcision (Genesis, chapter 17) and Jeremiah's covenant written upon the hearts of the people. (Jeremiah 31:31-39.)

Note D. Jabesh-gilead and the Men of Benjamin

Sometimes, by connecting scattered incidents, it is possible to discover interesting relationships among various groups. One such opportunity presents itself in the story of the Levite's concubine (Judges 19-21), and the subsequent difficulties of the city of Jabesh-gilead and the men of the tribe of Benjamin.

After the evil men of Gibeah had been responsible for the death of the Levite's concubine, her master cut her body in pieces and sent them as a summons to a conclave of all the tribes of Israel. The men of Jabesh-gilead did not respond, thereby making themselves liable to a serious penalty. Likewise, in the conference, the tribe of Benjamin failed to condemn the culprits of Gibeah, a city of Benjamin. For this reason the other tribes made war upon the tribe of Benjamin, and, after two disastrous attacks, succeeded in ambushing them, killing all the tribe except 600 men. The story assumes that the women of Benjamin were all destroyed.

Before the battle, the tribes had sworn by the LORD that they would not give their daughters as wives for the men of Benjamin. When after the decimation of the Benjaminites the others relented and wished to save the tribe from extinction, they did not dare to violate their oath. They therefore attacked the city of Jabesh-gilead, which was already due to be punished, killing all men and married women, and giving the virgins as wives to the men of Benjamin. Because there were not enough to go around, they had to be supplemented by others stolen from Shiloh.

Now Gibeah was the home of Saul (the Benjaminite who became the first king of Israel) both before and after his coronation. The number of incidents located there makes us realize how close to his home he stayed through most of his life. And, according to the older story of his selection, it was because he saved the city of Jabesh-gilead from Nahash, king of Ammon, that he was chosen king. (1 Samuel, chapter 11.) Also, the men of Jabesh-gilead were the ones who, after the final defeat of Saul, went at night through the Philistine lines and ripped his body from the wall of Bethshan where it had been nailed, taking it back to their own city where it was burned and the bones were buried. (1 Samuel, chapter 31.) Is it possible that Saul's mother, or some other ancestress, had been one of the virgins of Jabesh-gilead?

We also note that the Levite's concubine, whose assault had started the whole sequence of violence, came from Bethlehem in Judah—indeed, had probably left it only the day before her death. This was, of course, the city from which later David came. Also we find (2 Samuel, chapter 10) that David was a good friend of Nahash, the king of Ammon, whose defeat by Saul at Jabesh-gilead had resulted in the coronation of the first king of Israel. If we could be certain of 2 Samuel 17:25, which states that the daughter of Nahash was the sister of Zeruiah, there might even be a blood relationship between David and Nahash, though 1 Chronicles 2:13-16 denies this. Collecting all these facts, it seems quite possible that there was a long record of bad blood between the men of Benjamin (especially the inhabitants of Gibeah) and the citizens of Jabesh-gilead on one side, and the men of Judah (especially the inhabitants of Bethlehem) and the Ammonite king on the other side. This would help account for the bitter enmity Saul showed toward David, who eventually succeeded to Saul's throne. However, as suggested in the story of David (above, p. 92f), there were undoubtedly many shifts in the alliances of these men.

Note E.   The Composition of the Book of Isaiah

The first point of departure in treating of the composition of the Book of Isaiah is that mentioned above, p. 144, that the same writer would not have been a contemporary both of Uzziah in 740 B.C. and of Cyrus the Great shortly before 538 B.C. In keeping with this idea, it has long been the custom to consider that part of the book beginning with the fortieth chapter to be "Deutero-Isaiah" or "Second Isaiah." And since the references to Cyrus predicted the restoration of Jerusalem, the date assigned to it was shortly before the return to Judah after the captivity, in 538 B.C. But it became increasingly evident that the latter part of this section, though similar in style to the first part, was written against the background of Judah *after* the return from Babylon. Thus it became the custom to consider Isaiah, chapters 40—55, as Second Isaiah, and chapters 56—66 as "Third Isaiah."

But there are also many parts in the first half of the book which do not harmonize with the times of Isaiah ben Amoz, prophet and political adviser to kings Ahaz and Hezekiah. Chapters 13-23 are a series of oracles against foreign nations, some of which do not seem to be associated with Isaiah. For example, there is some attention paid to Babylon:

> And Babylon, the glory of kingdoms,
>   the splendor and pride of the Chaldeans,
> will be like Sodom and Gomorrah
>   when God overthrew them.
>   —Isaiah 13:19

Babylon had not yet become a free city in the time of Isaiah.

The section included in chapters 24-27 has many of the characteristics of apocalyptic writing, which began to develop much later than the time of Isaiah ben Amoz. This style portrays the LORD's hand in the destruction of the earth and the heavens, the reward of the faithful, and many other distinctive features. (See above, p. 247.)

> Behold, the LORD will lay waste the earth and make it desolate, and he will twist its surface and scatter its inhabitants.
>
> —Isaiah 24:1

> Open the gates,
>   that the righteous nation which keeps faith
>   may enter in.
> Thou dost keep him in perfect peace,
>   whose mind is stayed on thee,
>   because he trusts in thee.
>
> —Isaiah 26:2-3

Chapters 34 and 35 are twin poems, showing the picture of destruction and restoration, and are quite characteristic of late postexilic writing. Chapters 36-39 are copied almost word for word from 2 Kings. Assembling these observations, we have the following analysis:

Chapters	
1-12	Mostly the work of Isaiah ben Amoz.
13-23	Later oracles against various nations, only part of which are by Isaiah.
24-27	Very late, semiapocalyptic poems.
28-33	Partly at least by Isaiah ben Amoz.
34-35	Twin poems
36-39	Historical background, copied from 2 Kings.
40-55	Second Isaiah.
56-66	Third Isaiah.

Professor C. C. Torrey[1] considers chapters 34, 35 and 40-66, a series of poems, all by the Second Isaiah and all written long after the exile, portraying the return not only from Babylon, but from all other countries to which Israel had been scattered. Except for those who follow Torrey, most scholars analyze the book about as given above. Perhaps the first to do so was George Buchanan Gray.[2]

Some may fear that an "injustice" is done to other parts of the book by thus saying that they were not written by Isaiah ben

1. *The Second Isaiah* (New York: Charles Scribner's Sons, 1928).
2. *A Critical Introduction to the Old Testament* (New York, Charles Scribner's Sons, 1929, preface dated 1912).

Amoz and therefore are considered inferior. On the contrary, those who so analyze the book consider Second Isaiah by all odds the greatest part.

Note F. The So-called "Virgin" Passage

One of the most controversial verses in the Bible—or any place else—is Isaiah 7:14. As stated above (p. 144ff), after Isaiah had told King Ahaz that the countries which he feared would not injure Judah, and ordered him to ask for a sign to that effect, and the king had refused to request one, the prophet said:

> Therefore the LORD himself will give you a sign. Behold, a young woman shall conceive and bear a son [equally possible translation: is with child and shall bear a son], and shall call his name Immanuel [meaning "God is with us"]. He shall eat curds and honey when he knows how to refuse the evil and choose the good. For before the child knows how to refuse the evil and choose the good, the land before whose two kings you are in dread will be deserted. (Isaiah 7:14-16.)

The meaning of this passage seems quite clear. In a time of national emergency, Isaiah told the king that the LORD was giving him a sign that his country would not be overrun by the armies of Israel and Damascus. It was that a young woman would conceive, or else was already with child, and that, before the child was born, the military situation would be so improved that it would be the natural thing to name her child "God is with us." Moreover, before the child was old enough to know what was good to eat and what was not, the countries of Israel and Damascus would be deserted. Isaiah's amazing ability to judge political events is amply demonstrated by the passage. He gave the "sign" in 735 B.C. In 732 Damascus was completely subdued by Assyria, and Israel would have suffered a like fate, had she not offered to put upon the throne a king acceptable to Assyria. And there is nothing the least unusual about a name which includes the word "God." In the Hebrew, almost all proper names ending in "el" or "iah" or beginning with "J" are references to God. Indeed, even in our own language the name "Jonathan" (from the Hebrew) means "Gift of the Lord," as do all its derivatives such as John, Jean, etc., and the Greek equivalents Dorothy and Theodore (Gift of God).

The difficulty rests entirely in the translation of the other word. The Hebrew word in verse 14 means "young woman." It gives no indication whatever whether she is a virgin or married. There is a Hebrew word which does mean virgin, and it was in use before the time of Isaiah, but Isaiah did not use it. Some four or five centuries after Isaiah's time, his book was translated into Greek, and the translator *did* use a word which means virgin.

If the English translation is made from the work of this Greek translator, who lived over four hundred years after Isaiah, the translation is "a virgin will conceive," and many people consider it a prediction of the birth of Jesus to a virgin. If, on the other hand, we translate the word Isaiah used, it becomes "young woman," as in the Revised Standard Version. Furthermore, Isaiah said quite definitely that he was giving the LORD's sign to Ahaz, and it is most difficult to imagine that a prediction of a virgin birth, to take place nearly seven and a half centuries later, would have been of any material benefit as a sign to a king worried about the invasion of his country.

Note G. The Dead Sea Scrolls

It would seem that no book about the Old Testament can be written today without some reference to the so-called Dead Sea Scrolls. The following account is greatly oversimplified, but may present a description adequate for the purpose of this book.

In 1947 a group of manuscripts were found in a cave at the Wâdī[3] Qumran, near the northwest corner of the Dead Sea. According to one story some boys seeking to drive a goat out of the cave by throwing stones heard the breaking of a jar and, on investigating, found these ancient scrolls. By another account, the cave was being used in smuggling operations. According to Dr. Millar Burrows,[4] who was Director of the American School of Oriental Research at Jerusalem at the time of the discovery, there were six works represented by the scrolls found in the first cave at that time:

1. The Book of *Isaiah*—one complete and one partial manuscript
2. A *Commentary on Habakkuk*
3. A *Manual of Discipline,* containing regulations for a monastic order

3. A wâdī is the bed of a stream which, during part of the year, is completely dry.
4. Millar Burrows, *The Dead Sea Scrolls* (New York: Viking Press, 1955), p. 19, the best of the books written as yet upon this subject.

4. An Aramaic manuscript called, tentatively, the *Lamech Scroll*
5. Directions for a war between certain Israelite tribes and an enemy described as Edomites and other neighboring people, called *War of the Sons of Light with the Sons of Darkness*
6. Certain *Thanksgiving Psalms*

Some time after their discovery, most of these manuscripts came into the possession of the Syrian Orthodox Monastery of St. Mark in the Old City of Jerusalem, under the jurisdiction of Metropolitan-Archbishop Samuel. Others found their way to the Hebrew University, where the late Dr. Sukenik was professor of Archaeology. By this time communication between the two parts of the city, and elsewhere in Palestine, had become very difficult because of the war. Shortly afterward it was almost impossible.

Some manuscripts from St. Mark's Monastery, including the oldest one, a complete copy of the Book of Isaiah, were brought to the American School for evaluation and dating. As Dr. Burrows was in Baghdad at the time, the responsibility temporarily fell upon Dr. William H. Brownlee and Dr. John C. Trever. Dr. Trever had but recently done some intensive work in paleography—the study of ancient writings—and was probably the first one to estimate correctly the extreme antiquity of the Isaiah scroll. With Dr. Brownlee he photographed the whole of it and sent some prints to Dr. William F. Albright, who, like Dr. Burrows, had been one of his teachers. Dr. Albright promptly corroborated the date as probably the last quarter of the second century B.C. Examination of linen in which the scrolls were wrapped, both regarding the technique by which it had been woven and by the "carbon-14" method of checking the age of organic material by the rate of atomic disintegration, tends to corroborate the great antiquity of the scrolls.

Extensive search of other caves, sometimes by unauthorized natives, sometimes by experts, produced a great many more documents, most of them, however, being extremely small. The jigsaw puzzle process of fitting together these fragments—many the size of postage stamps—is now going on. However, no finds have been made which are equal in importance to the first great discovery.[5]

---

5. But manuscripts located in Cave IV, especially those of the Book of Samuel, throw great light upon the assumed Hebrew manuscript lying behind the Septuagint (Greek) translation of this book. For a textual scholar, it is difficult to imagine a more important discovery. See Cross, *op. cit.*, p. 653f.

Urged on by the appearance of the scrolls, and by the unusual subject matter of the *Manual of Discipline,* archaeologists have excavated a ruin nearby which had been thought to be an old Roman fort.   This ruin, Khirbet Qumran, was found to have been a building in the nature of a chapter house of some organization, occupied first in the latter part of the Hasmonaean period, this occupancy terminated probably by an earthquake—either in 31 B.C. or earlier.   A second occupancy was terminated possibly in A.D. 70 by Roman soldiers.   After that, it may have been the quarters of a small military detachment.   Pottery fragments, especially from the first two periods, and coins help to indicate the periods.[6]   The building originally included, among other rooms, a kitchen, dining room or meeting room, and a room for copying manuscripts, equipped even with inkwells.   The general agreement of scholars is that, at the time of the Jewish revolt, the monastic order occupying Khirbet Qumram hid their valuable library of manuscripts in nearby caves, first sealing them in jars, exactly as Jeremiah had done with the deed to the property he had purchased in Anathoth (Jeremiah 32:6-15).   There some of them had remained until 1947.

The *Manual of Discipline* gives a series of most severe regulations for the governing of just such a monastic order as that which seems to have made its local headquarters at Khirbet Qumran.   It is partly because these rules resemble what we know of the discipline of the Essenes, and partly because the Qumran group were so well organized, and so evidently part of a yet larger organization, that their identity with the Essenes is so generally assumed.   They are usually called the "covenanters" because of their great concern for the covenant of the law.

Especially in the commentary on Habakkuk there are a number of difficult references to a "Teacher of Righteousness," and to his opponents, the "Man of the Lie" and the "Wicked Priest" (possibly the same person).   Many different people have been suggested as the teacher of righteousness—from Onias III, the assassinated high priest of the time of Antiochus Epiphanes on. There have been some who believed that there was a tradition of such a teacher who had been murdered and whose resurrection was expected.   When first propounded, this theory caused considerable excitement, for it was suggested that the story of Jesus' crucifixion and resurrection were nothing but a projection of this supposed tradition.   That theory came from only one scholar,

---

6. Burrows, *op. cit.,* p. 67.

and has since been completely discarded. Indeed, one excellent student believes that the translation should be "Right Teacher" rather than "Teacher of Righteousness," i.e., one who correctly expounded the law, the important basis for their entire brotherhood.[7] Perhaps more to the point, however, is the fact that it cannot be proved that there *was* any return of this teacher expected.[8]

What, then, is the significance of the finding of the Dead Sea Scrolls? First let it be said that, for the average reader of the Bible, there is no startling change of thought indicated. Though the realm of scholarship has been thrilled as seldom before, the main results of the discoveries will continue right there—in the realm of scholarship. We now have manuscripts far more ancient than we had before—by almost a thousand years, for the Hebrew of Isaiah. And the most important thing they do is to substantiate what we had. It is almost unbelievable that scribes could have copied so accurately to produce the text we are now using.

A second significance is found in the manuscript *War of the Sons of Light with the Sons of Darkness*. Picturing a final war of the forces of Good with the forces of Evil, it gives us renewed emphasis upon the Israelite concern for "Last Things," which was of growing importance in the last years of the pre-Christian era. We do not have a complete picture of the thinking of the chosen people if we do not include such angles as this manuscript, and the final conquest of Evil at the Battle of Armageddon in Revelation (16:14-16). Some of this is reflected in the teaching of Jesus in the so-called "Little Apocalypse" of Mark 13.

The third contribution of the Dead Sea Scrolls which appeals greatly to the average reader is the outline of the organization of the covenanters (Essenes?) made by reading their *Manual of Discipline*. Here is an X-ray picture of a substantial group of devoutly religious men as they existed in the time of Christ. It was likely from just such a body of men that John the Baptist came, preaching a baptism of repentance for the forgiveness of sin—
"the voice of one crying in the wilderness:

Prepare the way of the Lord,
make his paths straight—" (Mark 1:2f).

---

7. Theodor H. Gaster, *The Dead Sea Scriptures* (New York: Doubleday & Co., 1956), pp. 5, 249, 251, etc.
8. Burrows, *op. cit.*, p. 330.

BIBLIOGRAPHY

This list of books has been made as short and useful as possible. Every book has a real contribution to make. It is not necessary, however, to read too many in the same area.

Commentaries

The Interpreter's Bible. New York: Abingdon Press, 1951-1957. 12 vols. The value of this recent series of commentaries cannot be overestimated. It is comprehensive enough for the scholar, but may be read with profit by the average reader.

Clarke, W. K. Lowther. *Concise Bible Commentary.* New York: Macmillan Co., 1953.

Eiselen, Frederick C., and Others. *The Abingdon Bible Commentary.* New York: Abingdon Press, 1929.

Gore, Charles, and Others. *New Commentary on Holy Scripture.* New York: Macmillan Co., 1928.

Peake, Arthur S., and A. J. Grieve. *Peake's Commentary on the Bible.* New York: Thomas Nelson & Sons, 1957.

Geography

Baly, Denis. *The Geography of the Bible.* New York: Harper & Bros., 1957.

Glueck, Nelson. *The River Jordan.* Philadelphia: Westminster Press, 1946.

Kraeling, Emil G. *Rand McNally Bible Atlas.* Chicago: Rand McNally Co., 1956.

Wright, G. Ernest, and Floyd V. Filson. *The Westminster Historical Atlas to the Bible,* rev. ed. Philadelphia: Westminster Press, 1956.

Archaeology

Albright, W. F. *Archaeology and the Religion of Israel,* 2d ed. Baltimore: Johns Hopkins Press, 1946.

——. *The Archaeology of Palestine.* Baltimore: Penguin Books, 1949.

258

Burrows, Millar. *What Mean These Stones?* New Haven: American Schools of Oriental Research, 1941. (Also available from Meridian Books, New York.)

Finegan, Jack. *Light from the Ancient Past.* Princeton: Princeton University Press, 1946.

Pritchard, James B. *Archaeology and the Old Testament.* Princeton: Princeton University Press, 1958.

Wright, G. Ernest. *Biblical Archaeology.* Philadelphia: Westminster Press, 1957.

History, Religion and Literature

Albright, W. F. *From the Stone Age to Christianity,* 2d ed. Baltimore: Johns Hopkins Press, 1946. (Also available from Doubleday Anchor Books, New York, 1956.)

———. "The Biblical Period" in *The Jews: Their History, Culture and Religion,* Vol. I, ed. Louis Finkelstein. New York: Harper & Bros., 1949. (Also reprinted for private distribution by Biblical Colloquium, Pittsburgh, 1950.)

Anderson, Bernhard W. *Understanding the Old Testament.* Englewood Cliffs, N. J.: Prentice-Hall, Inc., 1957.

Bewer, J. A. *Literature of the Old Testament,* rev. ed. New York: Columbia University Press, 1938.

Breasted, James H. *A History of Egypt.* New York: Charles Scribner's Sons, 1909.

Driver, S. R. *Introduction to the Literature of the Old Testament,* rev. ed. New York: Charles Scribner's Sons, 1913. (Also available from Meridian Books, New York, 1957.)

Mould, Elmer W. K. *Essentials of Bible History.* New York: Ronald Press, 1951.

Oesterley, W. O. E., and T. H. Robinson. *An Introduction to the Books of the Old Testament.* New York: Macmillan Co., 1934.

Olmstead, A. T. *History of Assyria.* New York: Charles Scribner's Sons, 1923.

———. *History of the Persian Empire (Achaemenid Period).* Chicago: University of Chicago Press, 1948.

Orlinsky, Harry M. *Ancient Israel.* Ithaca, N Y.: Cornell University Press, 1954.

Pfeiffer, Robert H. *Introduction to the Old Testament,* 2d ed. New York: Harper & Bros., 1941.

———. *The Books of the Old Testament* (abridged and simplified edition of his *Introduction*). New York: Harper & Bros., 1957.

Pritchard, James B. *The Ancient Near East.* Princeton: Princeton University Press, 1958.

Sloan, W. W. *A Survey of the Old Testament.* New York: Abingdon Press, 1957.

Wilson, John A. *The Burden of Egypt*. Chicago: University of Chicago Press, 1951. (Also available as *The Culture of Ancient Egypt*, University of Chicago Phoenix Book, 1956.)

The Dead Sea Scrolls

Burrows, Millar. *The Dead Sea Scrolls*. New York: Viking Press, 1955.
——. *More Light on the Dead Sea Scrolls*. New York: Viking Press, 1958.
Cross, Frank M. *The Ancient Library of Qumran and Modern Biblical Studies*. Garden City, N. Y.: Doubleday & Co., 1958.
Dupont-Sommer, A. *The Jewish Sect of Qumran and the Essenes*. New York: Macmillan Co., 1955.
Gaster, Theodor H. *The Dead Sea Scriptures*. Garden City, N. Y.: Doubleday & Co., 1956.
Rowley, H. H. *The Zadokite Fragments and the Dead Sea Scrolls*. New York: Macmillan Co., 1953.

Periodicals

There are two small magazines of great value in the field of archaeology. Both are published by the American Schools of Oriental Research, Box 93A, Yale Station, New Haven, Conn.:
Bulletin of the American Schools of Oriental Research, ed. W. F. Albright (for the scholar).
The Biblical Archaeologist, ed. G. Ernest Wright and F. M. Cross, Jr. (nontechnical, for the average reader).

INDEX

Aaron, 54, 59f.
Abel, 38f.
Abiathar, 100, 109, 113, 166, 238
Abigail, 101
Abimelech, 77-78
Abiram, 60, 62
Abishag, 112, 114
Abner, 102f.
Abraham, 32, 43f.
Absalom, 107-11
Achan, 67
Achish, 101
Adam, 35
Adonijah, 112f., 238
Ahab, 24, 126, 128-30, 140, 149
Ahaz, 136, 143, 149, 151f.
Ahijah, 119, 136
Ahimelech, 99
Albright, W. F., 247, 255
Alexander the Great, 219
Alt, Albrecht, 248f.
Amalek, 59
Amalekites, 94, 98, 101
Am-haarez, 239f.
Ammon, 43, 47, 105, 138
Ammonites, 79ff.
Amnon, 107f.
Amorites, 26f.
Amos, 15, 133, 136-39, 150, 153, 164, 191
Antiochus IV (Epiphanes), 220f., 256
Antipater, 237f.
Apocrypha, 244-45
Ark, 57f., 91f., 104
Asa, 126, 132
Asahel, 102
Ashtaroth, 90
Asshur, 25
Asshurbanipal, 40, 155, 158, 160
Assyria, 25, 134f., 144f., 149, 152, 158f.

Athaliah, 126, 135, 151

Baal, 21, 38, 76, 85f., 119, 126, 129f., 132, 134, 141, 148f., 151f.
Babel, 42
Babylon, 158f., 162, 182ff., 187, 199f.
Balaam, 61
  oracles of, 121
Barak, 21, 74
Barton, G. A., 26
Bathsheba, 106, 109, 113f., 149
Benjamin, 48, 50, 69, 97
Bethel, 21, 47, 92, 127, 137f.
Bethshan, 21, 95
Blessing of Jacob, 48, 121
  of Noah, 121
Brownlee, W. H., 255
Burrows, Millar, 254

Cain, 38f.
Cambyses, 200
Canaan, 41
Canaanites, 21, 27, 38, 73f.
  religion of, 84-86
Canon, 243f.
Centralization of worship, 154
Chemosh, 79f.
Chronicles I & II, 33fn., 224
Covenant Code, 121, 153f., 249
Creation, 33, 35ff.
Cyprus, 25, 142, 199f.

D history, 32, 62
Damascus, 21, 24, 27, 105, 116, 118, 129f., 134f., 138, 143f., 158f.
Dan, 23, 75, 127
Daniel, 222-23
Danites, 81, 83
Darius, 25, 200f., 223
Dathan, 60, 62

261

David, 21, 25, 97-111, 112f., 133, 149
Day of the Lord, 164
Dead Sea, 22f.
Dead Sea Scrolls, 169, 239, 254-57
Death, origin of, 38
Deborah, 21, 73-76
    song of, 120, 162
Decalogue, 56, 248f.
Delilah, 83
Deuteronomic editors, 64, 71, 127f., 176f., 195, 208
Deuteronomic reformation, 64, 151, 156, 165ff., 171f., 182
Deuteronomy, 32, 62, 151, 153-55, 207, 208f.

E history, 32, 150, 154
Ecclesiastes, 17, 228-29
Edom, 24, 35, 45, 47, 65, 105, 116, 138, 237
Eglon, 8, 73
Egypt, 26, 52, 115, 118, 158ff.
Ehud, 73
Elhanan, 98
Eli, 91f.
Elijah, 128-30, 131-32, 136, 149, 151, 213
Elisha, 131-32
Endor, 95
Ephod, 83
Ephraim, 32, 48, 79f., 124
Esau, 35, 45f.
Esdraelon, 20, 21, 73ff.
Essenes, 238, 256
Esther, 17, 212
Ethbaal, 129
Eve, 35
Exile, 181ff.
Exodus, 33, 52-63
Ezekiel, 161, 181-86, 207, 209, 215, 220, 238, 242
Ezra, 33fn., 206-207, 210, 220, 224

Fable of Trees, 78, 120
Fertility cult, 84ff.
"Fiat" creation, 35
Fleshpots of Egypt, 55
Flood, 40

Gad, 65
Galilee, 20
    Sea of, 20f., 23
Gamaliel, 76f.
Gath, 20, 101
Gaza, 20, 82
Genesis, 33, 62
Gezer, 22, 74
Gibeon, 22, 47, 68, 74, 116
Gideon, 72, 76-77, 79
Gilead, 24, 78f., 80
Gilgal, 65, 92
Gilgamesh, 40
Glueck, Nelson, 24
Goliath, 98
Goshen, 51, 55

Habakkuk, 162f., 256
Hadad, 118
Haggai, 200-201, 212
Ham, 41
Hammurabi, 27
Hananiah, 168
Hasmonaeus, Mattathias, 221
Heber, 74
Hebron, 21, 102, 108
Herod, 238
Hezekiah, 136, 145f., 149, 151
Hiram, 114f.
Hobab, 52f.
Holiness Code, 195, 207, 209, 215
Horeb, 56, 131
Hosea, 139-41, 144, 149, 150, 172f.
    children of, Jezreel, 20, 134, 140
    "Not my people," 140
    "Not pitied," 140
Huldah, 155
Humble, the, 239f.
Hur, 59
Hushai, 109

Ichabod, 92
Isaac, 44f.
Isaiah, 15, 141-47, 150, 242, 251-52
Ishbaal, 102, 117
Ishmaelites, 44, 49, 61
Israel, 123f., 143f., 158f.
Israelites, 28, 35, 48, 65
    religion of, 84-86
Ittai, 108f.

J history, 31, 36, 39, 41, 122, 150, 154
Jabal, 39
Jabbok, 23
Jabesh-gilead, 24, 69, 90f., 95, 249ff.
Jabin, 76
Jacob, 35, 45-48
Jael, 74
Japheth, 41
JE history, 32f., 64, 150, 154
JED history, 209
Jehoahaz, 160f.
Jehoiachin, 160, 168, 177, 199
Jehoiakim, 160, 167f.
Jehoida, 135f.
Jehoshaphat, 24, 126, 132, 151
Jehu, 129, 134-35, 140
Jephthah, 44, 78-81
Jeremiah, 15, 56, 140, 147, 154, 165-175, 242, 256
Jericho, 65, 66
Jeroboam I, 69, 118, 123, 126-28
Jeroboam II, 135ff., 140
Jerubbaal, 76-77
Jerusalem, 21, 74, 104, 151, 158ff., 185
Jesus, 190
Jethro, 52, 59, 62
Jezebel, 128-30
Joab, 102, 108ff., 113
Joash, 135f., 151
Job, 208, 229-33
Joel, 214
John the Baptist, 15, 238
Jonah, 214
Jonathan, 98, 105
Joseph, 43f., 49-51
Joshua, 33, 59f., 61, 64-69, 200, 241
Josiah, 155, 159, 160-62
Jotham, 78
Jubal, 39
Judah, 21, 22, 49, 74, 97, 124, 137f., 143f., 149, 154f., 158, 185
Judge, meaning of term, 72
Judges, 32, 64f., 71-86, 241

Kings, I & II, 32, 241
Korah, 60, 62

Laban, 46f.
Laish, 84
Lamech, 39, 120, 255
Lamentations, 192f.
Leah, 46, 48
Levi, 60
Levite, 83
Leviticus, 33, 62, 194
Lot, 44
Lots, casting of, 67, 93f.

Maccabaeus, 221, 237
Malachi, 15, 212, 242
Manasseh, 48, 65, 77, 149, 151f.
Manna, 58
Manoah, 81
Manual of Discipline, 256
Mendenhall, George E., 249
Meribaal, 102f., 109
Messianic hope, 203
Micah, 83f.
Micah, the prophet, 147-48, 150, 166
Micaiah, 136
Mice, 91
Michal, 98f., 103, 105
Mount Hermon, 22, 75, 84
Mount Gilboa, 21, 102
Mount Carmel, 20, 21, 129ff., 149
Moses, 52-63, 154, 173
Moab, 24, 43f., 47, 105, 138
Moabite stone, 128
Miriam, 55, 59, 120
Mizpah, 47, 92

Nabal, 100f.
Naboth, 130, 149
Nahash, 24, 90f., 250
Nathan, 105, 106f., 113, 119, 136, 149
Nazirites, 81
Hahum, 162
Nebuchadnezzar, 159ff., 168ff., 222
Necho, 159ff.
Nehemiah, 33fn., 204-206, 210, 224
Nile, 26, 54, 159
Nineveh, 25, 159, 162
Noah, 40f.
Nob, 99
Northern Kingdom, 124f., 143ff., 151, 153f., 164, 185
Numbers, 33, 62

Obadiah, 45, 213
Omri, 21, 124, 128, 149
Origins, stories of, 34-42
Othniel, 72

P history, 33, 62
Palestine, 19, 25, 71-88
Passover, 55, 132, 213
Patriarchs, 43-51
Pharisees, 238
Philistines, 20, 21, 28, 104
Potiphar, 49
Priestly history, 32f., 207, 209f.,
    215, 220, 233
Prophets, 89-90, 241
Proverbs, 208, 227-28
Psalms, 15, 208, 225-27, 242

Qumran Monastery, 239, 256

Rachel, 46ff.
Ramoth-gilead, 24, 126, 130, 134
Rehoboam, 115, 123, 126
Reuben, 49, 65
Ruth, 190, 210-212

Sadducees, 238
Samaria, 21, 22, 124, 128, 135, 138,
    145, 151
Samson, 71, 81-83
Samuel, 69, 72, 89-93, 97, 118, 241
    Book of, 32, 64, 133
Saul, 24, 93-96, 97, 117, 133
Scythians, 159, 165f.
Second Isaiah, 172, 181, 187-192,
    203
Sennacherib, 145f.

Septuagint, 244
Sheba, 110f., 123
    queen of, 115f.
Shiloh, 57, 69, 91f., 166
Shishak (Sheshonk), 26, 115
Sinai, 53, 55ff.
Sisera, 74f.
Solomon, 26, 112-22, 224-25
Southern Kingdom, 124f., 164
Spies, 60, 66, 67

Tabernacle, 57f.
Tamar, 107
Third Isaiah, 215
Torah, 15, 241
Trever, 255
Tubal-Cain, 34, 39
Tyre, 114f., 138, 149

United Kingdom, 117f.
Uzziah, 136, 142

"Virgin Passage," 253-54
Vulgate, 245

Wilderness, 58-61
Worship of the Lord, 151f.

Yahweh, 31, 53, 247

Zadok, 109, 113, 238
Zealots, 239
Zechariah, 201-202, 212, 242
Zedekiah, 161, 168, 182
Zephaniah, 164f.
Zerubbabel, 200
Ziba, 109

Neuropsychiatric Features
of Medical Disorders

CRITICAL ISSUES IN PSYCHIATRY
An Educational Series for Residents and Clinicians

Series Editor: **Sherwyn M. Woods, M.D., Ph.D.**
University of Southern California School of Medicine
Los Angeles, California

A RESIDENT'S GUIDE TO PSYCHIATRIC EDUCATION
Edited by Michael G. G. Thompson, M.D.

STATES OF MIND: Analysis of Change in Psychotherapy
Mardi J. Horowitz, M.D.

DRUG AND ALCOHOL ABUSE: A Clinical Guide to Diagnosis and
Treatment
Marc A. Schuckit, M.D.

THE INTERFACE BETWEEN THE PSYCHODYNAMIC AND
BEHAVIORAL THERAPIES
Edited by Judd Marmor, M.D., and Sherwyn M. Woods, M.D., Ph.D.

LAW IN THE PRACTICE OF PSYCHIATRY
Seymour L. Halleck, M.D.

NEUROPSYCHIATRIC FEATURES OF MEDICAL DISORDERS
James W. Jefferson, M.D., and John R. Marshall, M.D.

ADULT DEVELOPMENT: A New Dimension in Psychodynamic
Theory and Practice
Calvin A. Colarusso, M.D., and Robert A. Nemiroff, M.D.

SCHIZOPHRENIA
John S. Strauss, M.D., and William T. Carpenter, Jr., M.D.

A Continuation Order Plan is available for this series. A continuation order will bring
delivery of each new volume immediately upon publication. Volumes are billed only upon
actual shipment. For further information please contact the publisher.